The Arts of Performance
in Elizabethan and Early Stuart Drama

The Arts of Performance
in Elizabethan and
Early Stuart Drama

Essays for G. K. Hunter

edited by
Murray Biggs
Philip Edwards
Inga-Stina Ewbank
Eugene M. Waith

EDINBURGH UNIVERSITY PRESS

© Edinburgh University Press 1991
22 George Square, Edinburgh

Typeset in Alphacomp Garamond
by Pioneer Associates, Perthshire, and
printed in Great Britain by
Robert Hartnoll Ltd, Bodmin

British Library Cataloguing
    in Publication Data
The arts of performance in
    Elizabethan and early Stuart drama.
    1. Drama in English
    I. Biggs, Murray
    822.309

ISBN 0 7486 0266 6

CONTENTS

(v)

Claude Rawson

GEORGE HUNTER
A PERSONAL MEMOIR

I first knew George Hunter sometime in the late 1950s. I was just beginning my own teaching career. He had recently moved from his first job at the University of Hull to the University of Reading, where he became one of an outstanding group of Renaissance scholars brought there by D. J. Gordon, among them Philip Brockbank, Frank Kermode and J. B. Trapp. Gordon had recently created a small sub-department of Italian, which was then included within the English Department as an adjunct to its Renaissance interests, and which has since developed into one of the strongest departments of Italian in the United Kingdom. My wife Judy taught Italian literature there in those early days, and was thus a member of the extended English Department. Some years later, when both George and Judy had left Reading for other universities, George was invited to become the first Professor of English at the new University of Warwick. Like D. J. Gordon, though in support of a rather different academic programme, he sought to create an English Department with an Italian element in it, and remembered my wife's work at Reading. I became the special arrangement which had to be made if she moved to Warwick, and we were both appointed among the first lecturers at that University in 1965. I owed the position, and the start of a long friendship with George, to a joint appointment (more uncommon then than now) in which I was the less wanted partner.

George was born in Glasgow in 1920, and grew up there. He served in the Royal Navy throughout the Second World War, spent several years at Oxford working for his D.Phil., and taught at the Universities of Hull, Reading and Liverpool before going to Warwick.[1]

These experiences, in whatever proportion, evidently combined to form in him a distaste (undiminished by his own elevation to positions of academic and institutional importance) for what might be called English academic gentility: for affectations and pretensions of caste and smartness; for the oily rhetoric of authority and that preoccupation with the 'smooth conduct of business' which are designed mainly to preserve privilege or contain dissent; for wine-bores and unctuous committee-operators; for the phonies of radical chic (as later for the

(1)

thuggish ideologues who took their place). In 1964, in the quater-
centenary of Shakespeare's birth, he was invited, along with other
leading Shakespearean scholars, actors and directors, to a Buckingham
Palace Garden Party. His son Andrew, aged seven, reported the occasion
in a diary he kept for his English teacher at school: 'This morning my
Mum and Dad had an invitation to tea with the Queen. They are not
going as Dad says it will be ded boring.' The teacher found this utterly
beyond belief, and commented reprovingly in the margin: 'Andy! you
know I like the truth in your news books.'

Whether the teacher was more incredulous of the fact of the
invitation, or of its rejection, is not recorded. To anyone who knew
George, the story corresponded compellingly to his normal manner. It
was not done for show. I suspect that if it had not been for the comedy
of Andy's notebook, no one would have known. George sometimes
projected an unprofessorial image. He rode a bike to work, carried a
knapsack and occasionally wore a cloth cap. I believe that the
distinguished Head of the Department of English and Comparative
Literary Studies was sometimes mistaken for a porter or maintenance
man. It was not populist posturing, which he would have liked no better
than the more upmarket sort. He cycled for exercise or pleasure, or
perhaps to save petrol. If there was a model, it was perhaps the Larkin of
'Church Going', whose cycle-clips had become a bit of a cultural icon:
not in every way a close resemblance, but George would have admired
the decency and unpretentiousness, or anti-pretentiousness. There was
certainly no resemblance to Norman Tebbitt's bicycling exhortation of
later years, representing a less patrician style of Toryism than the one
George grew up disliking, but which he would have seen, I think, as the
expression of a thoughtlessness and arrogance of power quite as gross as
those it replaced. George wore his hair very close-cropped and the joke
among the campus Cavaliers was that he was passing as a Roundhead.
An anonymous woman student, unschooled in the imagery of the Civil
War, is reported to have enquired on a lavatory wall in the Library
whether 'Professor Hunter [was] really a Skinhead?'

In the early days of the University, George was thought of by the rest
of the professorial establishment not only as a rough diamond but also
as a trouble-maker. They did not at that time realise the extent to which
his brusque and forthright observations, and his impatience with the
manipulative exercise of committee procedure, were expressions of a
loyal commitment to the institution and the academic ideals on which it
had been, at least professedly, founded. And for the remainder of his

decade at Warwick he remained intransigent in his defence of these ideals and in his insistence on due process in University business. But his manner mellowed, and when, in the wake of a major institutional reorganisation, he was appointed Pro-Vice-Chancellor, he surprised many by his easy assumption of an authoritative and statesmanly urbanity. The forms that this took, however, were ones which reflected qualities he had always possessed, modified by the dignity of office: an easy approachability, a concern (in presiding over committees, for example) to avoid or minimise offence, an ability to compliment distinguished visiting speakers without affronting the intelligence of the audience. For even in his most adversarial days, George had been blunt, but never churlish, ungenerous or inconsiderate. And the change that was now taking place was not an acquisition of surface polish but the transfer to a public mode of the kindness and the caring decency which friends of George and Shelagh had always experienced in private, and which students clearly responded to in the context, neither private nor fully public, of departmental activity.

Catherine Belsey, now a distinguished professor, was a graduate student in the early years of the University, and has recently written a short memoir of that time:

> Professor G. K. Hunter was head of department. The conjunction of his rigorous scholarship and his astringent wit inspired awe bordering on panic, and it was only gradually that we realised how concerned he was, how kind to anyone who needed kindness. Later, when he supervised my thesis, the awe remained (I think I still have it) but the panic subsided, and it was only then that I began to realise how much he taught me — and what a great deal I had to learn.

What Belsey calls his 'astringent wit' was — and is — neither showy nor cruel. It shows itself not in epigrammatic flashiness but in a pondered awareness of the irony of things. It is well exemplified in the brilliant biographical sketches of successive generations of Humanists in the introductory chapter of *John Lyly: The Humanist as Courtier*, of which this account of Gabriel Harvey's career is one:

> At Cambridge Harvey showed the combination of brilliance and truculency which is commonly a feature of the upstart scholar, pulled up by his brains from an obscure background . . . Harvey's contacts with the court, when he actually made them, were (like other poor scholars') a disappointment to him. Little (or at any rate, too little) attention was paid to his gifts of intellect; he had not the

power of waiting till some great person deigned to notice him; he thrust himself forward in a series of much pondered-on, but ill-timed and tactless devices, and the court soon showed that it could do without his intellect more easily than he could do without its glamour.

The acuteness of this is more than that of the historical analyst of 'the tensions which were present in the Humanist outlook'. It also has something of that teacherly wisdom which is accustomed to observing, with a combination of sympathy and critical detachment, the characters and careers of notable students. It is simultaneously a vivid biographical statement, and an ironic reflection on some sadnesses and contradictions of the human comedy. Its blend of gravity, humane comprehension, and compassionate derision is Johnsonian: one would not have been surprised to come upon this passage in the *Lives of the Poets*. George is not, in personal temperament or social display, Johnsonian, and not given, like that other great student of the sixteenth century, C. S. Lewis, to those conversation-stopping triumphalisms which go by the name of 'talking for victory'. But in such a passage, he shares with Johnson a suspicion of brilliant paradoxical formulation and of the kind of sharply antithetical wit for which Lewis, consciously Johnsonian though he was, had an active predilection. When Lewis is quoted, in the same chapter on 'Humanism and Courtship', as saying that in Colet's plans for St Paul's 'the boys were to be guarded from every word that did not occur in Virgil or Cicero, and equally from every idea that did', George's gloss that this is 'somewhat unfair' has something to do, I suspect, with an instinctive distrust, similar to Johnson's, of the tendency of such starkly structured wit to be literally falsifying.

George's admiration for Humanist culture is often more amusing and less pompous than Lewis's denigrations: 'Erasmus and More do not seem to have thought of one another as "foreigners", and even such later Humanists as the Scaligers, or Lipsius, or Casaubon knew "the foreigner" only in the sense of "the boor", the man whose Latinity fell below an international standard of excellence, such as today applies only to hotel cuisine.' Compare Lewis's complaint, in a letter to the Italian priest Don Giovanni Calabria, penned in the starchy Latin they used as a common tongue, that the Humanists had impaired the possibilities of such communication: 'If only that plaguey "Renaissance" which the Humanists brought about had not *destroyed* Latin (and destroyed it just when they were pluming themselves that they were reviving it), we should then still be able to correspond with the whole of Europe.' Lewis is hardly at his best here, but the attitudinising self-deception of this cultural mythology was characteristic, and for a live yet critical sense of both past and present, and of the possibilities and limits of an intellectual pan-Europeanism, one might, on the evidence of these two passages, go to George rather than to Lewis.

A similar preference might be entertained for the passage at the end of George's book on *Paradise Lost*, where, after noting what he describes as the Cambridge attack on Milton which culminated in Empson's *Milton's God*, he continues:

> The first Oxford High Anglican counter-attack took its explicit stand on Christian premises. In Charles Williams's preface to the Oxford 'World's Classics' edition of Milton's poetical works (1940) and in C. S. Lewis's *A Preface to 'Paradise Lost'* (1942) the hieratic style of the poem is seen as the necessary expression of a joyfully ordered, ceremonial and hierarchical view of life, to which the Christian imagination naturally responds, and in whose terms Satan cannot be a hero but must be seen to be self-obsessed, absurd, boring. One certainly sees that he would have been excluded from a number of high tables.

There is also a kind of humour, wholly unaggressive, which runs as a more or less continuous thread through the information-packed pages of the book on Lyly, and which is also a feature of George's lecturing style:

> William Lily [grandfather of John Lyly, and author of the Latin grammar] died of plague in 1523 and was succeeded in his High Mastership [of St Paul's] by John Rightwise who succeeded also to his daughter Dionysia (Lily's will suggests that this was not achieved without compulsion). She, keeping the family and school traditions well aligned, subsequently married James Jacob, the school Usher, and so procured for John Lyly a set of uncles and aunts with names like Polydore and Scholastica. But though the family continued to be what Feuillerat has called it, '*une famille d'érudits*', the heroic quality of *making* traditions disappears from the scholastic world. Rightwise, says Anthony à Wood, was the most distinguished grammarian of his day (he means in England). He revised Lily's poem on the gender of nouns, and added a vocabulary to it. He took a troop of children to present a Morality before Henry VIII, and he may have written a play (*Dido*) which was performed at Cambridge. He led a useful and distinguished life, but it was the life of a follower rather than a leader.

A sense of large movements in intellectual history is rooted in specific information about institutional change, personal biography and family life, and in a feeling, always alert and never demeaning, for the comedy of individual detail: aunts with names like Scholastica, poems on the gender of nouns (respected as a reasonable mnemonic aid and simultaneously perceived as faintly preposterous), children performing a Morality before Henry VIII, led by 'the most distinguished grammarian of his day'.

This was the style, informative and witty, in which students heard George lecture at Warwick, though he lectured not on Lyly, but on Homer and Dante and Milton, on Chaucer and Wordsworth, on Sophocles and Shakespeare and Ibsen. Another difference was that his lectures were not biographical or historical, except incidentally. It was one of his points of principle that the study of literature was to be disencumbered from an apparatus of 'literary history' to which undergraduates were necessarily unresponsive and which, in his view, obstructed rather than enriched their experience of works of literature at that early stage of their studies. It was partly on such assumptions that the Warwick syllabus was grounded, and which made it one of several innovative developments in the teaching of English at British universities.

It was a time of innovation. The new universities were just beginning. Universities still basked in public esteem, and both political parties competed for public favour by promoting more and more university expansion. This was before the troubles of the late 1960s, when the public fell out of love with universities, and before the financial recessions of the 1970s, when it became financially as well as politically acceptable to curtail their growth. The dark age of triumphal philistine Thatcherism did not seem even a remote possibility. The new institutions had a prestige which for a time attracted some of the liveliest among the younger, or younger-minded, leaders of the profession. The opportunity of creating new departments from scratch, and setting up new syllabuses which challenged traditional conceptions of each academic discipline, brought George Hunter to Warwick as it brought David Daiches to Sussex, Ian Watt to East Anglia, Donald Davie to Essex, and Philip Brockbank to York.

In English Studies, the chief target for revision was the linear, monolingual syllabus which led, as the phrase was, from Beowulf to Virginia Woolf. In 'English at Warwick', which he contributed to a series on the Idea of an English School in *Critical Survey*, George spoke scathingly of 'the traditional Oxford tutorial process of starting modern literature at 1579, with an essay on *The Shepherd's Calendar*, and then working forwards chronologically to whenever modern literature ends at Oxford'. George was not, I think, an advocate of the one-to-one tutorial, or of some other Oxford habits, and on the limits of Oxford chronology he was exaggerating a bit: C. S. Lewis began his 'modern' tutorials with Skelton and Wyatt (the medieval part of the course did begin with *Beowulf* or earlier), and I remember early in my undergraduate career grinding out tutorial essays on *Ralph Roister Doister* and *Gammer Gurtons Nedle.* But the 'modern' ended, in my time (ten years before George wrote), not with Woolf but in 1830, so that what was overstated at one end may have been understated at the other. (Lewis was one of the more muscular opponents of bringing the Oxford syllabus any further into the nineteenth century.)

The objection George expressed was not to mere chronology: he preferred, on grounds of pedagogic efficacy 'a process which (within the same "period" assumptions) starts with its accessible authors — Marlowe, Webster, Donne — and then moves towards the relatively inaccessible Spenser and Jonson.' The alternative risked that unresponsive 'passivity' in students which he thought any 'course in English Literature which is controlled by the interest of historical development' had a tendency to encourage. Partly for the same sorts of reason, he opposed the compartmentalisation of authors into 'periods' and the restriction of relationships between major authors . . . to those possible within individual periods — Pope and Dryden, Pope and Swift. 'But what', he asked, 'of Pope and Byron, Pope and Milton, Pope and Boileau?' The last example illustrated another principle of dissidence from the old model, and its insistence on monolingual continuities: 'We have also sought to avoid the related restrictions imposed by the view that English literature is an isolated national phenomenon, that Eliot is more directly related to *Beowulf* than to Laforgue. It seemed to us that the power to read (with understanding) a good translation of Tolstoy or Pirandello is exactly the same power as is required to understand Shakespeare or Lawrence.' The remark about Laforgue, incidentally, contains a conclusive retort to cheap charges of indifference to historical connections.

Two consequences followed from this. The first was that major works of the Western literary tradition — the Bible, the *Iliad*, the *Aeneid*, the *Divine Comedy* — were taught in translation in a first-year course on the Epic Tradition; Tolstoy and Dostoevsky, as well as Stendhal and Flaubert, and Dickens and George Eliot, in a second-year course on the Novel; and Pirandello, along with some Greek, Spanish and French as well as English dramatists, in a final-year course on the European Theatre. This practice, more familiar in American than in

British universities, provoked strenuous exercises in eyebrow-raising, and self-appointed custodians of standards simpered with acidulous witticisms about a Great Books Course at Warwick. The programme did encounter problems, one of which was that it fostered a variant of the monolingual fixation it had been designed to subvert. Students sometimes commented, in their essays, on the stylistic features of Homer or of Dante, including alliteration and even punctuation, for all the world as though the poems had never existed other than in the form naturalised by Lattimore or John Ciardi.

One was struck too that when, after months of reading Genesis, the *Iliad*, the *Aeneid* and the *Divine Comedy*, students came to *Paradise Lost*, the first English poem in the Epic course, incomprehension first set in on a large scale: the older, foreign poems had been read (as they were sometimes vaguely imagined to have been written) in easy modern English, not the gnarled and difficult language that Milton perversely used. You could not wholly dispel such misprisions, though George had sought to neutralise the problem by making sure that the main instructors were competent in the original languages and capable of drawing informed attention to primary wordings. He also encouraged the use of, and comparison between, alternative translations, in order to convey not only the reality of a poem's non-anglophone origins, but also the idea that translations were as unstable as other interpretative acts.

The second feature of the abandonment of a monolingual conception of English Studies was the stipulation that all students in the Department must have experience in their first year of one foreign literature in its original language. In addition, students who chose a European rather than an American orientation in the continuation of their English degree undertook a 'comparative' study (genuinely comparative in the sense of being concerned with more than one literature, and not in the sense of talking about texts without reading any) of a topic or period in which two literary traditions interacted: Roman and English Satire, the Italian and English Renaissance Epic, French and Anglo-American Symbolist Poetry. It is here that the idea that 'Eliot is more directly related to *Beowulf* than to Laforgue' received its second and more vital refutation, in ways which produced, in the best students, a sharply specific sense of live literary interactions across national and linguistic frontiers.

Thus all students of English at Warwick had some active experience of a foreign language in their first year, and many beyond that period. This was no perfunctory 'language requirement', insisted on in the abstract by a general university regulation, but a matter of specific and directed engagement with literary texts, and of the live bearing of foreign works on the study of English ones. Those who came to Warwick with some knowledge of the school languages (Latin, French or German) were able to apply them at once. Others were taught Italian from scratch. Spanish was later introduced as an alternative, and both were open also to students who had one of the mainstream languages but opted to learn a new one. Some of the mainstream languages were, later still, added to the beginners' options. A feature of these beginners' courses in new languages, less common then than now, was that they were not aimed at diffused or unfocused objectives (including tourist situations in railway stations, restaurants and hairdressers' salons) but targeted specifically at the rapid acquisition of reading skills. The purpose was first and always the early attainment of a literary competence. One detects behind this project the aspiration which George had ascribed two or three years earlier, in his book *John Lyly: The Humanist as Courtier*, to the Latin grammar of William Lily, that product of a Humanist collaboration in which both Colet and Erasmus had taken part: 'The aim of "Lily's Grammar" was an extremely humane one: to take the pupils as quickly as possible to classical *literature* by cutting down to a minimum the rules that had to be learned.' A by-product of this, gradually created by skilled and innovative linguists at the University, was the development of some programmes of rapid language-teaching for reading purposes which had a successful application beyond the institution and beyond George's strictly literary objectives. But the *product*, in those early years, was the formation in the best students of a new and liberated literacy. This was naturally anchored in a first-hand experience of the national literature. But it was international in a sense that distinguished it on the one hand from doctrinaire monolingual provincialisms, whether of the Beowulf-to-Virginia Woolf variety or of a vulgarised Leavisism, and on the other from a superficial and modish cosmopolitanism, monolingual in all but gesture, parroting European sages without having read a word of what they really wrote.

It was also part of the Warwick idea that plays (both those taught in the European Theatre course, and those of English dramatists who figured in other sections of the syllabus) should be taught not merely as written texts, nor as documents in a mainly literary tradition, but as works performed in the theatre. Stage-history and the realities of theatrical production were emphasised from the beginning, on a scale which is again more common now than it was then. Peter Hall was in those first years an Honorary Professor, and gave a few public lectures which remain memorable after twenty-five years for the vivid detail of their exposition of the practicalities of Shakespearean production. Through him, and later through others, an active relationship was maintained between the Department's teaching, both undergraduate and graduate, and the Royal Shakespeare Theatre at Stratford-upon-Avon, which was only a few miles away. The first person brought in to teach the dramatic authors on a regular basis, other than George himself, was Germaine Greer, who, at Cambridge, had not only been writing her doctoral thesis on Shakespeare but had had active experience of stage performance and production. The tradition has been continued by a number of others, including Tony Howard, one of the earliest products of the undergraduate course, and subsequently a collaborator of Howard Brenton, whose own contributions to theatre at Warwick belong to a later time than George's but grew out of a context he created.

Anyone who has lived through the early years of a new university will know that they are unlikely to be remembered only for the serene fulfilment of intellectual or pedagogic ambitions. Some of the realities were harsh. People who came to work in freedom from older ways, and from the committees and bureaucracies which sustained them, found much of their time taken up creating new committees and bureaucracies. Everything had to be done from scratch, and committees were needed even to create committees. In the earliest years, numbers were very small, thus giving a sense of shared purpose and making it possible to know all one's colleagues, including those in other disciplines, and even their students as well as one's own. But it also meant that the same small group was on all the committees. The burden and the boredom were numbing, and the atmosphere could be intensely parochial.

The physical amenities were those of a building site. Bulldozers sometimes crashed into classrooms in mid-seminar. The campus was for several years a muddy swamp. As the buildings went up, they had all the usual teething troubles: heating systems leaked or seized up, people got stuck in lifts. Even when the first work was completed, Warwick was a bleak environment, an architectural scar on spacious acres of green fertile land. Buildings with white tiles gleamed in the sunshine (when the sun shone) like Brobdingnagian lavatories. The university was known in a neighbouring institution as the Loo on the Hill. The buildings won architectural prizes because they were built to photograph well from certain bends on a footpath, showing more or less decoratively through a few well-placed trees. Students complained that the landscape was depressing and the buildings ill designed for use, but the architect said that only architects were qualified to judge. Then the white tiles began to fall, causing hazards that architects thought beneath their notice and a new canker of ugliness they could not pretend to have planned. A new architect was called in, who found a new use for trees, thousands of them, to hide the buildings completely. It was said to be too expensive to buy trees of the right size in such numbers, so saplings were planted instead, sowing the seeds of a future concealment. The social geography was bad too. The site was hundreds of acres, the size of a large American campus, but the population was tiny, too small at that stage to make it economically and culturally self-sufficient. At the same time, there was no single urban focus in the neighbourhood. The University was stuck in the fields, between four different towns. In the evenings and at weekends the campus was a desert. Transport was difficult because, in those days, the region was prosperous in a quasi-American way. Everyone owned cars except those who didn't, so there was little public transport for students. If you lived on campus it was hard to get out, and if you lived in one of the towns there was no incentive, and no easy way, to get in.

Nevertheless morale was high. Academic standards in the University were strong, and hopes and ambitions were keen and energetic. In the English Department, George was assembling a group which included Harold Beaver, Bernard Bergonzi, Gay Clifford, K. W. Gransden, Germaine Greer and William Righter, an exceptionally broad spread of skills and interests. Our undergraduates were excellent, and several, like Elizabeth Heale and Jenny Mezciems, quickly became distinguished members of the profession. The graduate programme was flourishing. Kate Belsey was only one member, though an outstanding one, of a graduate community which was to make its mark in several fields of scholarship, including especially those fields of sixteenth- and seventeenth-century literature and drama in which George was one of the country's most sought-after teachers.

I will quote again from Kate Belsey's memoir, because it shows from the point of view of a student the atmosphere of intellectual excitement getting the upper hand over an unpropitious environment:

> Warwick was not a bit like Oxford. There were a couple of white Lego buildings in the middle of a ploughed field, miles from the administration buildings, and even further from the bus stop. One of them housed the Library, but there were hardly any books. Classes were at an unsocial 5 o'clock, so that part-time students could attend. And as the autumn term wore on, the long walk through the dank, dark evenings to wait for a slow, steamy bus to

Leamington, seemed to grow even longer and more arduous. We were the first MA students in English. We weren't sure what we were doing, or why. We weren't convinced that anyone knew. We weren't at all certain that we weren't guinea pigs in some monstrous experiment. I thought of giving it up. And the moment I contemplated the possibility of leaving, I realised that I was *having the time of my life*.

It's hard to say why. Professor G. K. Hunter was head of department. [There follows the description of George quoted earlier] . . . Other members of the department were less terrifying, but no less stimulating . . . There was a sense that something important was going on. A new department was being built up from first principles, and what it did mattered. There was no complacency, no resting on old laurels, no easy imitation of existing systems. And most exciting of all from our point of view, the staff were prepared to *listen*. We had the sense that we too could make a contribution to the construction of something new, and that what we said just might matter as well.

George's influence on the Department was enormous. Those colleagues who came, in the course of time, to press for changes in parts of the syllabus he had regarded as essential, retained (both before and after he himself had left) a sense not only of his personal wisdom and authority but of the rightness of the curriculum he had set up. I recall during one of the more embattled arguments over syllabus reform some of the founder-members suggesting that if certain fundamental components (notably the requirement for all students of some experience of a foreign literature in its original language) were going to be jettisoned, it was probably best to make a new start and create a model based on freshly reconsidered assumptions. But few wanted that, least of all the reformers: they were, they felt, developing the original model, not discarding it.

None of the younger colleagues whom he appointed, whatever course their professional development took, avoided being deeply marked by his influence, as a mentor and as an example. His range was wide, from classical antiquity to modern drama and film: this showed not only in his published writings, but in his conversation and in his ability to interest himself in the work of his colleagues. He lectured on almost everything, often at short notice because someone was ill or away. Whatever your own specialisation, he was likely to teach you something about it. For me, his essay on 'The Romanticism of Pope's Horace' had been a particular stimulus, even before I knew him. Many years later, when I was on a visiting appointment in the United States, a student submitted an essay plagiarised from it verbatim: he was one of the best students in the class, and had chosen fastidiously.

As a teacher and colleague, George believed passionately in literature as literature. He saw it in those days as needing to be freed, in the classroom especially, from the aridities of an old-fashioned conception of 'literary history', to which he frequently referred with mild contempt as 'lit. hist.' But he rejected, then as now, the complementary aridities of those who promoted a literature stripped of historical context, whether that context was literary or other. That he always understood the humane purposes of the contextual skills, of textual scholarship and of wide-ranging annotation, is evident from his work as an editor; that he is one of the best historians of literature has been obvious since his book on John Lyly and will doubtless be equally obvious in the volume he is now writing for the *Oxford History of English Literature*. His sense of historical process, of cultural and intellectual change, is masterful. The account of the passage from Humanism to Euphuism, through the successive generations of William Lily the grammarian, his son George, and his grandson John Lyly has a classic simplicity of outline without any trace of simplification. Its sense of the solidity and complexity of human lives and of the density of event and circumstance is always vivid, and I have already mentioned the virtuosity of its biographical encapsulations (not only of the Lily family).

Similar gifts seem to me to be evident in the studies, collected in *Dramatic Identities and Cultural Tradition*, of the alien or outsider figures of the English Renaissance, not only the generalised 'foreigners' of the encyclopedic 'Elizabethans and Foreigners,' but also the Moors, Jews, Italians and others who are the subjects of several companion studies. That these studies are also in some cases magisterial accounts of individual plays (especially *The Jew of Malta* and *Othello*) hardly diminishes their vividness and authority as 'portraits of an age'. They belong to a style of intellectual history that he has made so much his own as to amount to a Hunterian subgenre. Like all his historical writings, they are sharpened by an unillusioned awareness of continuities: in *Titus Andronicus*, he reminds us, 'Shakespeare has the doubtful distinction of making explicit . . . (perhaps for the first time in English literature) the projection of black wickedness in terms of negro sexuality.' This is no modish 'relevance': it is a flat constatation in a context concerned chiefly with what differentiates particular moments of the past from others, and from the present. One emphasis of all these essays is to distinguish the specific features of older xenophobias from those of our own time, sometimes to the added discredit of the latter.

The gifts shown in these writings were the characteristics also of the Warwick English course. They continue to inform his teaching and his conversation. They show his openness to large perspectives, and his awareness that expansive generalisation must always be subject to factual revision. He never uses facts to shut off ideas, without first seeking to enlarge or refine them. I have seldom sought information from him without learning more than the specific answer I was after. I also learned from our joint editorship of *MLR* and the *Yearbook of English Studies* how generous he was to new ideas and how quick to spot the merely modish, how thoughtful in his advice to authors and how fair in judgement. We divided our tasks at 1670. Broadly he was responsible for all material before that date, and for drama topics in all periods, while I dealt with non-dramatic literature after 1670. We rejected individually but accepted together: if either of us wished to publish a piece, the final decision would be a joint one. It was the easiest and the most instructive professional collaboration I have experienced, and when, some time after his move to the United States he found the work too burdensome to continue at a distance, I felt the loss keenly.

George left Warwick for Yale in 1976. He had long been courted by universities in the United States, and his decision to go was long in the making. He felt that he had done what he could at Warwick and that it was right to move on. Few if any shared this view, but there was no persuading him to stay. He was, and I believe remains, greatly missed. He became an Honorary Professor there, and more recently a Fellow of the Centre for Research in Philosophy and Literature, a unit at the University which was one of the few happy consequences of the reorganisation of universities under the Thatcher blight. He had many other and less local distinctions. In the United States he was made a Fellow of the American Academy of Arts and Sciences in 1978 and Emily Sanford Professor of English Literature at Yale in 1987. In the following year the British Academy named him a Corresponding Fellow. I left Warwick almost a decade after George did, and my professional peregrinations have since made me his departmental colleague for a second time. Times have changed in English Studies, and some of the hidebound philistinism which he used to fight against in the old guard has reappeared with surface variations in the new. It has been cheering to see him as doggedly embattled against the one as he had been against the other, and to admire the old intellectual rectitude, the decency, the freedom from rancour.

Note

1 Of the Liverpool days, Inga-Stina Ewbank writes: In Kenneth Muir's department at Liverpool George joined a group of distinguished Shakespeare scholars working in an ethos of unabashed delight in learning, writing and publishing. His book on Lyly was completed in this period, and several of the essays in *Dramatic Identities and Cultural Tradition* — the book dedicated to the memory of Ernest Schanzer, the Liverpool colleague to whom he was closest — were conceived or written, or both. I have always felt that I was particularly fortunate to start my teaching career with George as a senior colleague and model. Not that he turned seniority into authority, but that his zest for learning and teaching could not (and cannot) help being infectious. Most democratically we shared the dreaded K-course — early-morning lectures to General and Subsidiary students — and co-taught a Drama seminar course where we ranged from *The Oresteia* to *A Taste of Honey*. All students learned far more than was on the syllabus; and observing the effect on them of George's unique combination of scholarly integrity, wit and zest, I learned that, as he himself put it, 'when you teach literature, you also teach your own way of life'.

THE PERFORMANCE OF
SHAKESPEARE'S SONNETS

In an essay published in 1953, George Hunter singled out their dramatic quality as that which distinguished the sonnets of Shakespeare from those of his contemporaries.[1] Shakespeare's unique utilisation of traditional materials set up in readers and critics 'an overwhelmingly biographical reaction'. They felt that the poems had the substance of life. The Sonnets, 'expressing and concentrating the great human emotions of desire, jealousy, fear, hope and despair', achieved their specifically dramatic nature not by using the confessional mode but by creating the sense of relationship, 'the relation of one human heart to others', and by their verbal power, 'for ever creating in the mind of the reader *new* relationships'.

In 1976 Giorgio Melchiori, in his book *Shakespeare's Dramatic Meditations,*[2] called attention to Hunter's 'perceptive essay'. His purpose in that book was to isolate sonnets which were not dialogues and which were 'dramatic in a different way' (p. 30). Sonnets 94, 121, 129, 146, according to Melchiori, 'represent a conflict not between characters, their actions and their feelings, but *within* one character . . . The feelings and thoughts are actors in a performance played on the stage of the author's mind' (p. 30). In discussing 94, Melchiori saw Shakespeare employing a 'strategy' to 'suggest the tortuousness of meditation, an attempt at reconciling a mass of contradictions' (p. 64).[3]

These two conceptions of what is dramatic in the Sonnets are not far apart. Most readers would accept that 'the tortuousness of meditation', as the mind attempts to reconcile contradictions, is visible also in the dialogue sonnets and creates the sense of the relationship 'of one human heart to others'. The vividness with which interaction and self-division are presented in the Sonnets certainly justifies calling them dramatic. But there is a quite different way in which it can be argued that the Sonnets are dramatic; namely, that the individual poems are the constituent components of a drama. The claim would be that the whole sequence of 154 poems is a single coherent drama, acting out if not before our eyes then in a theatre of the mind the developing relationships among a group of people. The writer of the Sonnets, the dark woman, the lovely boy, and the rival poet are the persons of the drama. So, in a generic way of speaking, the Sonnets would be dramatic as the speeches in a play are dramatic. That they are also, in a colloquial way of speaking, dramatic, in that they vividly and freshly present personal and interpersonal conflict, is their means of fulfilling their generic task.

Of course, to call a series of sonnets handed round to be read by acquaintances and then printed in a book a drama is to take liberties with a term meant to indicate a performance staged by actors. Perhaps the truer generic analogy for the Sonnets would be the epistolary novel, which also comprises a sequence of units in the subjective mode. But the epistolary novel, though burdened by having to record past events, is itself already moving towards the condition of drama.[4] The Sonnets have the immediacy of performance: they create the moods and moments they record. Within and by means of the conventions of sonnet-writing, the protagonist tries to define himself in his relationship with others in the act of writing the sonnet. As we read the poem we are watching the poet weaving the fabric of self-constitution. It hasn't happened; it is happening. It is the immediacy of this activity of self-creation in the face of an unknown future, from unit to unit through the entire sequence, that allows us to call the Sonnets, in part and in whole, dramatic, and makes the phrase, the performance of the Sonnets, no catechresis.[5]

The poet is on a stage, seated at a table with a pen in his hand. His performance in writing his sonnets demonstrates to the audience the jarring confusion in which his sexual and economic needs, his spiritual aspirations and his literary ambitions intermingle. His naïve ardour to dedicate himself to the true and the beautiful is unsettled by his uncertainty of the holiness of the heart's affections, by his certainty that he does not wish to lose the patronage of the wonderful young aristocrat who has taken him up, and by his inability to forsake the woman he despises. Nevertheless, to try to locate the true and the beautiful in a person and to celebrate that person and his relationship with him in verse — *hic opus, hic labor est* — 'O let me, true in love, but truly write!' (21)

Of the four people involved in the drama, the poet, the dark woman, the shining youth, and the rival poet, only the poet appears on stage. And in the basic plot of mutual treachery, the rival poet drops out; he is a competitor not a traitor. The traitors are the woman, the youth, the poet, and the poet's pen.

The Sonnets stage what is essentially an improgressive situation; a situation in which time passes, many things happen, and nothing changes. Everything of importance in the Sonnets is going on at the same time. Certainly there was a time when the relationship of the poet

to his young patron was formal, deferential and distant; there was a
time when the patron first went to bed with the woman; there are
journeys, estrangements, reunions; winters come and go. But in these
sonnets, which so often invoke the remorseless motion of devouring
Time, time is a motionless monster. Doubt coexists with affirmation,
enchantment with disenchantment, love with hate, sexual desire with
sexless love. The whole force of the sequence is to deny that movement
and progress towards enrichment or impoverishment, happiness or
catastrophe, which the sequential motion of a performed play almost
inevitably provides. Time brings nothing about; the end is where we
started.

The drama of the Sonnets would therefore be almost unplayable in a
theatre. The circling repetitiveness of what we falsely call the 'sequence'
(or the 'two sequences') would challenge the skill of the most cunning
designer of improgressive drama. The 'performance' is for a reader. Its
power comes in the shock for the reader when the page is turned and
the next sonnet contradicts and denies everything that the last few
sonnets had been striving to assert (e.g., 87, 111, 121, 129, 147). And
this repositioning is itself temporary and precarious. Nothing lasts long.
No ground is ever gained that is not lost; nothing is learned that is not
forgotten. Every reader, searching for the stability of progress, feels as
he or she moves through the pages that 'we're getting nowhere' —
particularly when the great celebratory sonnets which conclude the
young-man sonnets are followed by the dark-woman sonnets where all
wounds bleed again.

No modern work repudiates and so successfully resists closure as
Shakespeare's Sonnets, which interrupt and abort every development,
contradict every statement. The daring of this work is in the paradox
that it is constructed out of self-contained poems the most obvious
feature of which is the emphatic, relentless closure of the final couplet.
The unsteadiness of these final couplets in performing their expected
task of rounding off the argument of a sonnet contributes strongly to
the instability of the collection as a whole. Each unit seeks but rarely
finds its own completion in a series of poems which cannot ultimately
find a point of rest.

On the floor of the stage is a litter of discarded sonnets, inadequate
for the task they were meant to perform: sonnets which turned against
the writer as he wrote or turned against the person they were supposed
to please. Sealing and despatching a sonnet is a comparatively rare
moment in the performance. And even those few sonnets (after the
initial 'marriage' sonnets) are double-tongued as the poet shares with

the audience a meaning which (it is hoped) the recipient will not perceive.[6]

The drama of the Sonnets, as Hunter said, has to do with relationship; as Melchiori said, it has to do with the self-division of the poet; but the heart of the drama is the conscience of the poet concerning the writing of sonnets. The protagonist is trying to arrange his life by ordering his relationship with two people; and the ordering agent is verse. 'O let me, true in love, but truly write!' Alas! 'truth proves thievish' (48). It keeps stealing his sonnets from him. The more honest the poem, the less possible to send it. And those which are impossible to send have their own dishonesty, satisfying his own self-esteem before they serve truth.

I begin with sonnets in which the poet turns against himself, becoming aware even as he writes of the falsity of his position. Optimistic propositions, shoring up the crumbling walls of his faith, end in disaster. Among these, 35 has classic simplicity ('No more be grieved at that which thou hast done'). The excuses based on nature-analogies roll out with the efficiency of a ticket machine until they nauseate the poet.

> All men make faults, and even I in this,
> Authorizing thy trespass with compare,
> Myself corrupting, salving thy amiss . . .

The sonnet recovers an equilibrium in images of court-room and civil war which 'justify' praising what should not be praised, and the poet eventually pacifies his self-disgust, now authorising his own trespass with compare.

The subject of 70 is the whispering that's going on about the youth's conduct ('That thou art blamed shall not be thy defect'). The link with 35 is in the repetition of 'canker' in 'sweetest buds'. But self-corruption comes now not with the tiredness of the image but with the brilliance of the analogy that slander is a crow whose black wings actually intensify the beauty of the sky they stain.

> The ornament of beauty is suspect,
> A crow that flies in heaven's sweetest air.

It is a close shave. The precariousness of the argument is emphasised by the poet's warning to the youth that he is only, as it were, buying him time:

> Yet this thy praise cannot be so thy praise
> To tie up envy, evermore enlargèd.

In an excellent discussion of this sonnet, Gerald Hammond points out that this means both that the youth cannot outface suspicion every time, and that the poet cannot forever exculpate the youth by means of metaphor.[7] The final couplet is a reversal rather than a completion:

> If some suspect of ill masked not thy show,
> Then thou alone kingdoms of hearts shouldst owe.

A sonnet which began with the boast that suspicion of wrongdoing enhances the youth's virtue ends by admitting that it clouds and stains him (compare 33). Worse, it is not virtue that is masked, but 'thy show', the external appearance of virtue (see the ending of 93). Suspicion is a veil preventing us from seeing what lies beneath, but that which lies immediately beneath is a veil preventing us from seeing what lies further beneath.

Sonnets fail to reach their advertised destination in many different ways. In 59 ('If there be nothing new, but that which is'), the poet is at his daily exercises of feeding his patron with verse, and he is worrying whether it hasn't all been said before. Wondering what poets of a past age might have said 'To this composèd wonder of your frame', the poet drifts into wondering whether people, as well as poems, were better in the old days. And then comes the disconcerting irrelevance of the couplet:

> O, sure I am the wits of former days
> To subjects worse have given admiring praise.

This gratuitous reassurance reveals the otherwise wholly unexpressed fear that what the poet is trying to provide is not a verbal image of the beloved but cosmetics for an unworthy subject.

A sonnet may run in quite the opposite direction. Wonder at the bewildering multifariousness of the youth in 53 ('What is your substance, whereof are you made') shades into perplexity about this inscrutable youth with the ominous note of 'all external grace'. But it cancels all that with the strained and inappropriate gallantry of the last line: 'But you like none, none you, for constant heart.'

The treacherous comparison, comforting and corrupting, frequently announces itself with some noise. Here is the sestet of 56 ('Sweet love, renew thy force. Be it not said'). The poet laments a falling away in the keenness of affection, presumably because of some separation:

> Let this sad int'rim like the ocean be
> Which parts the shore where two contracted new
> Come daily to the banks, that when they see
> Return of love, more blessed may be the view;

> As call it winter, which, being full of care,
> Makes summer's welcome, thrice more wished, more rare.

Hammond rightly calls this 'a conscious, deliberate act of poeticizing' (p. 142). In confirmation, we should add that the use of 'Let . . .' here provides a connection with a similar attempt at building up and romanticising a situation in the first scene of *Troilus and Cressida*:

> Tell me, Apollo, for thy Daphne's love,
> What Cressid is, what Pandar, and what we?
> Her bed is India; there she lies, a pearl.
> Between our Ilium and where she resides
> Let it be called the wild and wand'ring flood,
> Ourself the merchant, and this sailing Pandar
> Our doubtful hope, our convoy, and our barque.

The sense of rehearsing comparisons which glamorise the situation is increased if in the couplet of 56 we accept the emendation of 'Or call it winter', or 'Else call it winter' instead of the meaningless 'As call it winter' of the 1609 Quarto.

The stratagem is basically the same in 139, in which there is the announcement 'Let me excuse thee' (which we understand to mean, 'Let me excuse thee by comparing x to y'.) This perturbed, disjointed sonnet, with so many thoughts jostling each other and struggling for expression, is of key importance among those which are shown to be sliding out of the poet's grasp. The treason of poetry comes with a different accent in the dark-woman sonnets, but in both series the poet's greatest fear is of being seduced by fondness for himself or for the other into blurring the distinction between right and wrong.

> O, call not me to justify the wrong
> That thy unkindness lays upon my heart.
> Wound me not with thine eye but with thy tongue;
> Use power with power and slay me not by art.
> Tell me thou lov'st elsewhere, but in my sight,
> Dear heart, forbear to glance thine eye aside;
> What need'st thou wound with cunning, when thy might
> Is more than my o'erpressed defence can bide?
> Let me excuse thee: 'Ah, my love well knows
> Her pretty looks have been my enemies,
> And therefore from my face she turns my foes
> That they elsewhere might dart their injuries.'
>> Yet do not so; but since I am near slain,
>> Kill me outright with looks, and rid my pain.

In Hunter's sense, this is a brilliantly dramatic sonnet in the way in which the intimation of a deep and complex relationship is so sharply etched. As the sonnet is performed in our theatre of the mind, the poet is not in bed talking to the woman but at his table writing this sonnet. *She* is not inviting him to justify any wrong she has done him; he is talking to himself, trying to arm himself against the corrupting temptation to compromise and settle for less. The whole sonnet is a violent repudiation of the truce just achieved in the preceding sonnet 138:

> Therefore I lie with her, and she with me,
> And in our faults by lies we flattered be.

Now he can't stand his own lies, and he can't stand hers. She won't meet his eyes; better that she did, even if it finished the relationship. 'Let me excuse thee . . .' I could get us out of this (he writes) by pressing the poetry button. Ladies' eyes are full of danger; it's out of sheer compassion she's not looking me straight in the face. That kind of excuse is what 'to justify the wrong' means; and, at the cost of making Stephen Booth dislike this sonnet very much,[8] the poet meets and overcomes the complaisant offer made to him by his own poetic facility.

The phrase 'Let me excuse thee' calls us back to 42, one of the three sonnets in the young-man series which are there to remind us of the simultaneity of the events in the dark-woman series.

> Loving offenders, thus I will excuse ye:
> Thou dost love her because thou know'st I love her.

Here the tone is different, as the poet sardonically rehearses the patently absurd conceit which will 'justify the wrong': 'And both for my sake lay on me this cross.' Yet this sonnet also illustrates the instant readiness of the sonneteer's armoury to produce the material for self-corruption.

Straight from this armoury comes 92 ('But do thy worst to steal thyself away'). The poet will die if the young man's affection ceases — so he will never have to suffer the misery of being deserted; if he is not loved, he's dead. A nice conceit. But into this self-pitying absurdity a sobering thought intrudes:

> But what's so blessèd fair that fears no blot?
> Thou mayst be false, and yet I know it not.

It wouldn't work. I might not die because I might not discern that you have ceased to love me. The world of the poetic fancy of the quatrains and the unfanciful world of deception in the couplet are not commensurate, and the effect of juxtaposing them is comic. It's no good day-dreaming about dying when love ceases where *you* are concerned; I should never know the moment to die.

This sonnet 92, part of the great series on the separateness of seeming and being which includes 'They that have power to hurt and will do none' (94), is also one of the many sonnets which either slide out of the poet's grasp or have to be corrected or cancelled at the behest of fact. Where does 94 stand among these poems in which the poet seems at war with his own pen? Here is John Kerrigan's recent summary of its fluctuations: 'Its ironies are almost inordinate, an ebb and flow between approval and disapproval ambiguating the text, whose iterative patterns . . . offer a security which, in reading, dissolves'.[9]

Abundant in generality and parsimonious in particularity, the poem begins as a concessionary qualification to the couplet ending 93:

> How like Eve's apple doth thy beauty grow,
> If thy sweet virtue answer not thy show!

Only in one circumstance is the gap between being and seeming admissible, and that is when people of fearsome power do not use their power. It is this tactical concession which 'ruins' the poem's attempt to praise an uncontaminated purity. Once the pass has been sold regarding the inseparability of inside and outside, there is little hope of maintaining respect for these strong self-reliant men, for the shadow of hypocrisy gathers about the chilliness and calculation which so distressingly strays into the features of the paragons. The sudden switch to the summer's flower cannot save the day. The stern warning to his impulsive and gregarious patron to keep himself pure in detached aloofness simply does not work. The half-heartedness of the praise of the patron's anti-type proclaims that the patron has won. The poet, corrupted by affection, cannot make his verse say what it should. Sometimes the words in praise of the youth come too easily; here, arguments directed against the youth are not strong enough. The success of this brilliant poem is in its inadequacy.

With all these examples before us of a contest between the poet's self and his verse it is hardly surprising that a constant expressed theme of the Sonnets should be the failure of poetry to fulfil its tasks and achieve its objectives. 'O let me, true in love, but truly write!' Yet the poet's consciousness of the distance between language and its referents comes in oddly contradictory forms. Anxiety about finding words worthy of conveying his emotions and worthy of the person who inspires those emotions is countered by the confidence of his boast that his verse, by enshrining the youth's beauty, will confer immortality on the youth. And that confidence in the power and quality of his verse is balanced by the frequently voiced satisfaction that the more feeble his verse, the more genuine the feeling.

These contradictions make the drama of the Sonnets sometimes more like comedy than tragedy; especially in the poet's self-presentation in the 'rival poet' series, in which Shakespeare's poet so strongly resembles Sidney's Astrophil. Despising the 'strained touches rhetoric can lend' and the 'gross painting' to be found in the other poet's work, he can write:

> Thou, truly fair, wert truly sympathized
> In true plain words by thy true-telling friend.   (82)

It is enough, apparently, to say 'that you alone are you' (84), though the whole throng of the Sonnets denies the possibility of such a labelling.

> Let him but copy what in you is writ,
> Not making worse what nature made so clear . . .   (84)

The only thing clear about the young man is his mysterious inscrutability.

> What is your substance, whereof are you made,
> That millions of strange shadows on you tend?   (53)

The conventions of sonneteering, in Shakespeare's objectified poet, become not insincerity but the bricks of self-preserving self-presentation. The poet pictures himself as the honest broker whose untutored words convey the majesty of his subject, whose very slackness in sending poems becomes the even more honest tribute of silence.

> But that is in my thought, whose love to you,
> Though words come hindmost, holds his rank before.
>   Then others for the breath of words respect,
>   Me for my dumb thoughts, speaking in effect.   (85)

Against this self-image is set the image of the rival poet, and 'the proud full sail of his great verse/Bound for the prize of all-too-precious you' (86). The rival poet turns into an *alter ego*, resembling the poet of the Sonnets much more closely than his simple-hearted competitor does, whose 'glory' is 'being dumb' (83). The 'prize of all-too-precious you' is both the tangible reward of patronage and the higher non-financial success of matching words to their object. The competition between two rivals for favour assumes the shape of the conflict within the poet himself, the conflict between writing and gesture in performing 'the perfect ceremony of love's rite' (23).

The simplest position taken by the poet is that of a pure soul ardent in affection but conscious of the inadequacy of words to pay tribute to the wonder of the youth and so spread and perpetuate his perfection. (See, for example, 26, 'Lord of my love, to whom in vassalage', and 32, 'If thou survive my well-contented day'.) All his efforts are to improve his skill. The experience of being in love actually enhances his powers and improves his chances of matching word and object:

> O, give thyself the thanks if aught in me
> Worthy perusal stand against thy sight.   (38)

But this simple position becomes untenable at the thought that if his language had the power to capture the very truth of the youth's beauty, it would mean that he had lost sight of the youth. The truest poetry is the most feigning. We poets spend our lives trying to get it right, but if we ever get it right, we have ceased to feel. Stumbling inarticulacy, even silence, is a better guarantee of true feeling than rhetorical brilliance. This is the stage of the conflict shown in diagrammatic form in sonnets 78–86 as a competition between two poets.

And now the worry transfers from the adequacy of the medium to the adequacy of the object. The image of the loved one begins to lose its radiance. Endeavouring to match the beloved with words looks more like trying to polish the tarnished silver of an imperfect being. The effect of this stage of the conflict on the shape of the Sonnets we have already looked at in part. There are further major ramifications. Let us put the matter this way. First, words are too weak to represent the perfect object. Secondly, words are too strong, for they create their own objects, quite separate from the living human being and the lived relationships they profess to characterise. Thirdly, as the perfect human being declines into imperfection, words take on a new value. That whole rich vein in Shakespeare's Sonnets on the immortalising power of poetry derives from the poet's recognition of the shortcomings of the youth:

> Shall I compare thee to a summer's day?
> Thou art more lovely and more temperate.
> Rough winds do shake the darling buds of May,
> And summer's lease hath all too short a date.
> Sometime too hot the eye of heaven shines,
> And often is his gold complexion dimmed,

And every fair from fair sometime declines,
By chance or nature's changing course untrimmed;
But thy eternal summer shall not fade
Nor lose possession of that fair thou ow'st,
Nor shall death brag thou wander'st in his shade
When in eternal lines to time thou grow'st.
   So long as men can breathe or eyes can see,
   So long lives this, and this gives life to thee.   (18)

'I cannot find in nature', he writes, 'anything adequate to express you, because you, unlike everything else in nature, never fade.' Obviously, 'you' is the poetic image of the young man, not the young man himself. His summer is eternal only because he lives in eternal lines. The young man is inexpressible in terms of nature only because the poet is expressing him.

The infection which disqualifies the youth as the perfect object of love solves the otherwise insoluble dilemma of the rival-poet series. For that poetry which can never meet its object except by being false to it, having now a false object, may be true to its own ends (of celebrating perfection) by bypassing and transcending its object and creating in words an ideal surrogate, whose identity with the young man is assumed for the purposes of patronage only. Thus, by a circuitous route, Shakespeare's poet finds himself in the same enclosure with every other epideictic poet who had a conscience but was also short of money. 'That in black ink my love may still shine bright' (65). A Jesuitical equivocation allows the poet to signify by 'my love' either his beloved or an affection transferred to a less physical successor.

Some of the most wonderful love poems in the English language are therefore poems of deceit. Sent by the impecunious poet to his patron, assuring him of his devotion, they almost all contain a mental reservation. Sonnet 101 is crucial in the drama of the Sonnets:

O truant Muse, what shall be thy amends
For thy neglect of truth in beauty dyed?
Both truth and beauty on my love depends;
So dost thou too, and therein dignified.
Make answer, muse. Wilt thou not haply say
'Truth needs no colour with his colour fixed,
Beauty no pencil beauty's truth to lay,
But best is best if never intermixed'?
Because he needs no praise wilt thou be dumb?

> Excuse not silence so, for't lies in thee
> To make him much outlive a gilded tomb,
> And to be praised of ages yet to be.
>> Then do thy office, muse; I teach thee how
>> To make him seem long hence as he shows now.

Other sonnets have admitted slackness in performing the duty of sending sonnets (e.g., 76, 78, 100) but none is so candid as this. The great aim of the sonneteer being to locate truth within beauty, this is one of the points at which failure is admitted. The truth which has been celebrated is not genuine truth, but truth dyed in the beauty of the youth. That is, taking a hint from the dyer's hand in 111, it has been stained, contaminated, infected.[10] If the truth presented by the youth is a painted idol, so is the truth offered by poetry in celebration of the youth. The muse rightly protests that truth needs no colour — whether the false colours of the youth or the false colours of poetry. But in the couplet the poet callously applies the spurs to the reluctant muse. The muse is to be organised into providing an image of the youth ('make him seem') in which his radiant outside will be depicted rather than his true nature ('as he shows now').[11] It is in this way that the patron will 'outlive a gilded tomb'. The poet buries the corrupt young man in a tomb and builds a verse monument to an ideal:

> Thus have I had thee as a dream doth flatter:
> In sleep a king, but waking no such matter.

Sonnet 87 ('Farewell — thou art too dear for my possessing') is a violent envoy to the rival-poet series. The competition between eloquence and inarticulacy to provide the perfect ceremony of love's rite ends in saying good-bye to the young man. It was no more than a dream that he was the embodiment of what the poet's heart longed to embrace.

In *The Mutual Flame*, Wilson Knight said that 'the Sonnets record a progress through the bisexual adoration and integration to an eternal insight or intuition.'[12] It is no new thing to claim that the great celebratory poems which conclude the young-man sequence (e.g., 105, 107, 116, 123, 124) have their eyes fixed on something beyond the youth. 'Let not my love be called idolatry.' No indeed, for it is addressed 'to one, of one, still such, and ever so' (105) who is not incarnate in an English aristocratic playboy; rather 'a god in love, to whom I am confined' (110).[13]

> Then give me welcome, next my heaven the best,
> Even to thy pure and most most loving breast.   (110)

The poet can achieve honesty in his verse only by giving up the young man as the object of his verse, and the price to pay is the consequent dishonesty of pretending to continue to address his patron. In his fascinating no-nonsense study of Sonnet 29, John Barrell argued that the language of pure and refined love was so firmly established as the discourse of patronage that the poet who wished to express an authentic love for another person or for God was disabled by the contamination of the only language available.[14] But if poetry couldn't escape the routine uses and misuses of the language it employs we should never read it. By definition it decontaminates language. Shakespeare's Sonnets are a superb example of how tempting the tired conventions of discourse are, and how they may be transcended. Endlessly, Shakespeare, in the person of his creature-poet, shows his ability to bring vitality into a language which may well often be, as Barrell insists, a code for a purely economic relationship. But surely the master-stroke, in this drama of the Sonnets, is to make his poet pass off the most convincingly genuine expressions of authentic love as the discourse of patronage.

The happiness of shared love in the later young-man sonnets is depicted as a *redintegratio amoris* following mutual forgiveness in which the recognised faults of the one ransom the faults of the other (see especially 120). If the poet is speaking with a double tongue in his ecstatic celebration of love, it also has to be said that as with every single emotional and intellectual stance in the Sonnets, the reign of mutual forgiveness is very short. Pharisaical self-righteousness is a conspicuous feature of the dramatised poet. It is at its worst in the despicable attitude to the woman in the second series, but it is present also in the young-man series. Servile, obsequious, masochistic he may be in his relations with the young aristocrat, but, if he is constantly making allowances for him and forgiving him, it is from the standpoint of one who does not himself need forgiveness. His greatest fear seems to be that by overlooking the young man's indiscretions and sins, he should himself become corrupt. This high-minded mysophobia is quite abandoned in the 'return' sonnets, which depend upon the frank admission of fault — 'wretched errors' (119).

> Needs must I under my transgression bow,
> Unless my nerves were brass or hammered steel.   (120)

Yet by means of one of the most extraordinary of the many contradicting juxtapositions in the Sonnets, this humility and contrition is punctured with the arrogant god-like claim of 121: 'I am that I am.'

'Tis better to be vile than vile esteemed
When not to be receives reproach of being,
And the just pleasure lost, which is so deemed
Not by our feeling but by others' seeing.
For why should others' false adulterate eyes
Give salutation to my sportive blood?
Or on my frailties why are frailer spies,
Which in their wills count bad what I think good?
No, I am what I am, and they that level
At my abuses reckon up their own,
I may be straight, though they themselves be bevel;
By their rank thoughts my deeds must not be shown,
   Unless this general evil they maintain:
   All men are bad and in their badness reign.

It is difficult to see how one can give recognition to the greatness of this *unpleasant* sonnet unless one sees it in the dramatic mode; otherwise we shall find ourselves praising its angry pettiness as good in itself. In its lofty claim to righteousness, and in that righteousness a distinctiveness from other people, whom he despises, the sonnet does more than banish the Christian contrition of its predecessor. It gives to that contrition the feeling of the temporariness of a stance tried out in verse. The two sonnets 120 and 121 are therefore similar in relationship to 146 and 147; the sense that the religious submissiveness of 120 ('Poor soul, the centre of my sinful earth') is only a transient try-out is enforced by the shattering sequel in which the poet confesses that the fever of desire is incurable. Nothing that he can frame in writing satisfies the poet for more than a moment, and every repudiation is itself repudiated.

At the very highest point of his celebration of a love outgoing time and mortality, there is the insidious question whether this affirmation does not belong more to writing than to reality:

Love's not time's fool, though rosy lips and cheeks
Within his bending sickle's compass come;
Love alters not with his brief hours and weeks,
But bears it out even to the edge of doom.
   If this be error and upon me proved,
   I never writ, nor no man ever loved.   (116)

The fragility of the insights of 116 is less ambiguously and riddlingly expressed by the great weight of the sonnets to the dark woman which are still to come.

In the unstaged performance of the Sonnets, the reader is both actor and audience. The drama is there for every reader to see and share in, yet it is unborn because it has not come to the theatre. It is a drama in writing, not conveyed by the voices of actors, and that seems appropriate, because it is a drama about writing, about the failure of a writer to create himself, and balance his existence, through the medium of the pen. The protagonist in the drama, the poet, whose name like that of his creator is Will, is in a state of suspension, of unrealised, inchoate existence. His story is very gloomy, because something resembling honesty forces him to block every avenue by which he might escape into definition. There is a curious likeness between the text of the Sonnets and the manuscript of *Hamlet* — if we take that manuscript to be represented by the long 'good' Quarto of 1604. In that manuscript, Shakespeare shows Hamlet trying to create himself and find his being not by writing sonnets but in a course of action. The amplitude of his self-cancelling switches of moods and resolutions is much greater than in the shortened Folio version of the play — which may still be a longer text than any that was acted in Shakespeare's theatre. The theatre, perhaps, had to impose too much definiteness on what is essentially a study in indefiniteness. So there may be some advantages in not being born. The Sonnets rival *Hamlet* as a study in uncertainty and indefiniteness, and they might be said to be truer to their aim in that they are performed within the reader's mind and not on the stage.

Notes

1 'The Dramatic Technique of Shakespeare's Sonnets', *Essays in Criticism*, 3 (1953), pp. 152–64.
2 Oxford: Clarendon Press.
3 The idea that at least one sonnet was dramatic because it showed a speaker struggling with emotion as in a soliloquy was put forward by Richard Levin, 'Sonnet CXXIX as a "Dramatic" Poem', in *Shakespeare Quarterly*, 16 (1965), pp. 175–91.
4 See the excellent argument by Mark Kinkead-Weekes in *Samuel Richardson: Dramatic Novelist*, London: Methuen, 1973, ch. 10.
5 This essay is the resumption of an argument begun some years ago in a brief study of the sonnets to the dark woman in *Shakespeare and the Confines of Art* (1968). I suggested that the dark-woman sequence was 'a *dramatic* sequence in which the hero, a poet, restlessly turns to different poetic images of his own troubles'. None of them will serve. The Sonnets are 'shown to be separated from the life they pretend to

record'. Later post-structuralist approaches, by Joel Fineman in *Shakespeare's Perjured Eye* (1986) and by Howard Felperin in *Beyond Deconstruction* (1985), with their emphasis on the distance between rhetoric and persona on the one hand and lived life on the other, have offered unintended support to my argument.

6 See *Shakespeare and the Confines of Art*, p. 18.

7 *The Reader and Shakespeare's Young Man Sonnets*, London: Macmillan, 1981, pp. 121–4.

8 'What little life the poem has . . .'; 'Shakespeare may have written the poem for the sake of playing with words and constructions . . .' *Shakespeare's Sonnets*, New Haven & London: Yale University Press, 1977, p. 482.

9 The New Penguin edition of *The Sonnets and A Lover's Complaint*, 1986, p. 290.

10 See Geoffrey Hill's casual and inspired aside in *The Lords of Limit*, London: André Deutsch, 1984, p. 153, picked up by John Kerrigan, op. cit., p. 326.

11 See the valuable discussions of this sonnet by Hammond, p. 53, and Booth, ad loc.

12 London: Methuen, 1955, p. 104.

13 See further in my *Shakespeare: A Writer's Progress*, Oxford & New York: Oxford University Press, 1986, pp. 67–8.

14 *Poetry, Language and Politics*, Manchester: Manchester University Press, 1988, Ch. 1.

'SOFT, HERE FOLLOWS PROSE':
SHAKESPEARE'S STAGE DOCUMENTS

In what follows I shall be concerned primarily with those bits of paper that make an actual appearance as stage props in Shakespeare, not forgetting that we also often hear about *offstage* documents that figure significantly in the plays' action, such as the letters received by Cordelia, in *Lear* IV.iii.9–32, whose tearful reception of them is so movingly reported (in Q), or the letter substituted by Hamlet, on board ship, for Claudius' commission to England, ordering the deaths of Rosencrantz and Guildenstern, which Hamlet describes with such gusto to Horatio.

Setting aside, however, such documents, referred to but not seen, we find a considerable number (about eighty by my rough count) which appear as props but instead of being read out are merely pointed to or brandished for some purpose, or have their contents summarised or paraphrased. These often generate intense reactions among the characters involved. For instance, the letter addressed to Julia by Proteus in *TGV* I.ii.34–126, which Julia at first refuses to receive, commands Lucetta to remove, then retrieves from the floor where it has dropped, then tears to pieces, and at length reassembles as well as she can, vocalising only the address and the salutation. In *3 Henry VI* the letters received by Lewis, Margaret, and Warwick, during Warwick's visit to the French court, stir a variety of outraged and triumphant reactions in their recipients. In *Much Ado*, the final resolution of the prickly relations between Beatrice and Benedick hinges on 'papers' containing love sonnets that reveal their sentiments towards each other before all the company and thus constitute an irrevocable commitment. In *Richard III*, the Scrivener, who has drawn up the indictment of Hastings, denounces it as a fraud while in the very act of posting it; in the deposition scene of *Richard II*, Richard is pressed by Northumberland to sign the articles of accusation held before him; in *Julius Caesar*, Caesar's will, flourished before the people in the Forum, is summarised but not read, by Mark Antony. I find only one play in the canon — *The Two Noble Kinsmen* — in which no stage document is either brought forth or alluded to as playing a role in the drama.

To cite even these few examples is to insist on what may need little emphasis, Shakespeare's interest in the written as well as the spoken word. The action of his plays swarms with writings, and especially with epistles. Characters communicate with each other relentlessly through the post, and the post becomes in its turn a prime means of revelation, reversal, and surprise. 'Enter Octavius reading a letter' (*Ant* I.iv.1 SD), or 'Enter the King reading of a letter, at one door' (*Per* II.v.1 SD), or 'Enter Pisanio reading of a letter' (*Cym* III.ii.1 SD), or 'Enter a Messenger with letters' (*Ham* IV.vii.36) (Evans, 1974) — such directions become so habitual we scarcely notice them.

The characters display a marked penchant for documenting their activities. When Octavius wishes to disclaim responsibility for the conflict between himself and Antony, he invites the Egyptian messenger into his tent, in order to show 'How hardly I was drawn into this war, / How calm and gentle I proceeded still / In all my writings' (*Ant* V.i.74-6). They are forever handing each other written instructions, written notations, written memoranda of various sorts. Shakespeare, one suspects, would heartily agree with Jacques Derrida on one point: speech enjoys no mystical primacy or ontological priority over writing, but has co-existed with it as far back and as far wide as it is possible to track either. Certainly he keeps us — even as spectators — in a world in which writings have a continuing and commanding importance, are constantly being appealed to, commented on, argued over, approved, or repudiated. It is only the illiterate rebel Jack Cade who hangs the clerk who can write his name, and only the uncivilised Caliban who plots to destroy Prospero's books.

Documents may conflict with or compete with one another, as when Caesar holds both Artemidorus' petition and Decius Brutus' letter in his hands and must choose which of them to look at first, which to set aside. Needless to say, for the best of reasons he makes the wrong choice. Or they can, on occasion, prove incriminating: Goneril's letter to Edmund exposes her plot to get rid of Albany, and the inventory of Wolsey's wealth and his letter to the Pope precipitate his downfall. But Shakespeare nowhere implies the view of writing attributed by Derrida to Saussure, Levi-Strauss, and Rousseau — that it is something derivative, parasitic, and merely 'supplementary' to speech, and as such a degenerate and essentially corrupt form of language. It is capable of being abused, but then so is spoken language, as plays such as *Much Ado about Nothing, Othello* and others amply declare. It merely forms one vital strand in the continuous tissue of discourse of which the plays are composed.

A document is what Derrida would call a trace, a palpable residue partaking of the substantial existence of its writer. Hence no doubt the excitement with which the existence of a mere signature by someone who counts as much in the world as Shakespeare can be greeted; it takes on almost the character of a sacred relic, like the bones of a saint. And hence perhaps the physicality with which in the plays a document is often treated, as in the case of Julia, tearing her letter, only to reassemble it; Titus, affixing letters to arrows and shooting them up to the gods for justice; Orlando, hanging his verses on trees in Arden; Troilus, ripping up the letter from Cressida after her betrayal; or Goneril, vainly seeking to snatch her note to Edmund as Albany holds it up before her.

We are frequently reminded of the materiality of letters also when their seals are broken: opening them becomes either an act of intimate proprietorship or an invasion of privacy. As the Princess directs Boyet to read Armado's letter, she tells him to 'Break the neck of the wax' (*LLL* IV.i.59) — a fierce way of putting it. The seal itself becomes a kind of character, an intermediary whose substance, if violated, needs to be placated. Malvolio notices that the wax on his letter carries 'the impressure' of '[Olivia's] Lucrece, with which she uses to seal' (*TN* II.v.92-3). Thinking the letter meant for him, he addresses the intermediary with courtly politeness, 'By your leave, wax' (91-2). Hamlet, Edgar, and Imogen, likewise, each in their turn apologise for breaking the seal on correspondence, the first two with respect to letters not directed to them.

Certainly there is a paradox in the fact that Shakespeare, so notoriously indifferent to the printing of his plays, and apparently so unconcerned about writing letters — or, if he did write them, so careless about preserving them or those he may have received from others — should nevertheless in his plays be so endlessly and inventively preoccupied with written communication of all kinds, have worked it so profoundly into the blood and bone of his plots. Perhaps we may say about this paradox what we may also say of his lifelong fixation on the stage and on acting. Just as in this latter instance Shakespeare never loses sight of the material conditions of his art — the physical playing space, the live actors who inhabit it, the onlookers in the pit, and the hazards of performance — so he never loses sight either of the material conditions of composition, of ink and paper, wax and parchment, the marks on the page that must serve as the vehicle without which his plays cannot be transmitted to the theatre in the first place. Like his creation Armado he is intensely aware of the fact that his 'snow-white pen' is depositing tracks of 'ebon-coloured ink' on the page before him (*LLL* I.i.242-3). Not for nothing does the funeral monument in Trinity Church,

Stratford-upon-Avon, show him with a quill pen in his right hand and a
sheet of paper under his left.

One feature of a letter that differentiates it from an oral report is the
fact that it can be read only by the literate, by one who knows what the
system of signs on the paper means. Capulet's servant must appeal to
Romeo to read out the guest list for the ball, and Timon's Page must beg
Apemantus to inform him who is meant by the superscription of the
letters he carries. Moreover, since a letter does constitute a relic of its
writer, its authenticity may be subject to challenge and require
verification; the writer's identity may need to be established. Deception
is always possible, as in *Twelfth Night*, where Maria forges Olivia's
hand, knowing that her script resembles Olivia's so closely that 'on a
forgotten matter we can hardly make distinction of our hands'
(II.iii.160–1), a similarity that becomes the basis for the prank played
on Malvolio.

Letters are frequently interrogated as to the validity of their purported
signatures — so with Hamlet's letter to Claudius, Duke Vincentio's
letter (conveniently carried in his pocket) concerning his own imminent
return, Edmund's forged letter to Gloucester, alleged to have come
from Edgar, Posthumus' letter to Pisanio, and the letters of Antigonus
found with the infant Perdita, all of them truly or falsely said to be in
the 'hand' or 'character' of the supposed writer.

Turning to those documents read aloud on stage, in part or in whole:
out of a rough total of sixty-seven I count forty in prose and twenty-
seven in verse. These figures confirm a more casual impression that
most stage documents we hear are in prose. Of the prose documents,
twenty-six turn out to be letters, and fourteen documents of other sorts
— oracles, proclamations, petitions, instructions, inventories, etc. Of
the remainder, in verse, eighteen are letters and nine are epitaphs,
conjurations, inscriptions, and the like. Among the verse letters
themselves, two-thirds are love letters, compared to only about a fifth of
those in prose, this fifth itself being mostly clownish, like Armado's
letter to Jaquenetta, Falstaff's to Mistress Page, and Maria's forged
billet-doux from Olivia to Malvolio.

With the exception of love letters, then, the choice of prose or verse
seems often to be dictated more by momentary convenience than settled
policy, and Shakespeare tends to be casual about the distinction. In *All's
Well*, Bertram's letter to Helena, in which he specifies the impossible
tasks she must perform if she hopes to make him her husband, is in

prose, yet when a fragment from it is quoted in the final scene, again by Helena, it has been altered so as to conform metrically to the rest of the speech, in verse. Shakespeare, in short, has not scrupled to tamper with the wording of the phrase in order to bring it into conformity with its rhythmic context, though earlier he had seemed to be doing the opposite, casting the letter in prose in order to *distinguish* it from its context.

Cymbeline contains a more puzzling case. Pisanio, perusing the order from Posthumus commanding him to kill Imogen, reads aloud a few phrases from it, in verse. But when Imogen herself shortly reads the whole letter through, in prose, the part corresponding to that quoted by Pisanio is worded quite differently. Here we have first the fragment fitted into a verse context and then the complete text of the letter set in prose so that it contrasts rhythmically with the surrounding verse. In short, though the prose or verse of a letter will normally accord with that of its immediate metrical milieu, this cannot be taken as a rule of thumb. The markedly altered wording of the extract from Posthumus' epistle also suggests that Shakespeare is not concerned about meticulous quotation; he is quite ready to rewrite a passage in order to include information missing from the 'original' version, not bothering then to redo the original so as to make it conform to the 'revised' version.

Sometimes stage documents will ape legal or official jargon, either straightforwardly (as when Gloucester reads out the articles of contracted peace in *2 Henry VI*) or jocosely (as in Launce's oafish catalogue of his mistress's faults and virtues). One has the impression that by and large the stage letters are meant to provide a plausible approximation of their live counterparts, whether straightforwardly or parodistically. Angel Day's treatise on letter-writing, *The English Secretary*, supplies directions on how to address a variety of possible recipients, according to their rank and status: 'To the most reuerend Father in God, the L. Archbishop of Canterburie, or York, Primate of England, and Metropolitane his verie good grace. . . . To the high and mightie Prince, L. Duke of B. his most noble grace', etc. Shakespearian superscriptions often have a touch of parody about them, as in Armado's letter to the King: '"Great deputy, the welkin's vicegerent, and sole dominator of Navarre, my soul's earth's god, and body's fost'ring patron"' (*LLL* I.i.219–21). Hamlet addresses his missive to Ophelia with elaborate mock-courtesy, '"To the celestial and my soul's idol, the most beautified Ophelia"' (II.ii.110), and his note to the sovereign majesty of Denmark in terms that could hardly be more bitingly ironic: '"High and mighty"' (IV.vii.42).

At the same time, most of Shakespeare's stage documents display a tightness, a succinctness, a kind of coiled power, rarely found in comparable documents of the period. Of the two Shakespearian proclamations, that read out in *1 Henry VI* at the order of the Mayor of London, to quell the riot between the Duke of Gloucester's and the Cardinal of Winchester's men, declares, 'All manner of men assembled here in arms this day against God's peace and the King's, we charge and command you, in his Highness' name, to repair to your several dwelling-places, and not to wear, handle, or use any sword, weapon, or dagger, henceforward, upon pain of death' (I.iii.74–9). There is nothing unusual in this, and it may perhaps correspond fairly closely to historical instances of its kind, but among surviving proclamations of the sixteenth and early seventeenth centuries that resemble it in subject-matter, we usually find something more spun out and bureaucratic, something lingered over as though the proclaimer is reluctant to let the subject drop. Here is the start of the king's proclamation of 30 May 1607, which also has to do with unlawful assemblies, or, more specifically, with the 'suppressing of persons riotously assembled for the laying open of Inclosures'. It begins this way:

WHEREAS some of the meaner sort of our people did of late assemble themselves in riotous and tumultuous maner within our Countie of Northampton, sometimes in the night, and sometimes in the day, under pretence of laying open enclosed grounds of late yeeres taken in, to their dammage, as they say; The repressing whereof we did first referre only to the due course of Justice, and the ordinary proceedings of the Commissioners of the Peace, and other our Ministers in such cases: Forasmuch as Wee have perceived since, that lenitie hath bred in them, rather encouragement then obedience, and that they have presumed to gather themselves in greater multitudes, as well in that Countie, as in some others adjoyning, We find it now very necessary to use sharper remedies.

Wherefore, We will and command all Lieutenants, deputy Lieutenants, Sheriffs, Justices of Peace, Maiors, Bailiffes, Head-boroughs, Constables, and all other our Officers and Ministers to whom it may appertaine, if the said persons shall continue so assembled, after Proclamation made, or any such new Assemblies bee gathered in those, or any other parts of our Realme, immediatly to suppresse them by whatsoever meanes they may, be it by force of Armes, if admonitions and other lawfull meanes doe not serve to reduce them to their dueties. (Larkin & Hughes, 1973, vol. 1, pp. 152–3.)

And more, much more to the same effect. To be sure, the king's proclamation deals with a chronic national problem, the mayor's proclamation in *1 Henry VI* with an isolated local flare-up, and behind the king's proclamation as behind hundreds of other actual documents from the period there lie political necessities, or considerations of law or ceremony, which plainly exert a pressure for expansiveness and completeness that are lacking in their dramatic counterparts — all Shakespeare need do, essentially, is create a sufficiently convincing theatrical illusion — yet what strikes me at least about the Shakespearian proclamation is its conciseness and pointedness, its absence of waste words and rhetorical flourishes. It contains only the plainest, simplest announcement of the order, with just enough legal phrases — 'charge and command', 'wear, handle, or use', 'sword, weapon, or dagger', etc. — to make it sound official.

As for the proclamation of a holiday on Cyprus, to celebrate Othello's wedding, that is even more noteworthy, both for its subject-matter and its tone. Virtually all Elizabethan and Jacobean royal proclamations deal in restraints, in restrictions, prohibitions, and negative injunctions. They regulate the price of commodities such as wool, they specify the length of rapiers, they prohibit the melting down of coin, they outlaw seditious rumours, they ban controversies in religion, they order foreigners to leave England or English gentlemen to return to their country houses, they forbid preaching without licence, or the eating of meat in Lent, or the performing of unlicensed plays, or the use of pistols, or the export of armour to Russia, and the like. And they threaten stiff penalties, including death, for infringement. Except for an occasional 'licence' or 'injunction', never, so far as I have been able to discover, do they invite citizens to engage in public revelry; never do they suggest a setting aside of restrictions. Indeed, the only proclamations that deal with pastimes at all concern the queen's recreations, or the king's, and have to do with facilitating the royal hunt. They say nothing about the disports of the common people, to which they are plainly indifferent. (Larkin & Hughes 1973; Youngs 1976; Heinze 1976.)

As for the so-called *Book of Sports* issued by James VI & I in 1618, endorsing 'lawful' village games on Sundays after proper church-going, that seems to have sprung more from political motives — from a desire to rebuke militant Puritan magistrates and unruly 'Popish Recusants', to keep people from the ale-benches and the conventicles, and to toughen them physically in case they are needed to fight the king's wars — than from any generous or spontaneous wish to encourage popular diversions. (Govett 1890, pp. 27–45; Hill 1964, pp. 194–5; Brailsford 1969, pp. 101–2.) Like the proclamation against unlawful assemblies cited above, the *Book of Sports* spells out its decrees with much amplitude of historical reference and many a tedious 'whereas', with a leisure — doubtless determined by the conventions of the form — that Shakespeare's purpose could not have tolerated even if he had been disposed to adopt it as model.

Most of Shakespeare's documents occur in highly special dramatic contexts that have no precise counterpart in actual historical situations. But for a rough parallel, we might compare the surviving letter from Francis Tresham, warning Lord Mounteagle about the Gunpowder Plot, with Artemidorus' petition, in *Julius Caesar*, alerting Caesar to the conspiracy against him. Young Tresham, who had become, two weeks earlier, 'the last & most reluctant member of the gunpowder conspiracy', sent the following unsigned note to Mounteagle:

> My Lord, Out of the love I beare to some of your friends, I have a care of your preservation. Therefore I would advise you, as you tender your life, to devise some excuse to shift off your attendance at this Parliament. For God and man have concurred to punish the wickedness of this Time. And thinke not slightly of this Advertisement, but retire your selfe into your Countrey, where you may expect the event in safetie. For though there be no apparence of any stirre, yet I say, they shall receive a terrible Blow this Parliament, and yet they shall not see who hurts them. This counsell is not to be contemned, because it may doe you good, and can doe you no harme; for the danger is past so soone as you have burnt the Letter. And I hope God will give you the grace to make good use of it: To whose holy protection I commend you. (Akrigg 1962, pp. 72–3.)

Apart from the fact that this is an actual letter, we notice that despite its relative brevity, it is marked by a kind of wavering prolixity; it is filled with protestations of good will and concern for Mounteagle, and with intimations of urgency, but also it is deliberately and, as it would seem, fearfully vague. Trying to convey a sense of impending danger to an unsuspecting person, Tresham is attempting to do so while at the same time implicitly endorsing the principle behind the expected 'Blow' ('God and man have concurred to punish the wickedness of this Time'), hence disclosing as little as possible about the nature of the threat other than what is needed to spur Mounteagle to look to his own safety.

Shakespeare's stage documents rarely if ever reflect this degree of ambivalence; clarity in dramatic structure takes precedence over complexity of utterance. Tresham's letter reflects not only an actual situation but a dangerous one, imposing constraints on its writer that Shakespeare, aiming solely at theatrical effectiveness, did not need to bother with. Artemidorus' 'paper', read out to us, though not to its destined recipient, illustrates the difference sharply:

> 'Caesar, beware of Brutus. Take heed of Cassius. Come not near Casca. Have an eye to Cinna. Trust not Trebonius. Mark well Metellus Cimber, Decius Brutus loves thee not. Thou hast wronged Caius Ligarius. There is but one mind in all these men, and it is bent against Caesar. If thou beest not immortal, look about you. Security gives way to conspiracy. The mighty gods defend thee!
> Thy lover,
> Artemidorus'   (*JC* II.iii.1–10)

This petition, unlike Tresham's, is as sharp and cutting as a set of blades. Almost every phrase proleptically plunges a sword into Caesar's body by naming a trusted associate who stands ready to betray him. The language is drastically compressed: 'If thou beest not immortal, look about you. Security gives way to conspiracy.' 'Overconfidence', warns this last clause, or 'foolish unsuspectingness', both 'leaves the way open for' and 'will be overcome by' conspiracy.

Generalising, we can say that Shakespeare's letters, especially the prose letters, are nearly always notable for their incisiveness and brevity. Exceptions occur only when satirised characters, such as Don Armado or Falstaff, are being ridiculed for their stylistic extravagance. Serious letters are normally pared to the bone. So Antonio, in Venice, writing to Bassanio, in Belmont:

> 'Sweet Bassanio, my ships have all miscarried, my creditors grow cruel, my estate is very low, my bond to the Jew is forfeit; and since in paying it, it is impossible I should live, all debts are cleared between you and I, if I might but see you at my death. Notwithstanding, use your pleasure. If your love do not persuade you to come, let not my letter.'   (*MV* III.ii.314–22)

Alongside this laconic missive we may set an earlier epistle from Marlowe's *Edward II*, in which the king's emissary, the Frenchman Levune, briefs his master on recent events in France:

> My dutie to your honor praemised, &c. I haue according to instructions in that behalfe, dealt with the king of Fraunce his

lords, and effected, that the Queene all discontented and dis-
comforted, is gone, whither if you aske, with sir *Iohn of Henolt*,
brother to the Marquesse, into Flaunders: with them are gone lord
Edmund, and the lord *Mortimer*, hauing in their company diuers of
your nation, and others, and as constant report goeth, they intend
to giue king *Edward* battell in England sooner then he can looke for
them: this is all the news of import.

> *Your honors in all seruice*, Levune.

(Marlowe, 1925, 11. 1723–32)

This differs from Antonio's letter in that it rehearses tidings we already
possess, from the events of the very preceding scene. Edward may need
the information but we, the theatre audience, do not, so that dramatically
speaking it is redundant. At the same time Levune's implied boast that
he has effected the desired breach between Queen Isabel and the French
king is an irrelevancy the play can do without, Levune being a marginal
character whose fate does not concern us.

Antonio's letter, on the other hand, supplies us with vital intelligence.
The last we heard, in a colloquy between Shylock and Tubal, was the
rumour that his ships had miscarried, and that if it proved true, Shylock
was fully expecting to exact the penalty. Now we learn, from Antonio
himself, that he is in prison, care-worn and resigned, wishing only to
see Bassanio before he dies. Apart from the anaphora on 'my', the style
of the letter is as stripped down as simplifying rhetoric can make it. As
in the case of Artemidorus' petition, it is built mainly on a series of terse
parallel clauses: 'my ships have all miscarried, my creditors grow cruel,
my estate is very low, my bond to the Jew is forfeit'. It acquaints us both
with Antonio's present plight and with his deepening despondency, and
does so with an absence of anything resembling verbal bedizenment.

Something similar might be said of Bertram's letter to his mother
following his departure for Florence:

> 'I have sent you a daughter-in-law. She hath recovered the King
> and undone me. I have wedded her, not bedded her, and sworn to
> make the "not" eternal. You shall hear I am run away; know it
> before the report come. If there be breadth enough in the world I
> will hold a long distance. My duty to you.
> Your unfortunate son, Bertram.'   (*All's Well* III.ii.19–27)

Unlike Antonio's letter, this cannot be said to provide us with new
facts. But it does illuminate Bertram's inner state more piercingly. Like
Antonio's letter, it passes over the kind of explanatory or particularising

detail we would expect in an actual letter, but which a theatre audience already possesses. And as Antonio's letter brings his near-suicidal depression vividly before us, so Bertram's letter conveys even more stingingly than his behaviour at court the intensity of his detestation of his marriage. It is marked by unpleasant wordplay — 'She hath recovered the King and undone me. I have wedded her, not bedded her', 'sworn to make the "not" [homophonous with "knot"] eternal', etc. — as well as by a tinge of petulant schoolboyishness ('I am run away') and more than a touch of self-pity ('undone me', 'Your unfortunate son'). We notice too the churlish absence of any salutation or 'superscript' to his mother that would correspond to Antonio's 'Sweet Bassanio'.

The even more curt letter to Helena herself spells out the fantastic tasks she must perform if she hopes to claim him:

> 'When thou canst get the ring upon my finger, which never shall come off, and show me a child begotten of thy body that I am father to, then call me husband; but in such a "then" I write a "never".'
> (*All's Well* III.ii.57–60)

A moment later, Helena, continuing, reads the final cruel touch: '"Till I have no wife, I have nothing in France."' (74–5) The thought has again been strenuously boiled down, this time almost to a single periodic sentence, marked, or, as we may think, disfigured, by wordplay: 'in such a "then" I write a "never"' — 'write' here being a far stronger term than 'say' or 'speak', with the force of 'decree', 'ordain', or 'solemnly record', and used punningly in both metaphoric and literal senses, since Bertram is actually writing the note as he writes the word 'write'. In both instances, then, the letter serves as index to the mood and 'character' of its composer — pained, weary, and defeated in the one case, cold, hostile, and defiant in the other; in the one case unable to muster many words to adorn the harsh facts, in the other deliberately administering snubs by way of 'witty' brevity, and as conspicuously bent on rejecting the claim of the marital link as the first is on reaffirming the friendship bond.

In the plays of Ben Jonson also we sometimes find letters used as key elements, but Jonson customarily turns these into full-scale revelations of their writers. The letter sent by Lorenzo Jr.'s scapegrace companion in *Every Man In His Humour* brilliantly conveys the madcap trying to lure his friend to town for the day, and is marked by a kind of overflow of characterising detail, meant to be pungent and pleasurable in its own right.

With *Sejanus*, in an audacious stroke, Jonson makes the climax of the entire action turn on the reading of a letter. Starting from the recorded fact that Tiberius, living on Capri, contrived Sejanus's downfall by means of a long, ambiguous, but ultimately devastating message to the Senate, accusing his favourite of treason, with the result that Sejanus was arrested, dragged off, and executed within minutes — starting from this historical datum Jonson proceeds to imagine the letter itself and its reception as it is read out in the Senate — the hesitations and windings with which Tiberius manages to accuse and ensnare his victim while seeming to defend him, the bewildered reaction of the Senators as they struggle to make out their Emperor's drift, until at last, grasping his malign purpose, they hasten to heap insults of their own on the hated favourite to whom they have so recently toadied.

In both instances Jonson's method makes the letter the vehicle of a virtuoso piece of characterisation, much as he would do with a major speech. Shakespeare's procedure is the reverse. He severely excludes from his stage letters the very copiousness and flow of fancy with which he is so free in passages of dialogue. For a suggestive comparison we may look at one of the sample letters in *The English Secretary*. Day's purpose is to offer lessons in correct letter-writing, together with a plentiful supply of model epistles suited to various occasions. He works within a long tradition, going back to antiquity, which viewed letter-writing as a branch of rhetoric, and assumed that competence in the one enterprise meant following the rules and employing the strategies of the other. It assumed that letters should utilise all the devices of oratory, and it tended to ignore bare narration, description, or the reporting of objective fact. (See Ong 1971, pp. 23–47.)

Day offers the following 'epistle commendatorie' as a suitable letter of introduction:

> It may please your Lordship, This Gentleman the bearer hereof, with whom a long time I haue beene acquainted, and of his qualities and good behauiour haue had sounde and large experiment, hauing beene a good time a sutor vnto mee, to mooue his preferment vnto your Lordships seruice: I haue nowe at the last condiscended vnto, aswell for that I know your Lordship to be now presentlie disfurnished of such a one, as also that there shall hardlie be preferred vpon a sudden any one so meete as himselfe to supplie that place. And thus much by your pardo*n* and allowance dare I assure vnto you, *tha*t if it may please you in credit of my simple knowledge and opinio*n* to imploy him, you shal find that

besides he is by pare*n*tage discended from such, as of whome I
knowe your Lordship will verie well accompt of, hee is also learned,
discreete, sober, wise, and moderate in all his actions, of great
secrecie and most assured trust, gouerned in all companies
accordinglie: finallie, a man so meete, and to this present turne so
apt and necessarie, as I cannot easilie imagine howe you may be
serued better. Pleaseth your L. the rather for the great good will I
beare him, and humble duetie I owe vnto you, to accepte, imploie,
and accompt of him, I nothing doubt but your L. hauing by such
means giuen credit to my choice, shall finde him such, as for whose
good seruice, you shall haue further occasion to thinke well of mee
for him. Whereof nothing doubting, I doe refer both him and my
selfe in all humblenesse to your best and most fauorable opinion,
from my house in B. this of, &c.   (Day 1599, Sig. O3v)

This, it may be added, with all its irritating prolixities and redundancies,
its tiresome beating of the air, nevertheless belongs among the shorter
letters in Day's collection. And it is clear that a certain degree of
copiousness, of free-flowing eloquence, is precisely one of its aims. To
cite Frank Whigham in a similar connection, the letter-writer in question
'Seems to have seen here an occasion for the conspicuous expenditure
of words' (Whigham 1981, p. 868).

Shakespeare proceeds differently. Here is Dr Bellario, introducing a
young protégé of his to the Duke of Venice:

'Your grace shall understand that at the receipt of your letter I am
very sick, but in the instant that your messenger came, in loving
visitation was with me a young doctor of Rome; his name is
Balthasar. I acquainted him with the cause in controversy between
the Jew and Antonio, the merchant. We turn'd o'er many books
together. He is furnished with my opinion which, bettered with his
own learning — the greatness whereof I cannot enough commend
— comes with him at my importunity to fill up your grace's request
in my stead. I beseech you let his lack of years be no impediment to
let him lack a reverend estimation, for I never knew so young a
body with so old a head. I leave him to your gracious acceptance,
whose trial shall better publish his commendation.'

(*MV* IV.i.149–63)

Again we are struck, surely, by the austerity with which our master of
copia, our word-spinner *par excellence*, our immortal phrase-maker and

inexhaustible fount of imagery and analogy, here represses all
luxuriance, sticks severely to business and makes the letter interesting
without cutting a single rhetorical caper or extending it a jot past the
need of its basic purpose. One way he keeps it interesting is by making it
mysterious. We never learn what went on between Portia and Dr
Bellario. While seeming to tell everything, Shakespeare seems purposely
to be keeping us in the dark, not allowing us to suppose that we can ever
know the full history even in such an apparently simple situation.
Certainly he seems deliberately to be flouting the precepts of the letter-
writing manuals, ignoring the prescribed adherence to oratorical form,
dispensing with rhetorical expansiveness or anything resembling artful
persuasion.

The same is even more strikingly true if we compare the indictment
of Hermione, in *The Winter's Tale*, with any of a number of surviving
indictments from the same period in which high-ranking personages are
arraigned on comparable charges. Here, to begin with, is the indictment
of Hermione herself, read by an officer of the court:

> Hermione, queen to the worthy Leontes, King of Sicilia, thou art
> here accused and arraigned of high treason in committing adultery
> with Polixenes, King of Bohemia, and conspiring with Camillo to
> take away the life of our sovereign lord the King, thy royal husband;
> the pretence whereof being by circumstances partly laid open,
> thou, Hermione, contrary to the faith and allegiance of a true
> subject, didst counsel and aid them for their better safety to fly
> away by night.   (III.ii.12–20)

And here, for a first comparison, is the opening sentence only, which is
also the opening paragraph, of the indictment of Thomas Howard,
Duke of Norfolk, for his part in the 1571 rebellion against the crown:

> THE Jury present and say, in behalf of our Lady the Queen, That
> *Thomas* Duke of *Norfolk*, late of *Remming-Hall* in the County of
> *Norfolk*, as a false Traitor against the most Illustrious and Christian
> Princess *Elizabeth*, Queen of *England, France*, and *Ireland*,
> Defender of the Faith, *&c.* and his Sovereign Lady, not having the
> Fear of God in his Heart, nor weighing his due Allegiance, but
> seduc'd by the Instigation of the Devil, contrary to that cordial
> Affection and bounden Duty that true and faithful Subjects of our
> fair Lady the Queen do bear, and of right ought to bear towards our
> said Lady the Queen; and intending to cut off and destroy the said
> Queen *Elizabeth*, the 22d day of *September*, in the 11th year of the
> Reign of our said Sovereign Lady Queen *Elizabeth*, and divers

other Days and Times before and after, at the *Charter-House* in the
County of *Middlesex*, hath falsely, maliciously, and traitorously
conspired, imagin'd and gone about, not only to deprive, depose,
and cast out the said Queen, his Sovereign Lady, from her Royal
Dignity, Title, Power, and Government of her Kingdom of *England*;
but, also to bring about and compass the Death and final
Destruction of our said Sovereign Lady the Queen, and to make
and raise Sedition in the said Kingdom of *England*, and to spread a
miserable Civil War amongst the said Subjects of our said Lady the
Queen, and to procure and make an Insurrection and Rebellion
against our said Lady the Queen, his supreme and natural Lady;
and so to make public War within the Realme of *England*, contrary
to our said Lady the Queen, and the Government of her said
Kingdom, and to endeavour a Change and Alteration of the sincere
Worship of God, well and religiously establish'd in the said
Kingdom; and also totally to subvert and destroy the whole
Constitution of the said State, so happily instituted and ordain'd in
all its Parts; with divers Aliens and Foreigners, not the Subjects of
our said Lady the Queen, hostilely to invade the said Kingdom of
England, and to make cruel War against our said Lady the Queen
and her Dominions.   (*State Trials*, 1776, vol. 1, cols 83–4)

This endless sentence, with its rhetorical excesses, its absurd insistence
on attributing wicked motives to the defendant in every phrase and
every passing epithet, is only the first of four lengthy paragraphs. For
excess of a different kind we may look at the first paragraphs of the less
emotionally high-pitched indictment of Sir Walter Raleigh in 1603:

THAT he did conspire, and go about to deprive the King of his
Government, to raise up Sedition within the Realm; to alter
Religion, to bring in the Roman Superstition, and to procure
foreign Enemies to invade the Kingdom. That the Lord *Cobham*,
the 9th of *June* last, did meet with the said Sir *Walter Raleigh* in
Durham-House, in the Parish of *St Martin-in-the-Fields*, and then
and there had Conference with him, how to advance *Arabella
Stuart* to the Crown and Royal Throne of this Kingdom; and that
then and there it was agreed, that *Cobham* should treat with
Aremberg, Embassador from the Archduke of *Austria*, to obtain of
him 600,000 Crowns, to bring to pass their intended Treason. It
was agreed that *Cobham* should go to the Archduke *Albert*, to
procure him to advance the pretended Title of *Arabella*: from
thence knowing that *Albert* had not sufficient means to maintain

his own Army in the *Low Countries, Cobham* should go to *Spain* to procure the King to assist and further her pretended Title.

It was agreed, the better to effect all this Conspiracy, that *Arabella* should write three Letters, one to the Archduke, another to the King of *Spain*, and a third to the Duke of *Savoy*; and promise three things:

First, to establish a firm peace between *England* and *Spain*.

Secondly, to tolerate the Popish and Roman Superstition.

Thirdly, to be ruled by them in contracting of her Marriage.

(*State Trials*, 1, cols 212–13)

So much forms roughly the first quarter of the accusation. Here, instead of the overheated and inflammatory rhetoric of the Norfolk indictment, we find an indictment that consists chiefly of a minute spelling out of the alleged crime, filled with the particulars of secret meetings between conspirators, supposed locations and dates, purported quotations of what the suspects said to each other on those occasions, imputations of sinister purpose, and so forth. The Norfolk indictment buries the accused under a mass of injurious epithets, this second under a mountain of evidentiary detail. Neither, it is safe to say, would pass muster as a proper 'indictment' in any court of law in the English-speaking world today. Shakespeare, while exercising the utmost dramatic economy in his version of the basic formula, condensing it to a bare handful of the key points in the charge, manages to imply as stinging an attack on official injustice as we could possibly infer either from the passionate outpouring of invective against the wretched Norfolk or the elaborately trumped-up bill of particulars mustered against Raleigh.

To sum up, then: Shakespeare places a quite extraordinary reliance on *writings* in his plays, even where it almost seems as though he is dragging them in, looking for excuses to insert them. He weaves them deeply and inextricably into the verbal texture of the plays, whether in documents we actually see or those we only hear about, whether they are read out word for word or merely paraphrased, so that graphic communication becomes as natural and inevitable and indispensable a part of the verbal medium as its vocal counterpart. Perhaps we may trace this impulse in part to the fact that Shakespeare himself, like many of his contemporaries, seems to have lived in a whirl of documents. Along with his father and at least one daughter he found himself throughout his life repeatedly enmeshed in lawsuits, as well as in business transactions and Stratfordian politics, which required, and received, the fixity of scribal representation. And it is possible to imagine that as a result of living in such a world he instinctively tended to reproduce this feature of it, at least, in his plays.

Where his own invented documents contain prose, Shakespeare handles that prose with a wiry minimalism that bears little resemblance either to the songful lyricism of his earlier verse or the passionate complexities of the later. This would apply — except for their high density of wordplay — to such documents written in his own behalf as the dedications to *Venus & Adonis* and *The Rape of Lucrece*. Here too he seems deliberately to aim at effects of compression, and to shun all semblance of copious fluency. It seems at times almost as though he is consciously rebuking, by his own practice, the tendentiousness, the effusiveness, the self-indulgence and effective hypocrisy of most familiar varieties of prose — of letters, dedications, proclamations, petitions, indictments, ceremonial announcements of all sorts. If he is not doing so by providing lessons in restraint, he is doing so by way of parody, which comes to the same thing. Armado's letters to the king and to Jaquenetta, Falstaff's letter to Mistresses Ford and Page, brilliantly illustrate how *not* to utilise the implements of writing.

As for their effect on the dramatic context, most stage documents form a sharp contrast to their verbal surroundings. They alter the pace, they arrest our attention in unforeseen ways, and propel the narrative strongly forward, even as they more fully unfold the nature — the 'character' — of their writers. They endlessly activate and enliven the verbal domain of the plays. And so they end by making a major contribution of their own to the seemingly unending richness of the Shakespearian linguistic world.

References

Akrigg, G. P. V. (1962) *Jacobean Pageant, or The Court of King James I*, Cambridge, Mass.: Harvard University Press.

Brailsford, Dennis (1969) *Sport and Society, Elizabeth to Anne*, London: Routledge & Kegan Paul.

Day, Angel (enlarged edn., 1599), *The English Secretary or Methode of Writing of Epistles and Letters*, etc. London: C. Burbie.

Evans, G. Blakemore, H. Levin, A. Barton, F. Kermode, H. Smith, M. Edel, C. Shattuck (eds) (1974) *The Riverside Shakespeare*, Boston: Houghton Mifflin.

Govett, L. A. (1890), *The King's Book of Sports: A History of the*

Declarations of King James I and King Charles I as to the Use of Lawful Sports on Sundays, London: Elliot Stock.

Heinze, R. W. (1976) *The Proclamations of the Tudor Kings*, Cambridge: Cambridge University Press.

Hill, Christopher (1964) *Society and Puritanism in Pre-Revolutionary England*, New York: Schocken Books.

Larkin, James F. and Hughes, Paul L. (eds) (1973) *Royal Proclamations of King James I 1603–1625*, vol. 1 of *Stuart Royal Proclamations*, Oxford: Clarendon Press.

Marlowe, C. (1910, repr. 1925), *The Works*, ed. C. F. Tucker Brooke, Oxford: Clarendon Press.

Ong, Walter J. (1971) 'Oral Residue in Tudor Prose Style', *Rhetoric, Romance & Technology: Studies in the Interaction of Expression and Culture*, Ithaca: Cornell University Press, pp. 23–47.

State Trials (1776) *A Complete Collection of State Trials and Proceedings for High Treason and Other Crimes and Misdemeanours*, etc. 4th edn., vol. 1, London: T. Wright & G. Kearsley.

Whigham, Frank (1981) 'The Rhetoric of Elizabethan Suitors' Letters', *PMLA*, 96, pp. 864–82.

Youngs, Frederick A., Jr. (1976) *The Proclamations of the Tudor Queens*, Cambridge: Cambridge University Press.

Stanley Wells

STAGING SHAKESPEARE'S GHOSTS

Study of the arts of performance in Shakespeare's time takes on practical as well as academic significance as the likelihood grows that before long a reconstructed Globe theatre will become available for experimentation; and the discovery of remains of both the Globe and the Rose may do something to increase confidence in the authenticity of such a structure. If we are to make good use of a third Globe we shall need to think afresh about many matters extending from relatively straightforward ones such as exits and entrances, sightlines, use of upper levels, and stage furniture, to costumes, make-up, blocking, acoustics, music, and acting styles. Scholars and theatre practitioners jointly will seek to establish a range of possibilities which may be regarded as normative, but will also be conscious that certain kinds of character or types of action call for a differentiation that will set them off from the norm. One may think of happenings such as dumb shows, plays (or masques) within plays, processions, theophanies, and the like, and characters such as witches, jesters, and spirits, who by no stretch of the imagination can be expected to behave like even the theatrical manifestations of ordinary human beings.

I want to look at the ghosts in Shakespeare's plays with the aim of raising questions about styles of performance that may have been associated with their portrayal in the theatres of Shakespeare's time. Ghosts are so closely related to other supernatural manifestations such as spirits and apparitions as to raise problems of definition. Although *O.E.D.* traces the word 'ghost' back to the ninth century, its first instance under the definition 'an apparition, a spectre' is, surprisingly, in Shakespeare's *Venus and Adonis* (1593), when Venus 'chides . . . death' as 'Grim-grinning ghost, earth's worm' (l. 933). But it is difficult to see how this differs from 'The soul of a deceased person, spoken of as appearing, in a visible form, or otherwise manifesting its presence, to the living', said to be 'Now the prevailing sense' and traced back to the fourteenth century. It seems distinctive of a ghost to appear of its own volition, not (like the apparitions in *Macbeth*) at the behest of others. Although its appearance may be associated with abnormal states of mind in those who see it (as is Banquo's ghost) it must have some

(50)

claims to objective, non-hallucinatory reality; though (like the ghosts in *Richard III* and *Julius Caesar*) it may be associated with sleep, it must be not simply a dream vision (like that of Queen Katherine in *All is True*, or *Henry VIII*). The ghosts in *Richard III* escape disqualification under this clause on the grounds that for two men simultaneously to dream the same dream must be regarded as more than coincidence. So I shall restrict myself here to the ghosts in *Richard III*, *Julius Caesar*, *Hamlet*, and *Macbeth*, leaving their close relatives to another occasion.

Ghosts had entered English drama by way of translations of Seneca several decades before Shakespeare started to write, and a number of allusions to theatrical ghosts in the sixteenth and early seventeenth centuries have fostered preconceptions about them and have suggested that their representation may have been governed by convention. One of the principal pieces of evidence for the existence of a play about Hamlet before Shakespeare's is the allusion in Thomas Lodge's pamphlet *Wit's Misery* (1596) to one who 'looks as pale as the vizard of the ghost which cried so miserably at the Theatre, like an oyster wife, "Hamlet, revenge."' (p. 56). 'Vizard' has many meanings; a common one in this period was 'mask', though it could also mean a part of a helmet or simply a face. The allusion has helped to suggest that stage ghosts may have worn masks, but there is no clear evidence for this. The miserable crying clearly implies the wailing kind of vocal delivery traditionally associated with ghosts, who in *Julius Caesar* are said to 'shriek and squeal about the streets' (II.ii.24), and in the Induction to the anonymous play *A Warning for Fair Women* (1599) to come 'screaming like a pig half sticked' (l. 56). Ideas about the appearance of ghosts are often related to the concept that they have broken directly from their graves (*Contention* I.iv.20, *Measure for Measure* V.i.432) and can return 'to their wormy beds' (*A Midsummer Night's Dream*, III.ii.385). So they may be represented in their burial clothes (like Elizabethan grave sculptures), as is implied in the sarcastic reference, also in the Induction to *A Warning for Fair Women*, to

> a filthy whining ghost,
> Lapped in some foul sheet, or a leather pilch.
> (ll. 54–5).

(A pilch was 'a leathern or coarse woollen outer garment.') Use of a sheet is additionally substantiated in Middleton's play *The Puritan* (1606): 'we'll ha' the ghost i'th'white sheet sit at upper end o'th'table' (IV.iii.90–1) — often taken to refer directly to the apparition of Banquo's ghost in *Macbeth*, though R. V. Holdsworth (1990) has shown (in a recent article) that Middleton had already had a ghost 'Sit . . . at the upper end of a tavern-table' in *The Black Book* (1604), before *Macbeth* was written. And in Tourneur's *The Atheist's Tragedy* (1609), Languebeau Snuffe, preparing to disguise himself as a ghost, 'pulls out a sheet, a hair [that is, a wig], and a beard' (IV.iii.55). On the other hand some ghosts are explicitly stated to wear costumes of the living, not of the dead; Hamlet's father is the most obvious example, and later Brachiano's Ghost in Webster's *The White Devil* (1612) appears 'In his leather cassock and breeches, . . . boots, a cowl' (V.ii.120). The idea that ghosts are 'pale' (*1 Henry VI* I.ii.7) may refer either (or both) to the colour of their costume or to their bloodlessness; 'hollow' (*King John* III.iv.84) suggests decay and would be more difficult to represent on the stage. In *The Knight of the Burning Pestle* (1607) a ghost's pallor is comically simulated when Jasper enters with 'his face mealed' (V.i.4) — a primitive kind of make-up.

Ghosts sometimes simply 'walk' (*Winter's Tale* V.i.63, 80) but are often thought of as having a particular style of movement; in *Julius Caesar* we hear of 'gliding ghosts' (I.iii.63), and Macbeth compares Tarquin, with his 'ravishing strides', to a ghost (II.i.55–6). But Macbeth's comparison may be rather to Tarquin's efforts to remain unheard than to his gait; certainly in later stage tradition it became important for a ghost to move noiselessly: a nineteenth-century performer of Hamlet's deceased father was advised 'if thou didst never that dear father play before, see that your boots or shoes creak not. Macready, when he played the Ghost to Charles Young's Hamlet, wore list or felt slippers under his mail-clad feet. You have no carpet on the platform, recollect' (Sprague, p. 128). There is some evidence that the appearance of ghosts may have been enhanced atmospherically by the use of special effects. In *Locrine* (1591), for instance, is the stage direction *Enter the ghost of Corineus, with thunder and lightning* (V.iv.0), and according to the Induction to *A Warning for Fair Women*, when the ghost cries '*Vindicta*! Revenge, revenge!' 'a little rosin flasheth forth, like smoke out of a tobacco pipe, or a boy's squib' (ll. 59–60). (Powdered rosin could be blown through a candle flame or torch to simulate lightning (Lawrence (1927), p. 174).) Nevertheless, extant plays in which ghosts appear do not justify the assumption that they were conventionally accompanied by thunder and lightning. I have found no evidence for the use of music to increase the eeriness of a ghost's appearance, but this is not to deny the possibility.

Surviving allusions to the appearance of ghosts in Shakespeare's theatre certainly indicate distinctive styles of performance, but they cannot be regarded as prescriptive, and one has only to think of the difference between, say, the ghost of Hamlet's father and Banquo's ghost to realise that Shakespeare was not bound by predetermined convention, even though he may have drawn upon it. I want now to examine the dramaturgy of Shakespeare's ghost scenes in an attempt to discover how he made his ghosts ghostly and to consider some of the options open to those trying to reconstruct the early performance of those scenes. I shall assume the agreed basics of the Globe stage — a tiring-house wall with at least two apertures, a thrust stage which may have held a trap, and an upper acting level.

The first unequivocal ghosts in Shakespeare's plays are those in *Richard III* — eleven of them — and a fine body of men and women they are. They are associated with retribution, and their appearance is an important factor in making the closing scenes of *Richard III* the climax not only of the play but of the whole sequence of plays concerned with the Plantagenets, since they include the ghosts of two people — Henry VI and his son, Prince Edward — who have not appeared in the play and refer to events (such as the Battle of Tewkesbury) that reach backward into its pre-history. Shakespeare could have got the idea for these ghosts from either his reading or his playgoing. In *A Mirror for Magistrates* Richard says that he thought he saw the ghosts of all he had killed crying for vengeance around his tent, and in the anonymous *True Tragedy of Richard III* (surviving in a corrupt text printed in 1594) Richard has a long speech in which thirteen out of seventeen lines end in the word 'revenge', and in which he says

> Methinks their ghosts comes gaping for revenge,
> Whom I have slain in reaching for a crown.

The traditional association of ghosts with demands for revenge had been firmly established in English popular drama by the appearances of Revenge in person along with the ghost of the murdered Don Andrea in Kyd's *The Spanish Tragedy* (1587), and there are numerous other examples: in George Peele's *The Battle of Alcazar* (1589), for example, we find the direction '*Three ghosts crying* Vindicta' — apparently just a sound effect — and in the anonymous *Locrine* (1591) the ghost of Albanect cries 'Revenge! Revenge for blood!' and exits declaiming '*Vindicta, vindicta*' (III.vi.41, 54). Pre-Shakespearian ghosts betray their Senecan origins and have all benefited from a classical education; as F. W. Moorman (1906) remarks, 'though the ghosts of Richard's victims are Senecan in character, in that they are represented as spirits of vengeance . . . they depart from Seneca's manner in making absolutely no reference to the underworld of classical mythology' (p. 193). This in itself may warn us against associating them with conventional modes of presentation, and so may their style of speech, for there is nothing to suggest that these ghosts should shriek, squeal, or scream. They are dream-spectres, and Shakespeare sets the scene carefully for them.

Before they appear the pace of the action has been slowing down, the focus of the audience's attention narrowing, but we have also been made increasingly conscious of the duality of the action and of the division of the characters of the play into two parties, one headed by Richard, the other by Richmond, each associated visually with one of the stage doors. A mood of concentration and stillness is set up in preparation for the ghosts' arrival. The mood could be either sustained or broken by the method of their appearance.

It is commonly assumed that convention would have required them to arrive from under the stage through a trap-door. So, for example, Julie Hankey, in her 'Plays in Performance' edition of *Richard III* (1981), writes in her note on the entry: 'Elizabethan stage ghosts customarily rose up through the trap-door from under the stage, which represented the "kingdom of perpetual night" — where Queen Elizabeth knew King Edward had gone.' It is true that in later performances they customarily did so, that the directions to Colley Cibber's popular adaptation (1700) require them to do so, and that one of them is shown emergent (or descendent) in Rowe's frontispiece (1709), where seven ghosts, some dressed in winding-sheets, most with open mouths as if in the act of speech, and all with uplifted hands, are lined up around an understandably grumpy-looking Richard sitting asleep, his head propped on his hand, at a table.

But early texts of Shakespeare's plays require the ghosts simply to 'enter', there is no reference in their speeches to the classical — or any other — underworld, and the absence of directions for covering noises such as would be provided by thunder combines with the inappropriateness of such effects to the tone of the scene to suggest that traps were not used. As Gary Taylor writes in the Oxford *Textual Companion*, use of a trap 'might suggest that they all (including the innocent princes and "holy Harry") came from hell, and would create problems with exits if one ghost were going back down the trap while another was rising' (Wells and Taylor (1987), p. 247). Each ghost is required to address both Richmond and Richard who sleep on the main stage. The effectiveness of their speeches would be enhanced if the ghosts were placed above the sleepers; for this reason the Oxford edition conjectures that they should appear on the upper level, an arrangement that would be worth experimenting with.

The effect of the ghosts' speeches is cumulative; their heightened formality of both speech and action resembles that of a play within the play. In the Folio text they enter in the order approximating to that of their deaths; in the Quarto (which may be closer to performance) the Princes come on before Hastings — who died first — perhaps because one of the boy actors had to reappear as Lady Anne and could scarcely do so instantly. Each is required to address first Richard, then Richmond, which suggests that, whether on the main stage or on an upper level, they would be placed centrally. The unreal formality of this episode is emphasised by the fact that the ghosts of Rivers, Grey, and Vaughan appear together and speak their last speech in chorus, and the ghosts of the Princes speak the whole of their eight-line speech in concert. There is nothing to indicate how they were costumed except that each speaks a few words of self-identification, which would be particularly helpful if they were ghostlily garbed. A declamatory, perhaps even 'wailing' method of delivery is suggested by their incantatory, repetitive style: every ghost except Grey ends its apostrophe to Richard with the words 'Despair and die' (and even Grey says 'Let thy soul despair'); their speeches to Richmond, by contrast, dwell on themes of life and success, stress the idea of 'comfort', and associate him with virtue and heavenly protection. As W. H. Clemen (1968), who examines the style of this scene in great detail, remarks, 'the recurring pattern of incident and phrase emphasises the ritual and ceremonial, the supra-personal quality of the sequence and thereby heightens its effectiveness' (pp. 211–13). The episode reaches a climax in Buckingham's speech — the longest — 'in which rhyme and an accumulation of rhetorical devices help bring about a moment of heightened intensity at the close of their ghost scene' (Clemen, p. 213). Although most of the speeches have been in the play's prevailing blank verse there have been occasional rhymes, and Buckingham's climactic speech ends with three couplets. All these stylistic features provide cues for the actors.

The ghosts in *Richard III* serve to exemplify awakening aspects of Richard's conscience and to offer supernatural confirmation of Richmond as God's agent in a virtuous task. So far from being Senecan figures of vengeance, they never mention revenge (though their presence may implicitly suggest the concept). The originality of their function may have been matched by an absence of conventionality in their presentation.

In *Julius Caesar* the ghost of Caesar is presented even more subjectively. Shakespeare read about the ghost in North's translation of Plutarch, where the tale is finely told:

> So, being ready to go into Europe, one night very late, as he was in his tent with a little light, thinking of weighty matters, he thought he heard one come in to him, and, casting his eye towards the door of his tent, that he saw a wonderful strange and monstrous shape of a body coming towards him, and said never a word. So Brutus boldly asked what he was, a god or a man, and what cause brought him thither. The spirit answered him, 'I am thy evil spirit, Brutus, and thou shalt see me by the city of Philippi.' Brutus, being no otherwise afraid, replied again unto it, 'Well, then I shall see thee again.' The spirit presently vanished away, and Brutus called his men unto him, who told him that they heard no noise, nor saw anything at all.

In dramatising this incident Shakespeare is, as in *Richard III*, careful to arouse the audience's receptivity. The emotional tumult of Brutus' quarrel with Cassius is past, and the scene goes through successive slackenings of tension signalled initially by Brutus' call (like Richard before him) for 'a bowl of wine' (IV.ii.194, 220). Lucius brings wine and tapers, the reconciliation between the two leaders is strengthened by the news of Portia's death, and the need for sleep begins to be felt:

> The deep of night is crept upon our talk,
> And nature must obey necessity,
> Which we will niggard with a little rest.

Brutus calls for his nightgown and bids an affectionate farewell to Cassius, Titinius, and Messala. Harmony is succeeding discord, and is symbolised by Brutus' request for music. Lucius speaks 'drowsily'; Brutus, acknowledging that everyone is 'o'erwatched', calls on Varrus and Claudio to sleep in his tent. The focus is contracting, there is more talk of sleep, Lucius plays and sings himself to sleep, Brutus considerately takes the boy's instrument away from him and opens the book that he has found in the pocket of his own gown. Everything is done to concentrate attention on a single spot on the stage — the book that the seated Brutus is reading — before the ghost appears. Presumably the audience should see it first, before Brutus complains 'How ill this taper burns' — alluding to a superstition drawn, according to Moorman, from folklore and reflected also in Richard III's 'The lights burn blue' after his ghosts have gone. It seems quite certain that for this ghost to emerge head first from a trap would destroy all Shakespeare's careful preparation for the mystery of its appearance. Brutus at first doubts its reality:

> Ha! Who comes here?
> I think it is the weakness of mine eyes
> That shapes this monstrous apparition.

The word 'monstrous' comes from Plutarch — 'a wonderful strange and monstrous shape of a body' — and Brutus' 'It comes upon me', echoing Plutarch's phrase 'coming towards him', suggests a walking rather than an ascending figure (so Beckerman 1962, p. 204.)

If it is to do anything to live up to Brutus' description of it as a 'monstrous apparition' its appearance must differ from that of the living Caesar — and, incidentally, a ghostly sheet would make more difference to an actor in Elizabethan costume than to one wearing a toga. Its monstrousness might lie specifically in its resemblance to the murdered Caesar: it might even have been shown 'pointing unto his wounds' as Agamemnon's ghost was to do in Thomas Heywood's *2 The Iron Age* (1612); though the absence of explicit allusion to the assassination, and of guilt in Brutus' reactions, makes this unlikely.

Brutus' brief conversation with the ghost is remarkably close to Plutarch, and the ghost's style of speech is not strongly characterised; indeed, it says nothing but 'Thy evil spirit, Brutus', 'To tell thee thou shalt see me at Philippi', and 'Ay, at Philippi'. The one major change is that whereas Plutarch's Brutus sees simply a 'spirit', Shakespeare's sees unequivocally the ghost of Caesar: this is not stated in the dialogue of their encounter, but the Folio's direction reads *Enter the Ghost of Caesar* and later Brutus is to speak of it as precisely that — 'The ghost of Caesar' — seeing in its appearance a premonition of death (V.v.17).

The ghost departs quietly; and again there is no suggestion that machinery was involved. True, Brutus says 'Now I have taken heart, thou vanishest', but the word 'vanish' is used in a later play — Barnabe Barnes's *The Devil's Charter* (1607) — in a direction that refers explicitly to an exit through one of the stage doors:

> *He goeth to one door of the stage, from whence he bringeth the ghost of* Candie *ghastly haunted by* Caesar *pursuing and stabbing it; these vanish in at another door.*

(ll. 1952–5)

Later theatre practice has tried to turn Caesar's ghost into a spectacular rather than a mysterious figure: in the eighteenth century, for instance, its promise to see Brutus at Philippi is fulfilled; in added lines it boasts

'my three and thirty wounds are now revenged' and sinks down a trap
saying

> The Ides of March Remember — I must go.
> To meet thee on the burning Lake below.
>
>   (Cited Odell (1920), I.237.)

Some twentieth-century directors, too, have brought the ghost into the
final scenes: J. R. Ripley (1980) writes that John Barton, at Stratford in
1968,

> gave his ghost, in addition to the tent visit, two further appearances.
> Just after the farewells of Brutus and Cassius, his wrathful presence
> crossed the battlefield, and finally, as Brutus lay dead at the end of
> the play, he stood, gleaming, over the body, the last thing visible as
> the lights faded. (p. 266)

Treatments such as these bring the ghost closer to the Senecan revenge
figure; but although the naming of Plutarch's 'spirit' as Caesar's ghost
introduces an element at least of conscience — for this is the spirit of a
murdered man appearing to his murderer — Shakespeare's ghost is
essentially premonitory rather than vengeful, a fact that should be
reflected in the style adopted for its performance.

   Of all Shakespeare's ghosts, the most Senecan is the ghost of Hamlet's
father, who comes straight from the underworld (and talks of it
graphically) to incite his son to take vengeance on his murderer. We
know that this ghost had appeared on the English stage before
Shakespeare's play was written, and the loss of the earlier Hamlet play
makes it particularly difficult to assess the originality of Shakespeare's
treatment. Its most obvious extant dramatic forebear is Kyd's Ghost of
Andrea, but Shakespeare's ghost is far more closely integrated into the
dramatic structure. Unlike the ghosts in *Richard III, Julius Caesar*, and
Macbeth, it is the ghost of a character we have not previously seen, and
like Kyd's ghost it has things to tell us that are essential to the play's
exposition, but its first appearance is atmospheric rather than expository,
and again its entry is carefully prepared. As in *Richard III* and *Julius
Caesar*, the characters to whom it first appears are seated; it is night
time, but no one is asleep or even close to sleep. On the contrary, it is
the duty of Barnardo and Marcellus to stay awake, and Horatio has been
summoned specifically to see the Ghost. Its appearance is both expected
and dreaded, and the first reference to it — 'What, has this thing
appeared again tonight?' — establishes it as something beyond ordinary
human experience, and consequently difficult to name. Horatio,
Marcellus tells us, refuses to believe in its existence, and Horatio

confirms this with 'Tush, tush, 'twill not appear.' The dialogue moves into the narrative mode as Barnardo prepares to repeat his account of the Ghost's previous two appearances, creating a sense of expectation rather in the way that a conjurer will distract our attention from something he does not want us to see by telling us of something irrelevant to it; and expectation that we are about to hear a long story is increased by the way the narrator and his hearers settle down to it: 'Sit down a while', says Barnardo, and 'Well, sit we down', agrees Horatio. Where do they sit? Stools could have been set out in advance; or, if a throne of state was already in position (perhaps unlikely for a scene on the battlements), it could supply steps on which they might settle down; but perhaps they would sit on the front of the stage, focusing attention as far as possible from the tiring-house façade. W. J. Lawrence (1927) argued that the Ghost's entry must have been through a trap and that the three men would see it rising in front of them; others have followed him (Sprague (1944), p. 128: 'The Ghost's entrance, in Elizabethan productions, was unquestionably through a trap'; DeLuca (1973), pp. 147–50, etc.) Certainly anyone experimenting with a reconstructed Globe might wish to put this theory to the test. My own opinion is that it rests partly on a conditioned faith in the theatricality of the use of stage machinery for supernatural entries deriving from post-Restoration theatre practice and partly on an excessively condescending attitude to Elizabethan audiences; thus Lawrence writes: 'There can be little doubt that stage effects of this order were hugely delighted in by the mob and could have been omitted by the players only at their peril' (p. 105). More genuinely theatrical, to my mind, and more consonant with Shakespeare's use of an interrupted narrative, would have been the Ghost's silent appearance at one of the apertures in the tiring-house wall, initially unobserved by most of the audience as Barnardo directed their attention to 'yon same star that's westward from the pole'. In the text (Q2) closest to Shakespeare's manuscript the entry direction breaks Barnardo's narrative after the phrase 'The bell then beating one' ('tolling one' in Q1). Only the time that it takes to speak thirty-one lines has elapsed since we were told, ''Tis now struck twelve' — and modern productions, at least, often use this as a sound-effect to still the audience for the play's opening words — but since Marcellus is later to remark that the Ghost's previous appearances have been 'just at this dead hour' (I.i.64), it seems likely that an apparently coincidental stroke on a bell would have broken the listeners' concentration and signalled the Ghost's presence. Coleridge (1989), commenting on Barnardo's 'elevation of style', remarks on 'the interruption of the narration at the very moment when we are most intensively listening for the sequel, and have our thoughts diverted from the dreaded sight in expectation of the desired yet almost dreaded tale — thus giving all the suddenness and surprise of the original appearance' (p. 79).

The dialogue seems to imply that (as we might expect) the onlookers do not approach particularly close to the Ghost, which does not speak to them; it would be worth experimenting here, too, with an upper-level entry, which might thereby be the more unobtrusive.

If there was indeed a convention of costuming ghosts so that they appeared to have risen directly from the grave, the convention must have been broken here, for the onlookers immediately remark on the Ghost's resemblance to 'the King that's dead' and on its 'fair and warlike form': after its departure Horatio will refer directly to its costume: 'Such was the very armour he had on/When he the ambitious Norway combated.' Even if the Ghost is dressed in everyday clothes, it must be visually impressive if there is to be any correlation between its appearance and what is said about it. It apparently looks grim — 'So frowned he once . . .' — yet Horatio later claims to have discerned more sorrow than anger in its countenance, which was 'very pale'; it apparently carries a truncheon and must walk in a stately, dignified manner if it is to justify Barnardo's statement that 'it stalks away' and Marcellus' later reference to its 'martial stalk'. It is not impassive, for Marcellus can see that 'It is offended', presumably at the peremptoriness of Horatio's 'I charge thee speak'. (A recent Stratford ghost was walking towards Horatio at this point, then suddenly turned on its heel and stalked away rather more rapidly in a distinctly huffy manner.)

Horatio interprets this first appearance as premonitory — it 'bodes some strange eruption to our state'. After it has gone the onlookers sit again and Horatio embarks on an expository narration which again focuses attention and is again interrupted by the Ghost's appearance. The Folio omits Horatio's description of how, shortly before Julius Caesar's fall,

> The graves stood tenantless, and the sheeted dead
> Did squeak and gibber in the Roman streets.

Shakespeare may have felt that it was unfair to confront the actor playing a very different kind of ghost with such images; this ghost is not sheeted and does not 'squeak and gibber'; indeed its very silence on its first two appearances is among its most mysteriously impressive features. Here too it has been argued that the Ghost would have entered by the trap (Lawrence (1927), pp. 106–7; McManaway (1949), p. 315).

DeLuca's argument against this raises unnecessarily naturalistic considerations: 'Why should the Ghost have returned below at this time — especially when it is known to have been walking the battlements?' — but there is nothing in the text to suggest that its entrance is anything but unobtrusive, and it apparently approaches the onlookers — 'lo where it comes again!'. Horatio declares that he will 'cross it', a daring thing to do since it was supposed that anyone crossing a ghost's path was asking for trouble. Or perhaps he means that he will make the sign of the cross. (See Sprague (1944), p. 132.) The 'good' Quarto's stage direction *It spreads his armes* has caused problems. Dover Wilson among others took 'It' as a mistake for 'He', that is Horatio, but there is no evidence for this; Hibbard suggests that the Ghost's 'spreading of its arms is interpreted by Horatio as preparation for flight and leads to his cry, "Stay, illusion."'

The cock crows — an actual sound effect according to Q2's direction — before Horatio has finished questioning the Ghost, provoking its departure; W. J. Lawrence writes that 'from the producer's standpoint, no greater puzzle is presented anywhere in the entire Shakespeare canon than the difficulty of determining what was the exact "business" arranged for the situation developing out of Horatio's command, "Stop it, Marcellus."' The dialogue reads:

> MARCELLUS Shall I strike at it with my partisan?
> HORATIO Do, if it will not stand.
> BARNARDO 'Tis here.
> HORATIO 'Tis here.
> MARCELLUS 'Tis gone.

This is substantially the same in all three early texts. The good Quarto — the one nearest to Shakespeare's manuscript — has no direction for the Ghost's departure. The 'bad' Quarto directs *exit Ghost.* after Barnardo's ' 'Tis here'; the Folio has a similar direction after Marcellus' ' 'Tis gone'; but of course the placing of such directions in early printed texts is no reliable guide to the exact timing of the actions to which they refer.

Whether, as he wrote these lines, Shakespeare knew exactly what stage movement would accompany them we cannot tell. The closest parallel in the Shakespeare canon is probably the vanishing of the Witches in *Macbeth* (I.iii.77–8: 'The earth hath bubbles, as the water has,/ And these are of them. Whither are they vanished?') The fact that the *Hamlet* passage is exactly the same in all three early printed texts, two of them palpably influenced by performance, suggests that the lines

were made to work. Lawrence (1927), influenced by the actor Louis
Calvert, proposes that 'a double for the Ghost was adroitly provided.' He
imagines the first Ghost disappearing 'at one of the two widely separated
entering doors' as Barnardo cried ' 'Tis here' while the double
simultaneously 'came forth from the other door' — like figures on a
weather clock — then 'took a step forward and flung itself down the
suddenly yawning grave trap' (pp. 107–8). Current beliefs about the
area of the stage would require the Ghost to have taken a running jump
rather than a single step to reach the grave trap, and Lawrence himself
realises that if the Ghost 'had been arrayed cap-à-pie in real armour,
considerable danger would have attended the jump, a constant risk of
bruises and broken bones', and then demonstrates with characteristic
learning that imitation armour might have been used. McManaway
(1949), in an even more farcical scenario, imagined a single Ghost
jumping into the trap — 'to the delight of the groundlings' — as
Marcellus tried to stop it, then immediately rising 'through another
trap' only 'to vanish again through a trap to the bewilderment of all the
onlookers' (p. 315), and scarcely justifying Marcellus' later statement 'It
faded on the crowing of the cock' (I.i.138) and Horatio's that 'it shrunk
in haste away/ And vanished from our sight' (I.i.219–20). It has even
been suggested (French, 1964) that at this point the ghosts were
'figures painted upon canvas, stretched over a wooden framework'
which 'could have been mounted upon poles and merely thrust into
view from beneath the stage through a narrow slot' (pp. 94–5). Sabbatini
describes the construction of such a device in his *Pratica di fabricar
Scene e Machine ne' Teatri* (Ravenna, 1638, p. 20), and if its use in
Hamlet seems improbable to us, that may serve as a useful reminder
that the acceptable conventionalities of one generation may become the
outdated absurdities of the next. To me it seems that Shakespeare has
provided Marcellus' offer to strike at the Ghost with his partisan, as
well as the dispute between Barnardo and Horatio about the Ghost's
whereabouts, as a cover for the Ghost's quick exit through a stage-door
or arras. (See DeLuca, p. 151; Jenkins (1982), note to I.i.42). (Similar,
though wordless, action is needed at a later moment in the play when
Hamlet escapes from his captors on 'Hide fox, and all after': IV.ii.29–
30.) But Lawrence's theory has appealed to some modern directors;
indeed Peter Hall used three outsize ghosts in his 1965 Stratford
production. Certainly the dispute leaves ample opportunity for
experimentation in a reconstructed performance, and it raises the
fundamental question of principle as to the degree to which actors

attempting reconstructions of early performances should feel free to elaborate on the evidence supplied by the early texts. The scholarly nature of the enterprise would appear to dictate an austere rejection of stage business for which there is no evidence, yet it is difficult to believe that the Elizabethans would have been similarly austere. If, to cite an example from *Hamlet* itself, only the 1604 Quarto and the Folio texts had survived — as might easily have happened — we should lack the evidence supplied by the 1603 Quarto that Ophelia entered *playing on a Lute* in her mad scene.

By the time the Ghost makes its third appearance we are more accustomed to it, and its entrance is less impressively built up. We are on the battlements, 'it is very cold', and the time 'draws near the season/Wherein the spirit held his wont to walk.' (I.iv.6–7). Horatio sees it first — 'Look, my lord, it comes' (l. 19), and there is no evidence for (or against) the use of a trap. The Ghost's impressiveness is created for us by the vehemence of Hamlet's reaction (in the speech beginning 'Angels and ministers of grace defend us!', ll. 20–38), by its continuing silence in the face of Hamlet's demands and questions, by the 'courteous action' (l. 41) with which it repeatedly — at least four times — but still silently beckons Hamlet to follow it, and by Horatio's fear that it may 'tempt' Hamlet 'toward the flood', change itself into 'some other horrible form', and drive Hamlet mad, culminating in Horatio's and Marcellus' unsuccessful attempts to hold Hamlet back before he throws them off — 'By heaven, I'll make a ghost of him that lets me' (l. 62) — and leaves the stage with the Ghost (even Lawrence did not suggest a trap for their joint exit).

On their re-entry, doubtless by a different stage-door, the Ghost quickly satisfies Hamlet's and our desire to hear him speak. Responsibility for the impression that he makes passes now from the director to the actor. An adequate analysis of the style of the Ghost's speeches would form a study on its own; suffice it here to note that their formality, their long sentence structures and frequent enjambements, their intensity of utterance and the momentousness of their content cumulatively both justify and are enhanced by the Ghost's earlier silences.

The Ghost's final words in this sequence are (in the Folio):

Adieu, adieu, Hamlet. Remember me.

After having for so long been seen but not heard, he will shortly be heard but not seen as he calls upon Hamlet from the cellarage, so here if anywhere there might be a case for his descending down a trap. His final words vary in the Quartos and the Folio; Lawrence (1927), accepting Q2's

> Adieu, adieu, adieu! Remember me

suggests that the line 'was uttered while standing on a trap, and that with each *adieu* the spectre sank a little, and disappeared rapidly on saying, "Remember me."' (p. 110). This is shown happening in drawings by C. Walter Hodges in the New Cambridge edition of the play (ed. Philip Edwards, Cambridge, 1985), and Harold Jenkins (1982) supports the use of a trap here. Varying Lawrence's suggestion, DeLuca proposes that 'The ghost may actually descend a portable stair well moved up under the trap and take one step down as it utters each of the syllables of the final line' (p. 153). To me, either of these suggestions would seem more appropriate to a travesty of *Hamlet* than to a serious production, yet there is no way of firmly refuting them. I find more sympathetic G. R. Hibbard's (1987) note 'The Ghost's lingering farewell sounds far better suited to one making his exit through a door than to one about to disappear through a trap.' And in practical terms, as he points out, the actor 'has ample time in which to make his way into the cellarage from backstage before he has to speak again . . .'. It will be interesting, in a reconstructed Globe, to know whether the Ghost's cries from the cellarage will be muffled or resonated by the wooden sounding chamber.

The Ghost's final appearance is in the Closet scene (3.4), dressed, so the 1603 Quarto tells us, *in his night gowne*, which appears to mean some kind of dressing gown. By this point in the play the Ghost is, as it were, becoming internalised. The fact that it is not seen by Gertrude might be held simply to indicate her guilt. Partial sighting of a ghost also occurs in Thomas Heywood's *2 Edward IV* (1599), though there innocence is the reason that a messenger fails to see the ghost of Friar Anselm:

> thy untainted soul
> Cannot discern the horrors that I do. (Sig. V2v)

But it seems significant that it is only at the height of Hamlet's supremely eloquent and passionate invective against Claudius that the Ghost appears, as if it were truly, as Gertrude claims, 'the very coinage of [Hamlet's] brain' (l. 128). (See Anthonisen (1966): 'what we see here described is an episode of visual hallucinosis that hardly could be represented any better' (p. 245). Anthonisen also remarks 'the difference between Hamlet's hallucinatory experience in his last encounter with the ghost and the "epidemiological", shared experiences at the opening of the play' (p. 246).) Still, there is no question that Shakespeare intended it to be represented objectively. Again Lawrence argues for the use of a trap, and again a sudden appearance through a door or arras would seem more appropriate, if only because the precise timing of an entry in mid-sentence, on 'A king of shreds and patches — ', would be virtually impossible to achieve by hand-operated machinery. (It seems astonishing, nevertheless, that as recently as 1973 DeLuca could object to the use of the trap on the grounds that 'Gertrude's closet must be in the upper levels of the castle, meaning that the Ghost must rise through the floors and walls of several stories of the castle' (p. 153).) Even Lawrence admitted that the Ghost should walk off, on the evidence of Hamlet's

> Look how it steals away.
> My father, in his habit as he lived.
> Look where he goes even now out at the portal.   (ll. 125–7)

As A. C. Sprague (1944) put it, 'If the Ghost really did descend here — out of habit, as it were — one can only say that he should have known better' (p. 165).

The hallucinatory elements in the final appearance of the Ghost of Hamlet's father seem premonitory of the last unequivocal ghost in the Shakespeare canon, that of Banquo in *Macbeth*. We have already seen Macbeth experiencing, and analysing, an hallucination,

> a false creation
> Proceeding from the heat-oppressèd brain.   (II.i.38–9)

We have inhabited a world in which the boundaries between natural and supernatural are easily crossed and uncertain of identification. We have witnessed the murder of Banquo and moved with ironic speed to a scene of festivity for which a table and stools must be set. Macbeth has told us that 'Both sides of the table are even', which presumably means that both sides are full (though G. K. Hunter (1967) takes Macbeth to refer to the guests' 'even' (equivalent) response to the Queen). He himself will sit 'i'th'midst', which I take to mean at one end of the table. We have seen and heard Macbeth in surreptitious conversation with the First Murderer, who has said of Banquo

> Safe in a ditch he bides,
> With twenty trenchèd gashes on his head,
> The least a death to nature.

A degree of stylisation is inescapable in the presentation of this scene. The on-stage characters must ignore the Murderer's presence — as they must later ignore the Ghost's — and must seem not to hear his conversation with Macbeth; it would seem best to play this episode close to the stage door by which the Murderer comes and goes. After he has left, Lady Macbeth urges her husband to 'give the cheer', and we have the direction *Enter the Ghost of Banquo, and sits in Macbeth's place*. If the Ghost enters by a door it must be a different one from that through which the Murderer has left, and Macbeth must be looking away from it as the Ghost enters and sits with its back to him — for as Ross invites him to sit, all Macbeth can see is that 'The table's full.' The place reserved for him is occupied by a ghost; it is the ghost of an unburied man, so there is no naturalistic reason why it should wear grave clothes, though it might well be made up in such a way as to suggest the 'twenty trenchèd gashes' and to justify Macbeth's 'Never shake thy gory locks at me.' Its ghostliness is created principally by its trick of sitting in Macbeth's place, its silence, and the vehemence of Macbeth's reactions combined with the bewilderment of the other onlookers. It may reasonably 'glide', 'stalk', or move 'like a ghost' (as Macbeth has earlier said) 'With Tarquin's ravishing strides', but traps, thunder, or lightning effects seem inappropriate to a ghost that can create so devastating an effect on Macbeth by its mere presence and a shake of its head. Its exit is unmarked in the Folio, but must occur between Macbeth's 'If thou canst nod, speak, too!' (l. 69) and his 'If I stand here, I saw him' (l. 73). In Davenant's adaptation of 1663 *The Ghost descends*. The direction deserves respect, since Davenant's printing of the songs shows that he must have had access to a manuscript of the King's Men; still, he may have adapted its staging as much as its dialogue.

The Ghost enters for a second time as Macbeth drinks a health to Banquo and wishes for his presence at the feast. This second appearance of the Ghost is one of the few moments in Shakespeare's plays of which we have an eyewitness account of a performance in the Globe itself. Simon Forman saw *Macbeth* there on 20 April 1611 and wrote:

> The next night, beinge at supper with his noble men whom he had bid to a feaste to the which also Banco should haue com, he began to speake of Noble Banco, and to wish that he wer ther. And as he thus did, standing vp to drincke a Carouse to him, the ghoste of Banco came and sate down in his cheier behind him. And he turninge About to sit down Again sawe the goste of Banco, which

fronted him so, that he fell into a great passion of fear and fury. . . .
(Cited Wells and Taylor (1987), pp. 543–4.)

The Folio's direction for the Ghost's entry is merely *Enter Ghost*;
Davenant has *The Ghost of Banquo rises at his* [Macbeth's] *feet.*
Perhaps a trap was used in the Globe, too, but Forman's 'came and sate
down . . .' does not imply this. There is no indication to the effect that
the Ghost should sit on its second appearance, but equally no reason
why it should not do so. As Forman does not describe the Ghost's first
appearance, when it unquestionably does sit, we may allow for the
possibility that he has conflated the two, but his account deserves to be
taken seriously, and is a testimony to the power of the actor (presumably
Burbage) playing Macbeth; as Dennis Bartholomeusz (1969) remarks,
'The reactions observed, fear, the impulse to retreat, and fury, the
impulse to attack, indicate that the Elizabethan [*sic*] actor was bringing
complex feelings to the surface' (p. 8). We cannot claim a certain
allusion to *Macbeth* in the passage in *The Knight of the Burning Pestle*
(1607) in which Jasper, disguised as a ghost, threatens the Merchant:

> When thou art at thy table with thy friends,
> Merry in heart, and filled with swelling wine,
> I'll come in midst of all thy pride and mirth,
> Invisible to all men but thyself,
> And whisper such a sad tale in thine ear
> Shall make thee let the cup fall from thy hand,
> And stand as mute and pale as Death itself.   (V.v.22–8)

Still, the business of dropping the cup sounds entirely natural and has
been adopted by many subsequent actors (Sprague (1944), pp. 261–2).

Modern productions frequently leave this ghost to the audience's
imagination — an idea that goes back at least to the mid-eighteenth
century (Sprague (1944), p. 255). Those that bring it on often engineer
matters so that the audience is unaware of its presence until Macbeth
sees it, but this would have been difficult on Shakespeare's stage and
does not seem consonant with the Folio direction. If we wish to see the
play as Shakespeare's audiences saw it, Banquo's ghost must enter in
full view of the audience and must be as visible to us, and to Macbeth,
as the Murderer who has killed him. Earlier in the play, before Macbeth
had embarked on his life of crime, he had hallucinated a dagger; now
the presence that accuses him should seem as real as the Witches that
had tempted him.

It is perhaps too easy to assume that the apparent simplicities of the Elizabethan stage mean that a presentation of the plays in an Elizabethan style will be a comparatively straightforward matter. But although editors of the plays have examined their dialogue with minute care they have rarely paid equal attention to their stage directions, and as a consequence many of the problems related to their staging have gone unexamined. This is a result in part of the study of Shakespeare's plays as literary rather than as theatrical artefacts, and in part a recognition of the fact that the plays belong to the theatre of all ages subsequent to Shakespeare's own, and that later performances will require staging methods different from those of Shakespeare's time. Perhaps my discussion of Shakespeare's ghosts will suggest that the detailed examination of the texts necessitated by reconstructed performances is likely to throw up many theatrical cruces just as detailed examination of the plays' dialogue has thrown up literary cruces. An examination of the plays in the light of theatrical conventions of Shakespeare's time may be illuminating but is likely to show too that Shakespeare departed from convention, and re-moulded it, as often as he followed it. Reconstructed performances are bound to be experimental, and their results provisional; but they will be no less exciting for that.

References

Note. Dates of plays are from Alfred Harbage's *Annals of English Drama 975–1700*, rev. S. Schoenbaum (London: 1964). Quotations from Shakespeare are from *The Complete Works*, General Editors Stanley Wells and Gary Taylor (Oxford, 1986). Quotations from other early printed sources are modernized from reputable editions. I am grateful for assistance from Dr R. V. Holdsworth and Professor Marvin Rosenberg.

Anthonisen, Niels L. (1966) 'The Ghost in *Hamlet*', *American Imago* 22, pp. 232–49.
Bartholomeusz, Dennis (1969) *Macbeth and the Players*, Cambridge.
Beckerman, Bernard (1962) *Shakespeare at the Globe*, New York.
Clemen, W. H. (1968) *A Commentary on Shakespeare's Richard III*, London.
Coleridge, S. T., ed. R. A. Foakes (1989) *Coleridge's Criticism of Shakespeare: A Selection*, London.
DeLuca, Diana Macintyre (1973) 'The Movements of the Ghost in *Hamlet*', *S.Q.* 24, pp. 147–54.
French, J. N. (1964) 'The Staging of Magical Effects in Elizabethan and Jacobean Drama', unpublished Ph.D. thesis, Birmingham.

Hankey, Julie, ed. (1981) *Richard III*, Plays in Performance, London.

Hibbard, G. R., ed. (1987) *Hamlet*, The Oxford Shakespeare, Oxford.

Holdsworth, R. V. (1990) *'Macbeth* and *The Puritan'*, *Notes and Queries* N.S. 37.2, pp. 204–5.

Hunter, G. K., ed. (1967) *Macbeth*, New Penguin Shakespeare, Harmondsworth.

Jenkins, Harold, ed. (1982) *Hamlet*, The Arden Shakespeare, London.

Lawrence, W. J. (1927) *Pre-Restoration Stage Studies*, Oxford.

Moorman, F. W. (1906) 'Shakespeare's Ghosts', *MLR* 1, pp. 192–201.

McManaway, James G. (1949) 'The Two Earliest Prompt Books of *Hamlet*', *PBSA* XLIII, 288–320.

Odell, G. C. D. (1920) *Shakespeare from Betterton to Irving*, 2 vols, New York.

Ripley, John (1980) Julius Caesar *on Stage in England and America, 1599–1973*, London.

Sprague, Arthur Colby (1944) *Shakespeare and the Actors*, Cambridge, Mass.

Wells, Stanley, Gary Taylor, *et al.* (1987) *William Shakespeare: A Textual Companion*, Oxford.

Eugene M. Waith

KING JOHN, HENRY VIII, AND THE ARTS OF PERFORMING SHAKESPEARE'S HISTORY PLAYS

There is a certain logic in printing *King John* and *Henry VIII* in the same volume, as is done in the Bantam and Signet editions, for example, even though the two plays are widely separated in the chronology of Shakespeare's plays and although they deal with unrelated periods of history. Unrelated, that is, except for the fact that both kings had been seen as staunch opponents of the Pope. To a reader of these contemporary editions a more cogent reason for the pairing may be that these are the two history plays that are not parts of either tetralogy. They also have had somewhat parallel stage histories, in that both enjoyed a period of considerable popularity in the eighteenth and nineteenth centuries, when they were coveted vehicles for actors and lent themselves to the spectacular staging then favoured by actor-managers. In recent years they have been performed less frequently and have received considerably less critical attention than the two tetralogies.

The fact that they were formerly more admired raises interesting questions about taste, intellectual climate, theatrical practice, and finally the nature of the plays themselves. While touching on all of these questions I intend to concentrate on the last one: do these plays differ significantly from the other history plays in structure or in the kind of theatrical effect apparently aimed at? In considering these questions it will be useful to look first at some of the reasons for twentieth-century preferences among the history plays and then, by way of sampling some different approaches to them, to examine the comments of two critics in the latter part of the eighteenth century, during that period when *King John* and *Henry VIII* were ranked more highly than they now are.

Richard III and the Henry IV plays (especially *1 Henry IV*) seem to have been perennial favourites. There is abundant evidence of the popularity of *Richard III* from Shakespeare's time to the present, though it has to be said that from 1700 until far into the nineteenth century the play seen on the stage was the adaptation made by Colley Cibber in 1700 (Young 1954, pp. xlvi–lxi), bits of which even affected Laurence Olivier's film version. During the eighteenth century *Richard III* ranked third among Shakespeare's plays in popularity on the stage, exceeded only by *Hamlet* and *Macbeth* (Hogan 1952–7, 2, 716). The enormous fascination of the role of Richard III, whether in the play as Shakespeare wrote it or in Cibber's version, is one obvious reason for this continuing success, as the appealing role of Falstaff is for the only slightly lesser popularity of *1 Henry IV*, from which a 'droll' was performed after the closing of the theatres in 1642 and illustrated on the frontispiece of *The Wits* (1662) with figures of Falstaff and the Hostess (Bevington 1987, pp. 66–85). In this century the role has continued to attract first-rate actors.

Interest in character, long a staple of Shakespearian criticism, and the theatrical equivalent — the desire to recreate interesting characters on the stage — thus account in part for the undiminished enthusiasm for these two histories, but specifically historical concerns have also played an important part. The scholars who are beginning to be called the 'Old Historicists' (a term which sometimes seems to suggest the 'Old Pretender'), notably Lily Bess Campbell and E. M. W. Tillyard, related Shakespeare's histories to Elizabethan historiography and the political thought of the time. The title of Miss Campbell's book, *Shakespeare's 'Histories': Mirrors of Elizabethan Policy* (San Marino, CA: Huntington Library, 1947), reveals her conviction that Elizabethan spectators understood the histories as lessons for their time and comments on recent or current events. Both Campbell and Tillyard made much of the 'Tudor myth' that the deposition of Richard II led to the civil wars which were ended only by the victory over Richard III of the man who ascended the throne as Henry VII, the first Tudor king (Tillyard 1944, pp. 59–61). *Richard III* fitted well into this scheme, which also revived interest in the Henry VI plays, leading up to *Richard III*. The strictly historical parts of the Henry IV plays also benefited from this approach, putting more emphasis on the growth of Prince Hal into Henry V. An influential book by John Dover Wilson, *The Fortunes of Falstaff*, suggested a morality-play structure for the Prince's growth, with Falstaff as the Vice. *Henry V*, recommended in times of war by its patriotic theme, but often castigated as chauvinistic, could now be seen somewhat differently as part of this grand design.

The case of *Richard II* is particularly interesting for reasons which will soon become apparent. One of the least popular of Shakespeare's plays in the eighteenth century (like the Henry VI plays, never performed during the second half of the century), it was revived early in the nineteenth century by Edmund Kean in a much altered version by R. Wroughton. Hazlitt considered Kean's Richard a lamentable misinterpretation of Shakespeare. Later, Charles Kean mounted the play as a spectacular historical pageant, adding a great scene of

Bolingbroke's triumphal entry into London (Child 1968, pp. lxxxiii–
lxxxviii). In 1903 Beerbohm Tree's production rivalled Charles Kean's in
splendour, but the much more frequent performances of the play which
followed in this century were of a completely different kind. It was the
role of the second Richard that began to attract actors such as John
Gielgud and Maurice Evans. As the stage history makes clear, this was
not a role that appealed strongly to actors of the eighteenth and nineteenth
centuries. It may have been in part their styles of acting that gave them
a preference for the third Richard, flamboyantly active and villainous
rather than indecisive, self-dramatising, and finally pitiful. The interest
of our century in psychology undoubtedly helped to make such roles as
Richard II appealing. Gielgud, who played it in 1929 and again in 1937,
characteristically saw the challenge of both psychological subtlety and
musical verse. He noted that in the second half of the play Richard's
'inner character begins to be developed in a series of exquisite cadenzas
and variations. In these later scenes, the subtleties of his speeches are
capable of endless shades and nuances, but (as is nearly always the case
in Shakespeare) the actor's vocal efforts must be contrived within the
framework of the verse, and not outside it. Too many pauses and
striking variations of tempo will tend to hold up the action disastrously
and so ruin the pattern and symmetry of the text' (Gielgud 1963, p. 28).
It was, as J. C. Trewin wrote, 'a part in which he achieved an agonised
splendour' (Trewin 1964, p. 157). To this sort of interest in the play
the proponents of the 'Tudor myth' soon added another, since *Richard II*
is firmly linked to the three plays that follow it.

It may at first seem strange that *King John*, written at about the same
time as *Richard II* — possibly between that play and *1 Henry IV* — and
also presenting an indecisive, weak sovereign, should not have enjoyed
an equal success in this century. Their stage histories have been
precisely opposite, *King John* losing the popularity it had in the
eighteenth and nineteenth centuries while *Richard II* achieved a
popularity it had not previously had. The lack of any full development of
John's 'inner character' may partially explain the neglect, and Gielgud's
phrase, 'the pattern and symmetry of the text', taken out of context and
given perhaps a fuller meaning than he intended, suggests another
reason. To both critics and directors in recent times *patterns* of meaning
are eagerly sought after, whether they are seen as lessons, ideas, or
dominant themes. Tillyard observes that *King John*, like *1 Henry VI*,
deals 'with French deceit' and contains 'long scenes of siege-warfare in
France', but 'lacks unity'; though it is 'a wonderful affair, full of
promise and of new life, as a whole it is uncertain of itself' (Tillyard

1944, pp. 217, 232, 233). The lack of structural unity, of which Tillyard complains, is directly related to the absence of the sort of overarching theme that he found in *1 Henry VI*, also an episodic play, and in the succeeding plays of the first tetralogy. He omitted *Henry VIII* from his book partly because he did not think it was all by Shakespeare, and, as he continued, 'Anyhow, *Henry VIII* is so far removed in date from the main sequence of History Plays that its omission matters little to the argument of this book' (Tillyard 1944, p. viii). Not only removed in date, one might add, but, like *King John*, lacking the sort of unifying theme that Tillyard found in what he called 'the main sequence' — i.e. the two tetralogies.

The directors of history plays were often influenced by approaches such as Tillyard's or Dover Wilson's. One of the most ambitious enterprises was Peter Hall's and John Barton's staging of the two tetralogies (with the Henry VI sequence reduced to two plays) for the Royal Shakespeare Company in 1964. In the programme for *Richard II* (for the plays were given in the order of historical chronology) one reads, under the heading 'The Cycle of a Curse', about 'the curse pronounced upon Bolingbroke's usurpation of the tragically weak Richard II', and about Richmond, 'whose subsequent coronation as Henry VII and marriage to Elizabeth (of York) was to reconcile the rival houses, lift the curse, and introduce the stability of the Tudor succession'. In the programmes of the next plays are such headings as 'The Morality tradition and the rejection of Vanity' and 'Education of a Prince'. The programmes of the Henry VI plays (which had already been mounted the previous season) also point to the motif of the curse on the House of Lancaster, explaining that 'The plays are therefore an intricate pattern of retribution, of paying for sins, misjudgements, misgovernments. . . . So the selfish instincts of men must be checked — by Parliament, democracy, tradition, or religion — or else the men of ambition will misgovern the rest.' In an interview printed in the programme for *Richard III* Hall and Barton acknowledge their indebtedness to Tillyard, Dover Wilson, and others.

What concerns me is neither the identification of the scholar-critics who influenced Hall and Barton nor the validity of the historical views they adopted. For my purposes it is less important that Tillyard's views are now largely discounted than that they provided most of the structure for a notably successful production of these history plays. It is understandable that in this age of directors the perception of a grand design should be especially appealing, whether the design is the one Tillyard saw or some other, and the plays in the two tetralogies clearly have more of this appeal than do *King John* or *Henry VIII*. The parallel neglect of the two plays may be attributed in part to this lack of thematic coherence.

What was it, then, that appealed so strongly to both actors and critics in the eighteenth century? The popularity in the theatre of various Shakespeare plays relative to each other can be gauged by glancing at C. Beecher Hogan's table of performances in London. There one finds that among the history plays *Henry VIII* came third, after *Richard III* and *1 Henry IV* (and thirteenth among all the plays). *King John* came sixth among the history plays, following *2 Henry IV* and *Henry V* (and twenty-second among all the plays). The Henry VI plays were seldom performed in the first half of the century and never in the second half. *Richard II*, performed twenty-five times in the first half, when *King John* was performed 113 times, was left on the shelf for the remainder of the century.

The comments of Francis Gentleman, actor, playwright, very much a man of the theatre, throw some light on this theatrical record. The publisher, John Bell, asked Gentleman to write introductions and notes for the acting editions he published in 1773–4 as *Bell's Edition of Shakespeare's Plays*. What Gentleman liked about *Richard III* in Cibber's adaptation, of which he thoroughly approved, is clear in the first words of his introduction: 'There is no passage or personage in English History, better chosen for the drama, than what we find in the following piece; whatever doubts may arise as to the real character and figure of our Third Richard, Shakespeare was most undoubtedly right to make him a confirmed, uniform villain: nothing in the median way would have been half so striking on the stage' (Gentleman 1773–4, vol. 3, *Richard III*, p. 3). Theatre, not history, was what mattered. He was less enthusiastic about *1 Henry IV* despite 'many striking Dramatic characters and incidents', and deplored the mingling of 'mirth, and some very low of its kind, with sadness'. He admired 'Falstaff's luxuriance' and the depiction of the 'Prince of Wales's pleasures', but believed that the play would never 'please the ladies' (vol. 4, *1 Henry IV*, p. 3). He returned to this point in his final comment: 'yet we are sorry to say, that the want of ladies, and matter to interest female auditors, lies so heavy on it, that through an excellent Falstaff only, can it enjoy occasional life' (p. 74). He found many speeches by the king 'much too long' and was glad that they had been 'judiciously abridged' (p. 5). The play, as we have seen, enjoyed considerably more than 'occasional life', but Gentleman may have been right in thinking that its success in the theatre depended heavily upon the excellence of the Falstaff. Samuel

Johnson, as reader rather than spectator, concluded his comment on the two parts of the play with an almost rhapsodic tribute to Falstaff, so that his estimate of what is outstanding in the play is not unlike Gentleman's (Johnson 1765, 7, p. 522).

In his introduction to *Henry VIII* Gentleman 'ventured to say' that 'no other dramatic writer could have drawn the king, queen, and cardinal, with such forcible and chaste propriety' (vol. 3, *Henry VIII*, p. 3). He was again bored by tediously long speeches, which he thought should be cut in performance, but he responded to Buckingham's farewell. He wrote: 'Buckingham, in this scene, if a proper degree of manly, dignified pathos is supported, must gain the actor credit, and give the audience pleasure' (p. 25). About Wolsey's farewell he was downright enthusiastic: 'If Shakespeare had never written a line more, than this admirable soliloquy [III.ii.350–72], and the excellent scene which follows, they were sufficient to stamp him an eminent author. Never was there a finer, or more philosophical a picture, of fallen ambition, brought to reflexion by a just reverse of fortune. . . . This speech requires an excellent orator, to do it justice; yet, it is so exquisite in itself, that a tolerable one, may seem respectable' (pp. 50–1). In his concluding comment he observed 'that however nervous and pathetic several scenes of this play are, the success in representation, unless before a very sensible audience, depends chiefly on decoration, and splendour of show' (p. 72).

The scene that Johnson most admired was the second scene of the fourth act, where Queen Katherine makes her dying speeches to her attendants and the ambassador from the emperor: 'This scene is above any other part of Shakespeare's tragedies and perhaps above any scene of any other poet, tender and pathetick, without gods [the scene was usually played, as it is printed in Bell's edition, without Katherine's vision], or furies, or poisons, or precipices, without the help of romantick circumstances, without improbable sallies of poetical lamentation, and without any throes of tumultuous misery' (Johnson 1765, 8, p. 653). He was well aware that the play held the stage 'by the splendour of its pageantry. . . . Yet pomp is not the only merit of this play. The meek sorrows and virtuous distress of Catherine have furnished some scenes which may be justly numbered among the greatest efforts of tragedy. But the genius of Shakespeare comes in and goes out with Catherine. Every other part may be easily conceived, and easily written' (p. 657). John Philip Kemble told Boswell that when Johnson asked Sarah Siddons which Shakespearian role pleased her most, she said 'that she thought the character of Queen Catherine in *Henry the Eighth* the

most natural', and that Johnson, agreeing, then promised to 'hobble out
to the theatre' whenever she performed it — a promise he was unable to
keep (Boswell 1934, 4, p. 242).

The responses to *Henry VIII* by the man of the theatre and by 'the
great Cham of literature' are strikingly similar. One notices how much
value both of them attach to the pathetic. Johnson defined it in his
Dictionary as 'Affecting the passions; passionate; moving', and Jean
Hagstrum shows that he associated it with 'effusions purely natural' in
his discussion of Dryden's drama, which he found deficient in this
respect. Shakespeare's portrayal of the pathetic was one of his chief
excellences, and Hagstrum cites the comments on Queen Katherine as
an example (1952, pp. 137, 139–40). The reported exchange with Mrs
Siddons seems to make the same point. Gentleman uses the word in the
same sense when he speaks of scenes that are 'nervous [i.e. forceful] and
pathetic', two of which are the farewell scenes of Buckingham and
(especially) Wolsey. Gentleman is also characteristically concerned with
the oratorical skill by means of which the actor will make these scenes
moving. For both critics the great virtue of *Henry VIII* is the portrayal
of the passions in certain dramatic moments. An admirer of John
Fletcher cannot avoid remarking on the considerable irony that both
Gentleman's and Johnson's examples of Shakespeare's supreme achievement are probably the work, wholly or at least in part, of his
collaborator.[1]

King John, it will be recalled, was performed less frequently in the
eighteenth century than five other history plays, but Gentleman's
comments show that parts of the play had a powerful appeal. He began
his introduction with the assertion that '*King John* most certainly
deserves to live on the stage, but they must be a very good set of
performers who can sustain it.' Then, noting the unevenness of the
play, he wrote that 'where the Author appears himself, he is thoroughly
so; where he slumbers it is near sound'sleep' (vol. 3, *King John*, p. 3).
He found the role of the king a difficult one: 'The character of King
John, except in two scenes and a few speeches, lies heavy on the actor;
who therefore requires great judgement, with deep and strong
expression, to assist the author; dignity of person and deportment are
also necessary' (p. 5). The Bastard's part also presented a challenge:
'The bastard, Faulconbridge, is as odd a personage as any author ever
drew; and Shakespeare has given him language equally peculiar with his
ideas; a bold, blunt utterance, with spirit, and a martial figure, may do
him justice on the stage; we utterly condemn that tendency to the
ludicrous, which some capital actors have given to this character' (p. 7).

He reserved his highest praise for Constance in the third act, where she hears how she and her cause have been betrayed: 'Our author, who took very little pains in general with female characters, there being no performers of that sex upon the stage in his time, has however roused his genius in favour of Constance; he has entered into, and expressed her complaints in a most masterly manner; the ideas through the whole of this scene, are happily pathetic; they appeal so successfully to the heart, that even common feelings must submit to their force' (pp. 25–6). The next scene, in which John lets Hubert know that he would like Prince Arthur killed, was an example of an opportunity for the actor of the king's part: 'It is impossible for words to express, or imagination to paint, a finer representation of dubious cruelty, fearful to express itself, than this address of John's to Hubert exhibits; the hesitative circumlocution, with which he winds about his gloomy purpose, is highly natural and the imagery exquisite. To do this scene justice, requires more judgement than powers: a jealous eye, deep tone of voice, and cautious delivery, are the outlines of what should be' (p. 35). The final scene of this act elicited another comment on Constance and another piece of advice on acting: 'Though Constance's grief before the battle, appears very powerful to sympathizing passions, yet upon the loss of her son there is a tincture of despair, mingled with such an increase of sorrow, that the scene grows rather too trying for refined sensations. The actress who performs this part, has here occasion for uncommon expression of grief; her features should be the living type of sorrow, and her voice capable of breaking harmoniously into the stile of expression, which a flood of anguish occasions' (p. 38). There is ample evidence that eighteenth-century actresses, including Mrs Siddons, made the most of the opportunities offered by this role and succeeded in moving their audiences.

From this sampling of eighteenth-century comments emerges a certain way of looking at these plays. As in all periods, they are evaluated by the man of the theatre in terms of theatrical opportunities, but in appraising serious (as opposed to comic) scenes, Gentleman places much more emphasis than would his opposite number today on moving the passions, and, in the scenes which he discusses at greatest length, the chief passion to be aroused is pity. Johnson's response to Katherine's final scene suggests that he looked to be moved in the same way. What is conspicuously absent is any concern with the ideas that might give thematic coherence to these history plays. Presumably actor-managers were less concerned than today's directors with dominant ideas or themes, and even a literary critic such as Johnson did not demand this kind of coherence. Hagstrum shows how he gradually shifted from an Aristotelian emphasis on structure to the view that Shakespeare's plots were finally justified by the succession of interesting incidents (Hagstrum 1952, pp. 127–8).

From this approach to drama *King John* and *Henry VIII* stood to gain in competition with other Shakespearian plays and specifically with the other history plays. All the histories have, in varying quantities, eminently playable roles and effective scenes, many of which can be staged with spectacular pageantry. The two non-tetralogy plays proved in many productions to abound in these assets, surpassing the Henry VI plays and *Richard II*. What they lacked, but what was not demanded of them, was a different sort of structure. No particular interpretation is needed to reveal the links which provide more unified structures for the tetralogies and for individual plays within them, and such structures lend themselves to the thematic interpretations which have appealed to many twentieth-century readers and directors.

The structural differences can easily be demonstrated. *1 Henry VI*, which admittedly is an episodic play, is nevertheless held together not only by concern with the war in France but even more by insistence on the quarrels among the English nobles which lead to the defeat of Talbot and the loss of French territory — Somerset and York, especially in the Temple Garden scene (II.iv), which prepares for 'York and Lancaster's long jars'; Gloucester and Winchester (III.i); Gloucester and Suffolk (V.v). The War of the Roses, thoroughly prepared for in Part 1 (whether or not it was written first), occupies the second and third parts. In Part 2, arguably the most coherent of the three, a frequent narrowing of focus to the ambitions of Richard Plantagenet, Duke of York, contributes to an impression of unity. Richard, Duke of Gloucester, the future Richard III, provides, perhaps less successfully, the unifying influence for the third part, and completely dominates the final play in the tetralogy.

In *King John*, as Tillyard and others have noted (1944, p. 217), historical themes left over, as it were, from *1 Henry VI*, seem to be present — the war against France and the lesson that domestic quarrelling will lose the war, while, as the Bastard puts it in the last lines of the play, 'Naught shall make us rue,/If England to itself do rest but true' (Shakespeare 1989, V.vii.117–18). It is only in the second part of the play, however, that internal dissension arises, and it comes as a surprise that the chief spokesman for patriotic dedication should be the Bastard, whose cynical observations on 'commodity' (self-interest) have provided a jaundiced view of the political scene. In the first part of the play a more important issue, as J. L. Simmons says, seems to be that of the legitimacy of succession, for both the king and the Bastard (1969, pp. 58–60).

In the Elizabethan play which was probably Shakespeare's source, *The Troublesome Reign of King John*,[2] as in the earlier *King Johan* by John Bale, the king's resistance to Catholic domination is an important theme (see Bullough 1966, p. 9), but in Shakespeare's play it is markedly less so (Simmons 1969, pp. 58–60). Here a potentially unifying theme is ignored as is the possibility of making the king's role more central. In the second part of *The Troublesome Reign* John is given several long speeches, including a soliloquy, in which he reveals more of his motivation and of his anguished feelings than he ever does in *King John*. Just before his submission to Pandulph he is given lines that combine self-revelation, the anti-Catholic theme, and prophecy of the reign of Henry VIII:

> Thy sinnes are farre too great to be the man
> T'abolish Pope, and Popery from thy Realme:
> But in thy Seate, if I may gesse at all,
> A King shall raigne that shall suppresse them all.
>   (2, 278–81; Bullough 1966, pp. 123–7)

Nothing in *King John* corresponds to these speeches.

A long scene in *The Troublesome Reign* is devoted to the English nobles' complaints about John's tyranny, as they plan to join the invading French forces (Part 2, Scene 3). They are answered by the Bastard with a strong speech urging obedience to John, but they proceed to swear allegiance to the Dauphin. The scene in Shakespeare's play which most nearly corresponds to this one (V.ii) skips the discussion of domestic politics and opens with the nobles joining the French. Once again historical matter is skimped.

What is notably augmented in *King John* is the pathos of Constance's situation in those scenes which Gentleman admired. Also the king, though robbed of his agonised repentance and prophecy, is given a gripping scene in which he, as if hardly daring to speak directly, gradually lets Hubert know that he wants young Arthur out of the way. In *The Troublesome Reign* the matter is briskly dispatched in six lines. Shakespeare gives the scene in which Hubert attempts to carry out these orders a different character by making Arthur a small boy instead of the young man he seems to be in *The Troublesome Reign*. And a telling detail distinguishes Shakespeare's depiction of the defection of the English nobles: Salisbury, their spokesman in both plays, is made to weep as he tells the Dauphin that they will fight with the French. In all these instances the scenes in *King John* have more of what Gentleman and Johnson called the 'pathetic'.

A succession of moving scenes seems to have proved an acceptable alternative to thematic continuity in the eighteenth century. In a somewhat comparable fashion, the Royal Shakespeare Company production of *King John*, directed by Deborah Warner at The Other Place in Stratford-upon-Avon in 1988, moved from one sort of excitement to another. In a boisterous (some thought too boisterous) rendition of the role of the Bastard, so emphasised by Shakespeare, David Morrissey contributed importantly to the impression of energy exuded by the production as a whole, and notably manifest in the rapid pacing. Susan Engel made the most of the grief and bitterness of Constance in speeches that were all the more effective for having no competition from the minimalist staging.

This approach could lead to more productions of *King John* and also of *Henry VIII*, which depends, above all, as the Prologue makes clear, on an appeal to the emotions. 'I come no more to make you laugh,' he says (Shakespeare 1971, Prologue, l. 1), presumably referring to Samuel Rowley's fanciful play about Henry VIII called *When You See Me You Know Me* and staged some years earlier. He continues:

> Things now
> That bear a weighty and a serious brow,
> Sad, high, and working, full of state and woe,
> Such noble scenes as draw the eye to flow,
> We now present. Those that can pity here
> May, if they think it well, let fall a tear;
> The subject will deserve it. Such as give
> Their money out of hope they may believe
> May here find truth too.   (ll. 1–9)

It is a more serious play, designed to elicit tears rather than laughter; it is also true to history. The priorities could not be stated more plainly. A major concern, according to the Prologue, is to be the falls of the great and famous:

> Think ye see
> The very persons of our noble story
> As they were living; think you see them great,
> And followed with the general throng and sweat
> Of thousand friends: then, in a moment, see
> How soon this mightiness meets misery.   (ll. 25–30)

The big scenes of Buckingham's farewell, Wolsey's farewell, and the trial and death of Queen Katherine amply fulfil the expectations aroused by the Prologue, and theatrical appeal of a different sort characterises a number of other scenes. Johnson noted that the play kept possession of the stage 'by the splendour of its pageantry'. His words remind us of the masque, so much in vogue at the time of this play and so obviously an influence upon it. Not only are there the masquers at Wolsey's banquet (I.iv), but also the spectacles of the coronation of Anne Bullen (IV.i), Katherine's vision, as she lies dying (IV.ii), and the baptism of Elizabeth with the prophecy of her reign and that of James I (in the last scene). This ending of the play is especially masque-like, for in the last act the play veers from its depiction of calamitous changes of fortune to the king's rescue of Cranmer from the plotting of his enemies and then to the description of the golden age to come with Elizabeth and James.

In the BBC television version of *Henry VIII*, directed by Kevin Billington in 1979, the effect of the spectacular scenes is inevitably much reduced, and the emphasis placed on individual characters, often seen in close-ups. The whispered intrigues at court are arguably more effective on the television screen than on a large stage. With the eighteenth-century views of the play in mind, it is interesting to note that Claire Bloom succeeds in making of Queen Katherine's ordeal the most affecting moments of the production, particularly in her spirited encounter with the two cardinals (III.i) and in her death scene (IV.ii). But the low-keyed and relatively naturalistic delivery dictated by this medium deprives these scenes, and those of Buckingham's and Wolsey's farewells, of some of the rhetorical power which actors on a stage could give them, especially if they paid attention to what Gielgud called 'the pattern and symmetry of the text' — that is, to the insistent rhythms of the verse. What is missing in this screen production is what was most admired in the eighteenth century. Claire Bloom's performance might well be described in the words Thomas Davies used about Mrs Pritchard, to whom he greatly preferred Mrs Porter. He wrote:

> Mrs Pritchard's Queen Katharine has been much approved, and especially in the scene of the trial. She certainly was in behaviour easy, and in speaking natural and familiar; but the situation of the character required more force in utterance and more dignity in action. Mrs Porter's manner was elevated to the rank of the person she represented (Davies 1785, p. 385).

Returning to the same point in his comment on Katherine's death scene, he wrote:

> During this truly-pathetick scene, the behaviour of Mrs Pritchard,

the representer of Katharine, was respectable; but her best efforts could not reach the grace and dignity of gesture, much less the heart-touching tenderness, of Mrs Porter. In this actress it was observed, that a very bad voice did not obstruct the forcible expression of excessive grief (p. 421).

Like *King John, Henry VIII* seems to have been designed primarily to work on the feelings of its audience, and its demands for pity are even more insistent. With considerably more spectacle than the earlier play it also elicits wonder, and for the patriotic appeal to England to 'rest but true' to itself it substitutes a splendidly comforting view of the immediate past and of the present. Neither ending can have the same effect on an audience today as it was expected to have on the audience for which it was written, but that earlier effect is still accessible to the imagination. As for the emotional scenes on which the reputation of both plays appears to have rested in the times of their greatest popularity, they can be made as affecting as ever in the right sort of performance.

Notes

1 This is not the place to argue for Fletcher's participation. I have given some of my reasons for believing in it in *The Pattern of Tragicomedy in Beaumont and Fletcher* (New Haven: Yale University Press; London: Oxford University Press, 1952), pp. 118–24, and have discussed stylistic differences between Fletcher and Shakespeare in my edition of *The Two Noble Kinsmen* (Oxford, New York: Oxford University Press, 1989), pp. 9–23.
2 It is generally considered the earlier play, though Ernst Honigmann has argued that it derived from *King John* in his Arden edition of that play (London: Methuen, 1954), pp. xi–xxxiii.

References

Bevington, David (1987) ed., Shakespeare, *Henry IV, Part I*, Oxford: Clarendon Press.
Boswell, James (1934) *Boswell's Life of Johnson*, ed. George Birbeck Hill, rev. L. F. Powell, 4 vols., Oxford: Clarendon Press, 1934.
Bullough, Geoffrey (1966) *Narrative and Dramatic Sources of Shakespeare*, ed. Geoffrey Bullough, vol. 4, London: Routledge; New York: Columbia University Press, 1966.
Child, Harold (1968) 'The Stage-History of *King Richard II*' in Shakespeare, *King Richard II*, ed. J. Dover Wilson, Cambridge: University Press.
Davies, Thomas (1785) *Dramatic Miscellanies*, London.

Gentleman, Francis (1773–74) in *Bell's Edition of Shakespeare's Plays*, 9 vols., London: J. Bell.

Gielgud, John (1963) *Stage Directions*, London: Heinemann.

Hagstrum, Jean H. (1952) *Samuel Johnson's Literary Criticism*, Minneapolis: University of Minnesota Press; London: Cumberlege; Oxford University Press.

Hogan, Charles Beecher (1952–7) *Shakespeare in the Theatre: A Record of Performances in London, 1701–1800*, 2 vols., Oxford: Oxford University Press.

Johnson, Samuel (1765) 'Notes on Shakespeare's Plays' in *Johnson on Shakespeare*, ed. Arthur Sherbo, Yale Edition of Samuel Johnson, vols. 7 and 8, New Haven and London: Yale University Press, 1968.

Shakespeare, William (1971) *King Henry the Eighth*, ed. A. R. Humphreys, Harmondsworth: Penguin Books.

Shakespeare, William (1989) *King John*, ed. Albert Braunmuller, Oxford, New York: Oxford University Press.

Simmons, J. L. (1969) 'Shakespeare's *King John* and its Source', in *Tulane Studies in English*, 17, pp. 53–72.

Tillyard, E. M. W. (1944) *Shakespeare's History Plays*, London: Chatto & Windus; New York: Macmillan, 1946.

Trewin, J. C. (1964) *Shakespeare on the English Stage 1900–1964*, London: Barrie & Rockliff.

Young, C. B. (1954) 'The Stage-History of *Richard III*' in Shakespeare, *Richard III*, ed. J. Dover Wilson, Cambridge: University Press.

A. D. Nuttall

SOME SHAKESPEAREAN OPENINGS:
HAMLET, TWELFTH NIGHT, THE TEMPEST

It is said that those musical works which begin with a high distant call on the French horn are very hard on the performers. Openings are naturally anxious affairs, but horn-playing is peculiarly vulnerable to nervous tension; a catch in the breath issues in a horribly audible false note. Shakespeare knew from working experience that first lines are similarly charged with anxiety for the performers. This area of potential defeat he turned, like several others, into a field of victory. The actor playing Barnardo in the opening scene of *Hamlet* finds that, in addition to the usual hazards of uttering the first words of the play, he is being supplied by a dramatist who has chosen, as it were, to live dangerously on his behalf: to have him tremble for a fraction of a second on the edge of farce. *Hamlet* begins, not with the Ghost of Hamlet's father, but with the ghost of a joke:

BARNARDO Who's there?
FRANCISCO Nay, answer me. Stand and unfold yourself.

A change in the shading — or the lighting — could transform this, swift as it is, into a familiar comic routine. The sentry, issuing his sonorous challenge, is answered not by a stranger but by a fellow sentry whom he has come to relieve. If the comic structure were more emphatic, we could say that Barnardo is first made a fool of and then, with marvellous rapidity, the same treatment is extended to Francisco (for *he*, absurdly, challenges Barnardo). One might infer that, since Barnardo has not yet formally taken over from Francisco, he is not yet on duty and that his first words are therefore not a sentry's challenge but a civilian's (alarmed) enquiry. Even if this is the case, the words fall into the pattern of the sentry's challenge (Francisco in reply immediately points out that Barnardo has, so to speak, stolen his line); the point is rendered finer still by the fact that Barnardo *is* a sentry, coming to take up his post.

Directors often complain about the way modern audiences laugh at the conclusion of *The White Devil*. It is possible that they always did. Webster in the address to the reader prefixed to the published version complains that the first audience failed to understand him. The 'ignorant

(84)

asses' at that dismal performance (at the Red Bull in Clerkenwell?) in 1612 may well have angered the author as much by their laughter as by their unresponsiveness. A fine control of the 'horrid laughter' appropriate to revenge tragedy may always have been difficult. William Empson thought that the special mystery of *Hamlet* arose from an initial technical problem of just this kind: that Shakespeare was asked to write a new version of Kyd's (?) old play, to please an audience which, while it was genuinely enthusiastic, was 'tickle o'th'sere' (that is, slightly *too* ready to laugh); Shakespeare's response was to 'pipe off' the laughter in episodes of histrionic pastiche, retaining all the while a power to freeze all those smiles by confronting the audience with something it could not begin to understand.

I have described the opening of *Hamlet* as if the dramatist has deliberately doubled the anxiety of the actor by tripping him up, on his first entrance. There is a sense, however, in which *scripted* mistakings relieve the pressure on the actor. As soon as the audience intuits that all this is part of the play, is authorially designed, the faint absurdity becomes not his but that of the character he is playing. The first horn-call of *Hamlet* is flawed, but the composer has decreed that it should be so. It is hard, indeed, to avoid a sense of theatrical self-reference in Francisco's third speech. 'You come most carefully upon your hour' (I.i.6), but, as I have argued elsewhere (Nuttall 1988), Shakespeare has already, in the first two words, mobilised both laughter and laughter-killing fear. By the time the play is over we know that the question, 'Who's there?', was in a manner prophetic, for standing behind Francisco, in the darkness, is a dead king, a most potent negation, having the power to undo the social fabric of Elsinore, to involve others in his own un-being. Perhaps since we know from Lodge's *Wit's Misery* (1596) that the old play of Hamlet contained a ghost (Lodge, 1963, vol. IV, p. 62), Shakespeare could count on thoughts turning in that direction at the very first words of the play. Before he uttered the first words of the drama, did Barnardo glimpse something or someone *other than Francisco?* Yet, in any case, the answers supplied by the ensuing action are non-answers, for the essence of the Ghost is that he has no essence. We therefore never really move from the interrogative mood of Barnardo's first speech to an indicative resolution. His question remains truer than other people's answers.

Thus, even as the actors enter the public arena of the theatre, emerging with creaking of boards and rustling of costumes in broad daylight before a crowd of onlookers, a sense is created that we are somehow able to watch the passing of these same figures from the

familiar world into the unintelligible world of death. It is often alleged
(though with decreasing confidence) that the Elizabethans had no
doubts about life after death. Shakespeare relies in this play on our not
knowing what death means; on this radical uncertainty the entire
shadow-fabric of the drama is raised. Whereas Lear says, 'When we are
born, we cry that we are come/To this great stage of fools' (IV.vi.182–
3), the stage on which the actors arrive at the beginning of *Hamlet* is
the dark obverse of that to which Lear alludes. The audience itself, in a
good production, experiences a disembodying fear. The laughter is
stillborn.

It may be that the artistic practice of beginning not at the obvious
first term of a series but part-way through is a Greek invention.
Aristotle had only scorn for the low poet who thought artistic unity
could be attained merely by recounting 'all the things that happened to
Theseus' (*Poetics*, 1451a), and Horace was never so Greek-minded as
when he coined the approving phrase, *in medias res* (*Ars Poetica*, 148).
After the Greek example even those poets with the strongest drive
toward a Hebraic natural origin (Milton, say) have felt obliged to avail
themselves of the peculiar dynamic of the *in medias res* opening.
Spenser defers to it completely in the opening of his thoroughly
Elizabethan *Faerie Queene*. Note that I exclude here those Greek
tragedies that begin at a point within a known, inherited myth, since in
such cases there may well be no disorientation at all. It may be said that
the distinction between Homer and Sophocles is a little elusive, since
the *Iliad* begins at a certain point in the Trojan story and *Oedipus Rex* at
a certain point in the Theban story. But no one in antiquity records any
sense of surprise at the customary Greek tragic playing off of plot
against myth. Individual plays could have disorienting openings.
Aeschylus' *Agamemnon* begins, notoriously, with an apparently empty
stage, but then the watchman, lying dog-wise on the roof, is suddenly
noticed (Denniston and Page, 1957, p. xxxi). But this is a special
theatrical effect. The surprise does not flow simply from the fact that the
play begins at a late point in the Trojan story. The most majestically
developed English drama of the Middle Ages, the great cycles of
mystery plays, exhibit a powerful impulse to begin from the 'deep'
beginning of all things. Such a beginning must be from that which has
no prior beginning. The York Cycle opens with the soliloquy of God, a
soliloquy which is also an announcement of self-hood. The playwright
has no thought of plunging *in medias res*. Instead he finds that he must
stress not so much the immortality of God as his 'birthless-ness':

I am gracyus and grete, God withoutyn begynnyng,
I am maker unmade, al mighte es in me . . .
(Beadle, 1982, p. 49)

We are here as far as one can well be from the artfully interventionist
opening of, say, *Othello*.

The epic *in medias res* opening remains, so to speak, the central feat
of formal art, against the ordinary logic of a 'natural beginning'.
Meanwhile, however, outside the canonical lineage of epic, other less
assertive modes of initial disorientation were developed. Chaucer's
Book of the Duchess opens not so much *in medias res* as *in medias
sententias*; the reader, who seems rather to overhear than to hear, is
admitted to a stream of rambling reflections on the horrors of insomnia.
It is instantly clear that the reader is not being *addressed*: rather one
senses that this monologue may have been going on for some time. In
Shakespearian drama it is fairly common for plays to begin in mid-
conversation. When figures enter talking, the presumption is that they
were talking before they entered.

Ask an ordinary, educated person how *King Lear* begins and you will
probably receive the answer, 'The play begins with an old king dividing
his kingdom.' In fact it begins, not with the ceremonial entrance of the
king, but with a low-key, gossiping exchange between Kent and
Gloucester. One needs to be fairly alert to take in the drift of the first
words of the play: 'I thought the King had more affected the Duke of
Albany than Cornwall.' The actor is given very little in the way of a
formal send-off by the dramatist — not even the stiffening tempo of
verse. It may be said that the first thirty lines or so of *King Lear* are
mere 'filler', designed to occupy the time in which an unruly audience is
settling down (corresponding, perhaps, to an orchestral tuning-up). But
the lines contain important information, concerning both the political
world of the play and the question of Edmund's parentage. *The Winter's
Tale* begins, in a somewhat similar fashion, with gossiping courtiers.
All this suggests (after all that we have said about unwanted laughter) a
surprisingly docile audience, which will fall silent at the first appearance
of the actors — even when those actors (in this contrasting strongly
with most late medieval drama) appear strangely negligent of their real-
life auditors, to be wholly preoccupied by their own concerns. It may be
that the audience was brought to order very simply, by a trumpet-call or
the striking of a staff upon the stage. In which case the notable thing is
Shakespeare's studious exclusion of the event from the inner texture of
his frame. As far as I know, the surviving evidence (for example,

Dekker's *The Gull's Hornbook*) points to an association of trumpets with formal prologue openings but tells us nothing about 'low-key' openings. (Chambers, 1923, vol. IV, p. 367; vol. II, p. 542).

Such a style of opening is the reverse of rhetorical: though Shakespeare, the master-rhetorician, knows very well that people can be made to listen with a different sort of attentiveness to words which they conceive to be addressed, not to them but to someone else. The queer false privacy of proscenium arch theatre is already well developed, on the projecting stage of Shakespeare's Globe. In like manner, it is surely a mistake to think that the *scripted* 'improvisations' of the figures labelled A and B in the text of *Fulgens and Lucrece*, or the irruption of Ralph from the audience in *The Knight of the Burning Pestle*, are a simple continuation of the sort of improvisation achieved by the young Thomas More. William Roper tells how 'at Christmas-tyde the boy More would sodenly sometimes steppe in among the players, and never studyeng for the matter, make a parte of his owne there presently among them, which made the lookers-on more sporte than all the plaiers beside' (Roper, 1935, p. 5). The behaviour of this brilliant, loved and applauded little boy contrasts strongly with that of the children in More's own *Utopia*, written years later: they are required to stand at table, keeping absolutely quiet, waiting to be given food by the adults (More, 1965, p. 142). One may guess, moreover, that the actors, perhaps, did not feel so warmly about little Thomas. *Scripted* pseudo-improvisation, meanwhile, presupposes a high degree of docility in both actors and audience. But such audiences (as we know today) can still laugh in the wrong places.

It will be evident that *Hamlet* does not conform exactly to what we have described as the *in medias sententias* mode. Instead of an overheard continuity we have a pivotal movement (one sentinel replacing another), crisis replacing stasis at the very inception of the drama. Nevertheless, we enter the world of the play *after* the first two appearances of the Ghost, though before its crucial encounter with the Prince. The further development whereby ordinary disorientation is suddenly extended into absolute mystery (life appropriated by death) might be supposed something essentially tragic. Yet there is a curious equivalent in comedy.

Twelfth Night opens, indeed, with a major chord, struck by the fantastical Duke in melancholic soliloquy, but at I.ii the play has what might be called a secondary opening:

> VIOLA What country, friends, is this?
> CAPTAIN This is Illyria, lady.

> VIOLA And what should I do in Illyria?
> My brother, he is in Elysium.

Barbara Everett has said of this exactly what needs to be said: 'Illyria is a name and a place that from the first maintains its own mocking half-echo of Elysium, a place of death as well as of immortality' (1985, p. 295). 'Illyria' may draw on other remoter echoes — 'idyll', 'delirium' (both words extant in English in Shakespeare's time, neither used by him), but Elysium is the word he planted in our minds. Viola, as she makes her first entrance on the stage, is half-bewildered by a strange thought: that she ought to be — perhaps is — dead. Barnardo in *his* opening, nerve-stretching speech, was instantly wrong-footed on a point of personal identity. Viola is similarly wrong-footed but this time even more fleetingly, on a question of context, which in its turn throws into question her own identity as distinct from her brother's. In *Hamlet* we have a lurking emissary from beyond the grave; Viola wonders conversely why she has not followed her drowned brother, and then, with the echoic word 'Elysium', the dramatist plants the further, fainter thought that Viola may herself be a new arrival in a place of (strangely happy) death. In both plays our responses are quickened by a sense of death as an alternative world, eerily coinciding with the palpable unreality of dramatic performance (creaking boards, Illyrians). Yet what I earlier called the fictional 'lighting' of the scene is indeed quite different. *Hamlet* begins in an imagined darkness, *Twelfth Night*, I.ii, in strange brightness. It is noteworthy that so complex a feat of emotional overlapping can be accomplished with such simple language, yet it is so. 'Illyria', while it echoes 'Elysium', also figures as its living antithesis, so that the dominant character of the situation for her is its incongruity.

It is easy to 'hear' in 'What should I do in Illyria?' an echo of *Et in Arcadia ego*. Erwin Panofsky in his famous essay on the phrase (1955) did not succeed in tracing it back before Guercino's pastoral death's head, which may belong to 1623, the year of the Shakespeare First Folio. Panofsky argued that, by the rules of Latin syntax, the phrase properly means, not 'I too have lived in Arcadia', but 'Even in Arcadia, I (death) am' (p. 296). Anne Barton (1972, p. 164) cited the Latin phrase, and the two great Poussin paintings in which it occurs, with reference to the momentarily disorienting intrusion of the idea of death towards the end of *As You Like It*. Yet it is in the early, marvelling sequence in *Twelfth Night*, in which Viola finds herself new-lighted in Illyria, like the sea-stained Odysseus in Phaeacia, that Shakespeare comes closest to the cadence of the Latin phrase.

It may seem that my argument has doubled back and consumed itself, the transcendent world of the dead now cancelled by a bright land of happy, living persons. But we must not allow the proper ambiguity of the scene to be lost. Elysium, like the Christian Heaven, is itself ambiguous: a place of dead people; a place where people find, to their joy, that they never died. Thus Viola's marvelling at the incongruous brightness of her surroundings does not automatically or unequivocally enforce the 'corrective' answer, 'She never died at all.' In a student production of *Twelfth Night* directed by Edward Kemp in Oxford in 1987, Viola entered Illyria at the beginning of I.ii by appearing over a wall and descending a ladder into the world of the play. Although we can be reasonably certain that the original Elizabethan actor did no such thing, the device caught very exactly and economically the 'liminal' feeling of the scene. With her first words Viola crosses some magic threshold.

Shakespeare has found a way to turn the nervousness of the actors and the uncertainty of the audience to account. His method is to involve both parties in far larger uncertainties. Performances, *qua* performances, are real physical events, making clamorously importunate demands upon our senses, yet at the same time the events displayed are not real events. This paradox of absence-in-presence is so familiar as to be normally almost unnoticeable. But Shakespeare reactivates the latent oddity by associating it with other antitheses: life/art, waking/dream, being/unbeing, life/death. These in their turn can release further paradoxes: art may be more vivid than that quotidian existence, the undiscovered country may be lit by a brighter sun than shines on us. That is why, instead of employing some dramatic equivalent of the *in medias res* opening of classical epic, he finds his way, via various versions of what I have called the *in medias sententias* opening, to an entry not so much into the midst of (known) things as *between things*, or between whole orders of things. The ordinary indeterminacy of Elizabethan and Jacobean staging, with its rudimentary scenery and correlatively high demands upon the imagination of the audience, is made the vehicle of an ontological indeterminacy.

With *Twelfth Night* we allowed the notion of an opening to extend as far as I.ii. With *The Tempest* we must allow it to extend still further into the play. We begin *fortissimo*, with a crashing of chords. We are plunged in the centre of the storm which gives the play its name. The over-riding voice is that of the tempest itself, not of the human agents. There is here no difficulty over the securing of audience attention since, according to the Folio stage direction, the first thing we hear is thunder. I suspect that the force of this particular audacious opening has been paradoxically diminished by the rise of electronic wizardry in the twentieth century. In some present-day productions of *The Tempest* the sound effects are so overwhelming as to turn the actors into twittering, almost inaudible ghosts of themselves; the original *coup de théâtre* is intolerably coarsened.

The dialogue is as informal, as lacking in overt rhetorical address, as the low-key gossiping openings we have already noticed, but here the human agents, for all their shouting, are further reduced, to mere confused panic. At line 62 comes the cry, 'We split, we split, we split!', and the audience knows that the ship is wrecked. Can we say that at the beginning of the play we *see* the ship wrecked? The question is of some interest because it turns out later (V.i.224) that the ship is perfectly all right (whether because magically reconstituted or because the wreck was some sort of illusion, James, 1967, p. 30). It is virtually certain that the King's Men did not contrive to overturn the stage at this point. The trap was too small to have been of any use. Instead we may suppose that they relied on the auditory sense. In this they could be reasonably secure: in drama of the period the authority of the ear is higher than that of the eye. Irwin Smith writes that when a nocturnal scene was presented at the candle-lit Blackfriars theatre, all the artificial illumination was unchanged, though the character (night-shirted, carrying *his own* candle), would speak of darkness (1964, pp. 302–3). Audiences were educated to respond to verbal indications of action or situation (which is why the 'Dover Cliff' episode in *King Lear* is so disorienting — Edgar's vertiginous speech compels, as it were, an excess of assent). 'We split!' will therefore be believed. Moreover the words may well have been accompanied by some sound as of rending timber. The slightly odd Folio stage direction a couple of lines before, *A confused noise within*, has usually been taken, since Capell's commentary, to refer to the quick-fire exclamatory speeches which immediately follow, but it is just possible that it points to some non-human sound effect — say, a creaking. At IV.i.138, the masquing spirits heavily vanish *To a strange, hollow and confused noise*. There the noise is almost certainly inhuman. It must be weird and a little alarming — a piece of Jacobean avant-garde theatre. Further, the moment at which the spirits 'heavily vanish' may place some strain on our earlier confidence that the stage itself did not move. After all, we are dealing with a play which post-dates the leasing in 1608 of the second Blackfriars theatre (candle-lit performances, 'transformation scenes'). What if, both in I.i and IV.i, Shakespeare once more succeeded in exploiting a technical problem — this time the presence of some over-ingenious mechanism — either by deliberately throwing away the oil-can or by 'covering' with some louder noise, to induce yet another species of disorientation? In I.i, however, the sailors are all, manifestly, still in place *after* the confused noise has been heard. It may also be salutary to recall G. F. Reynolds (1940, p. 43) on the scene in *The Two Noble Ladies* (1619–23) in which two soldiers crossing a river are drowned in full view of the audience; we could easily have inferred from the text some minor miracle of illusionism but we happen to know how it was done: two Tritons entered and dragged the soldiers away.

With the beginning of I.ii we pass into the alternative shock of a strange tranquillity, from the wreck to the unhurried conversation of father and daughter. The contrast of 'volume' is so marked as to make us doubt momentarily the reality of what we just 'witnessed'. This intuition is reinforced as Miranda tells us, in her first speech, that the whole episode may have been an effect of (Prospero's) art. All this, to be sure, operates at the subordinate level only; the dominant impression is that Miranda has witnessed, as we have witnessed, a shipwreck.

Yet a certain 'ecphrastic colouring' persists in the speech — a sense, that is, that we are listening to the description of a work of art rather than a reaction to a real disaster. 'O I have suffered/With those that I saw suffer' (I.ii.5–6) somehow suggests what we in the twentieth century have learned to call 'audience-empathy'. The disaster with 'no harm done' (I.ii.14) succeeds in anticipating various psychological explanations of the pleasure of theatrical tragedy. The way Miranda gazed at 'the brave vessel,/(Who had, no doubt, some noble creature in her)' (I.ii.6–7), and the way she gasped at the fate of the 'poor souls' (l. 9), seems not wholly unlike the way Leontes' soul is pierced by what he takes to be a statue of Hermione (*Winter's Tale*, V.iii.34). We may think also of the speech of the third servant on the painting of Daphne, in *The Taming of the Shrew*:

> Or Daphne roaming through a thorny wood,
> Scratching her legs that one shall swear she bleeds,
> And at that sight shall sad Apollo weep,
> So workmanly the blood and tears are drawn
> (Induction, ii, 56–9).

The special oxymoron of 'weep' and 'workmanly' is absent from Miranda's speech, but 'by your art' is only a few lines away.

Meanwhile the sense we found in *Twelfth Night* of passing through death by water to another world recurs here. The life of the Island is not our life. When in II.i the castaways enter, as Viola entered in I.ii, amazed to find their bodies and their clothes intact, they see the Island differently: one sees lush greenery while another sees a barren landscape (II.i.54–6). Once more, Shakespeare exploits the visual indeterminacy of Jacobean scenery. There is a line in Virgil which is commonly assumed to describe the condition of the dead:

> *Clausae tenebris et carcere caeco*
> (Shut up in darkness and a blind prison.)
> (*Aeneid* VI.734)

In fact it is uttered by one of the inhabitants of Elysium (which has *a larger sky* than ours, VI.640) to describe the inhabitants of *our* world. When Prospero invites Miranda to cast her mind back to 'the time before' (I.ii.39), to the real, living world of Milan, the image is not, as we might have expected, of a far-off, brilliantly illuminated picture, watched from the shadows by exiled spirits. Instead we have the line that haunted Keats:

> What seest thou else
> In the dark backward and abysm of time?
> (I.ii.49–50)

The dream-island is brighter than the political reality.

In *The Tempest* the threshold between sleep and waking is exploited to the same end, becoming indeed a place of transit where we may feel the dream could cross. The wakings in the play all lay stress on the equivocal character of perception at such moments: we may think here of Gonzalo and others at II.i (the arrival in this strangely transposed Elysium), and the sailors in V.i. Miranda compares her dim memory image of the ladies who attended her with a dream (I.ii.45), and Prospero, in the play's most famous speech, finally links the ideas of sleep and death ('our little life/Is rounded with a sleep', IV.i.157–8). The effect is rather of a cycling movement than of a linear imaginative drive to an unequivocal resurrection. Caliban, after all, having woken, cried to dream again. At the end of *The Tempest* the pastoral pattern, whereby a golden world, having been applauded, is at last eagerly exchanged for a return to court, is followed.

This essay discerns no single 'law' or 'deep structure' in Shakespearean openings, though it has been concerned with a certain pattern of affinity, by which even plays as generically opposite to one another as *Hamlet* and *Twelfth Night* may be linked. Shakespeare who endlessly recycles his imaginative intuitions rarely if ever repeats himself. The

drift of this essay has been to find a strange equivalence between the
world of the dead and various versions of Fairy Land. One may think of
the medieval poem, *Sir Orfeo*, in which the ancient story of Eurydice
undergoes a Celtic transformation, so that she is carried off to the world
of the dead by *a band of fairies*. In Shakespeare, none of it will, so to
speak, keep still. If the eye is allowed to wander, it will notice that in *A
Midsummer Night's Dream* my notion of 'lighting', whereby an initially
tragic conception is altered by a simple increase in illumination, is
entirely overthrown, since in the *Dream* the silvan pastoral is made
nocturnal. Shakespeare is not even thrifty enough to confine his
openings to the beginnings of his plays. In *The Merchant of Venice*
there is a secondary opening, at the end of the play, into the 'old money'
lovers' Paradise of Belmont, once again nocturnal but now lifted high in
the air, above the sordid traffic of Venice, a little nearer the ever-
singing stars. I have pursued my reason not to a conclusion but to a
bardolatrous *O altitudo!* Meanwhile, it all has its funny side:

> SIR ANDREW Begin fool. It begins 'Hold thy peace.'
> FESTE I shall never begin if I hold my peace.
> SIR ANDREW Good, i'faith. Come, begin.
>
> (*Twelfth Night* II.iii.66–8)

References

All references to Shakespeare are to *The Riverside Shakespeare*, ed.
   G. Blakemore Evans *et al.*, Boston: Houghton Mifflin, 1972.
Aeschylus (1957) *Agamemnon*, ed. J. D. Denniston and D. Page, Oxford:
   Clarendon Press.
Aristotle (1972) *Poetics*, introduction, commentary and appendices by
   D. W. Lucas (the corrected reprint of the edn. of 1962), Oxford:
   Clarendon Press.
Barton, Anne (1972) '*As You Like It* and *Twelfth Night*: Shakespeare's
   Sense of an Ending', in Malcolm Bradbury and David Palmer (eds.),
   Shakespearean Comedy, Stratford-upon-Avon Studies, 14, London:
   Edward Arnold, pp. 160–80.
Beadle, Richard (1981) ed., *The York Plays*, London: Edward Arnold.
Chambers, E. K. (1923) *The Elizabethan Stage*, 4 vols., Oxford: Clarendon
   Press.
Empson, William (1980) '*Hamlet*', in his *Essays on Shakespeare*,
   Cambridge: Cambridge University Press, pp. 79–136. This essay is a
   revised version of '*Hamlet* When New', *Sewanee Review*, 61 (1953),
   pp. 15–42, 182–205.

Everett, Barbara (1985) 'Or What You Will', *Essays in Criticism*, 35, pp. 294–314.

Horace (1901) *Q. Horati Flacci Opera*, ed. E. C. Wickham, rev. H. W. Garrod, Oxford: Clarendon Press (no page nos.).

James, D. G. (1967) *The Dream of Prospero*, Oxford: Clarendon Press.

Lodge, Thomas (1963) *The Works of Thomas Lodge*, 4 vols. (a re-issue of the Hunterian Club edition, Glasgow, 1883), New York: Russell & Russell.

More, Thomas (1965) *Utopia: The Complete Works of St Thomas More*, vol. IV, ed. Edward Surtz and J. H. Hexter, New Haven: Yale University Press. This edition, begun in 1963, is still incomplete.

Nuttall, A. D. (1988) '*Hamlet*: Conversations with the Dead', Annual Shakespeare Lecture to the British Academy, *Proceedings of the British Academy*, 74, pp. 53–69.

Panofsky, Erwin (1955) '*Et in Arcadia Ego*: Poussin and the Elegiac Tradition', *Meaning and the Visual Arts*, New York: Doubleday, pp. 295–320. This is a revised version of '*Et in Arcadia Ego*: On the Conception of Transience in Poussin and Watteau', *Essays Presented to Ernst Cassirer*, eds. Raymond Klibansky and H. J. Paton, Oxford: Clarendon Press, 1931, pp. 223–54.

Reynolds, G. F. (1940) *The Staging of Elizabethan Plays at the Red Bull Theater, 1605–1625*, Modern Language Association of America, General Series, no. 9, London: Oxford University Press.

Roper, William (1935) *The Lyfe of Sir Thomas More, knyghte*, ed. Elsie Vaughan Hitchcock, Early English Text Society, no. 197, London: Oxford University Press. This work was written about 1556 and first printed in 1626.

Smith, Irwin (1964) *Shakespeare's Blackfriars Playhouse: Its History and Design*, London: Peter Owen.

Virgil (1969) *P. Vergili Maronis Opera*, ed. R. A. B. Mynors, Oxford: Clarendon Press.

Robert Weimann

PERFORMING AT THE FRONTIERS OF REPRESENTATION: EPILOGUE AND POST-SCRIPTURAL FUTURE IN SHAKESPEARE'S PLAYS

The recent interest in a new model of Shakespeare criticism raises a host of practical and theoretical questions, among which the relationship between the representation of textual 'meaning' and the circumstances of performing practice appears to be quite central. As the unhelpful opposition between text-centred and stage-centred approaches is being challenged, timely suggestions are made for coping with what W. B. Worthen has called 'the text/performance dichotomy'. If this dichotomy has for many years continued to be an impediment, not to say embarrassment, the time has come to question this dichotomy and to do so at the 'center of the disciplinary ambiguity that characterizes performance criticism *as* criticism' (Worthen 1989, p. 442). It is at this centre that the relationship between textual representation and theatrical institution needs to be explored in terms of both their reciprocity and non-identity.

Once the text/performance dichotomy is suspended, the arts of performance need to be revisited at that crucial point where dramatic language and cultural practice, representation and existence, can be seen to interact. Such interaction is important in any theatre culture; in Shakespeare's case they appear to be vital and especially consequential. For here we have particularly intense and subtle transactions between roles and actors, between what is represented and performed and what (and who) is doing the representing and performing. In the Elizabethan theatre the act of performance effectively assimilates the crucial but precarious site on which the awareness of social occasion and the uses of theatrical signs tend to interact in a particularly compelling fashion. There is tension as well as complicity between the fiction in the text and the historical realities of its production and reception. The basic level on which such interlocking space operated appears to have been connected with the peculiar potential of the Elizabethan platform stage itself: at one moment this stage was able to project the dramatic locality of a throne, a tent, a house, a battlefield as some *locus* of textual fiction and dramatic illusion; at another moment this *locus*, the swift medium of representation and symbolisation, collapses into the material reality

(96)

of a neutral (nonrepresentational) platform stage in bright daylight. Similarly, at one moment a representing actor is strictly and consistently a symbol of a represented role and, at another moment, his symbolisation collapses (or at least is diminished), as the representation of a fictitious role gives way to the reality of an actual common player as, perhaps, some well-known agent of public entertainment.

In a theatre where transitions such as these are especially frequent and efficient, it seems imperative for us to approach the arts of performance in terms of a non-classical concept of mimesis which allows for wide and open frontiers of representation. In other words, we have a mimetic practice that, historically speaking, cannot be defined in terms of either the Senecan tradition or its humanist adaptations (see Hunter 1978). In the popular tradition, as I have suggested (Weimann 1985), mimesis is not at all a unified practice but one which is conducive to quite heterogeneous degrees of representational closure or rupture. As the boundary of textually pre-scribed space is an open one, the more complex 'purpose of playing' in the Elizabethan theatre appears effectively to cope with, even to thrive on, the non-identity between performance and script, between the actor's body and the author's language, between theatrical symbols and dramatic meanings. But this non-identity does not preclude a strong element of reciprocity between them. Shakespeare, as we know, set out as someone acting *and* writing *in* the theatre; between his acting and his writing there was continuity as well as difference, and the links and gaps between them must have helped to make relations between script and performance flexible and dynamic as well as secure. As the prologue to *Troilus and Cressida* suggests, the concerns of 'author's pen' and 'actor's voice' (l. 24), although not identical, were viewed together. No better education for a dramatist than to assist at the very crossing-points of the spoken (the performed) and the written word, especially when the area of complementarity between them was informed and constituted by the needs of a highly experimental, but broadly based cultural institution aspiring to national excellence.

Hence it is not too much to say that the language of dramatic representation in Shakespeare's theatre is radically contaminated by certain cultural purposes of performance, so much so that it appears quite unhelpful to proceed on the basis of any 'simple distinction between stage-centered and text-centered reading' (Berger 1989, p. xiii). To assume such a distinction can be especially misleading when the performed play is being described as a 'realization' of the written play. Even though the dramatic text precedes the performance text and in several important ways constrains the production through the pre-figuration of action, 'character,' setting, yet by itself the written text is radically incomplete. As Keir Elam (1980, p. 209) notes, the dramatic text, and especially the one in Shakespeare's theatre, is 'conditioned by its performability . . . is determined by its very need for stage contextualization'. In the words of P. G. Publiatti (cited by Elam), the 'linguistic text' should not be viewed as a text 'translatable into stage practice', but rather as 'a linguistic transcription of a stage potentiality which is the motive force of the written text'. As dramatic writing and theatrical production in several vital respects appear to condition one another, the cultural uses of performance in their turn must not be studied in isolation from either the dramatic text or the stage and its potentiality. It is in this twofold context that the difference between performance and representation needs to be examined with a view to defining areas of both discontinuity and continuity between them more closely.

These provisional points of definition and approach must suffice to suggest some theoretical framework within which the purpose of performance in Shakespeare's theatre can be explored against what I have called the frontiers of representation. For that, I propose first of all to look at the endings of several of Shakespeare's plays as arguably the most conspicuous area of complicity between the representational language of dramatic fiction and the social and cultural function of the Elizabethan playhouse. The idea is to study the extent to which the arts of performance are inscribed in, and yet transcend, the discourse of dramatic fiction. My point of departure is in those concluding lines where the language of dramatic fiction is imperceptibly surrendered or playfully adapted to the social occasion of theatrical communication, where the reality of that occasion transforms the representation of dramatic roles into the actor's performance of his own self-embodiment.

What in this connection seems most noteworthy is the trajectory by which the representational discourse of dramatic dialogue collapses into the projection of what may be called some post-scriptural or non-textual future after the play is ended. This future, in terms of its cultural use and social space, is not marked by emptiness; rather, it is achieved by and makes viable some unstable pattern of alliance between popular entertainment and public memory. Before the audience is about to applaud, the concluding lines, as it were, send the play out into the world, and they do so by accommodating the passing fiction to some sense of the actual circumstances of its production and reception.

What, then, from the present point of view deserves first of all to be studied more closely is the space in which (and the movement by which) the text of dramatic representation becomes most vulnerably tangential with cultural activities and historical occasions. But at the very point where the representational signs of theatrical fiction are suspended, the arts of performance can continue to serve some anticipation of the oral and mnemonic uses of the play's post-representational future.

To begin with, these post-scriptural dimensions of the play's future can best be assessed in terms of what nonfictional uses of public memory or collective emotion are inscribed in the text itself. There is, through the imperfect closure of the play's ending, a point where the fiction finally collapses and the text is being made to refer beyond itself, as when the 'story' is offered (not to say urged upon) the audience as something to be completed or so to be (re)told that it 'must/Take the ear strangely' (*The Tempest*, V.i.312). The image of some memorable action or person ('of whose memory/Hereafter more' — *Timon* V.iv.80ff.) lives on in the process of its collective reproduction. In more than one sense, the public impact and, if one may say so, the cultural potential of the Shakespearian text were inseparable from the form of its incompleteness. The oral form of its delivery, as well as its reception in reality, involved some distinct rites of memory which could collide with, or be fortified by, the 'rights of memory', those unforgotten claims in fiction that Fortinbras, in close conjunction with 'the rite of war' saluting Hamlet's 'passage' (V.ii.381ff.), invokes. Over and beyond the textual version it was possible 'To *hear* the rest untold' (*Pericles* V.iii.85) and 'to have more *talk* of these sad things' (*Romeo and Juliet* V.iii.306) after the play is ended.

The text in the theatre, serving both to project and to respond to potent prefigurements of public memory, is an agent of that memory itself: 'yet he shall have noble memory,/Assist.' (V.vi.154f.). These concluding words in *Coriolanus* appear so to link the representation of a dramatic fiction and its appropriation by an actual audience, that whatever authority the script at the crucial moment of its ending retains is being used to stimulate cultural involvement in the nonfictional world at the gates of the theatre. The call to 'Assist' does provide a cue to carry the body off-stage, but this fictional activity associated with 'three o' the chiefest soldiers' (149) might well be coextensive with a call for audience participation: in Elizabethan theatrical practice the conclusion of this text again is achieved in collaboration with its *assisting* audience.

If this points to the limits of representation (and already suggests the need for a concept of mimesis large enough to comprehend non-fictional uses of performance) the projection of the play's post-scriptural future can involve other means and strategies among which the use of an epilogue appears foremost. The epilogue, as it were, serves gracefully to intercept and/or extrapolate whatever rupture the trajectory from dramatic fiction to cultural reality may have to cope with. As in the play's ending the representational language of dramatic dialogue collapses, the epilogue in its own conventional form rehearses (and condenses) the transition from dramatic script to theatrical institution. Through the use of this convention, Shakespeare's theatrical represent-ations can, to a certain extent, organise and even celebrate their own successful collapse in the hoped-for applause of a judging audience.

In this connection the language of Shakespeare's epilogues is particularly revealing in that their performance articulates and, at the same time, gracefully helps to displace a sense of contingency, vulnerability, and incertitude in confronting the gap between players and spectators; in fact, there is the attempt to stylise the desperate kind of pleasure to be derived from playfully coping with the gap. Although, as Rosalind says at the end of *As You Like It*, 'a good play needs no epilogue' (Epilogue, 5) this function of the epilogue appears to be best served when that gap is playfully suspended. At that point the movement from the represented world of the playful fiction to the representing world of the Elizabethan playhouse is, through performance, turned into the awareness of a metamorphosis in whose achievement the audience is invited or even 'conjured' to participate:

> It is not the fashion to see the lady the epilogue: . . . What a case am
> I in then, that am neither a good epilogue, nor cannot insinuate
> with you in the behalf of a good play! I am not furnish'd like a
> beggar; therefore to beg will not become me. My way is to conjure
> you; and I'll begin with the women. I charge you, O women, for the
> love you bear to men, to like as much of this play as please you; and
> I charge you, O men, for the love you bear to women — as I
> perceive by your simp'ring none of you hates them — that between
> you and the women the play may please. If I were a woman, I would
> kiss as many of you as had beards that pleas'd me, complexions that
> lik'd me, and breaths that I defied not; and, I am sure, as many as
> have good beards, or good faces, or sweet breaths, will, for my kind
> offer, when I make curtsy, bid me farewell.

The transition is remarkably effected when the actor speaking as yet from within the role of Rosalind begins the epilogue by saying 'It is not the fashion to see the lady the epilogue.' But as he proceeds, he is gradually distancing the assimilated role, making his own cultural and sexual embodiment supersede whatever representation overlapped with the public dissolution of dramatic fiction. So he begins the epilogue by associating himself one last time with the represented 'lady' only to end up by pledging, 'If I were a woman, I would kiss as many of you as had beards that pleas'd me' (16). The transition, then, is from fictional representation to theatrical reality, from the assumed identity of the *role* of 'the lady' to the reality of the *body* of the boy actor who congenially establishes the true nonrepresentational identity of his gender by saying, 'If I were a woman.' But since such statement involves the supreme irony of finally counterpointing, by rehearsing yet again, the comic changes of gender, the theatrical effect is so much more than that of a mere transition: in conclusion the play provides some precariously built-up tension between both worlds, the one associated with the fiction of the text, the other associated with its *actual use in society*. For one brief moment, before the illusion of the role vanishes and the world of the play finally surrenders to the world of existence, the arts of performance must confront and cope with the gulf between the two.

This gulf constitutes the site on which the sexual, social, and semiotic divisions in the performance of Shakespeare's boy-heroine are re-negotiated at the end of the play. As a result, her/his representational status as some naturalised gendered subject finally explodes. The represented confusion involved in the fiction of cross-dressing is transformed into the actual histrionic energy of performance. It is the energy by which a young male actor excelled at the arts of performing highly complex images of continuity and discontinuity between who was represented and who was doing the representing. In this process of 'characterisation', the dominant notions of gendered difference are profoundly, and yet with great tact and charm, interrogated. As Jean Howard (1988, p. 435) has noted, since the epilogue reminds us that Rosalind 'is played by a boy, the neat convergence of biological sex and culturally constructed gender is once more severed'. But when the language of the epilogue seems about to challenge the imagery not just of gendered but of social difference ('I am not furnished like a beggar'), this difference stops short of being disrupted. The reason may well be that the represented signs of precious costume so envelop some handsome representing body that they preclude the social underside of the final metamorphosis of character back into actor.

However, the image of the beggar, so important in Lear's madness as a sign of limits in the representation of order, rank, and royalty, *can* be used to suggest the radical exhaustion of dramatic fiction. In the epilogue to *All's Well*, 'The king's a beggar,' and the achieved difference in this metamorphosis conveys at least a modicum of that actual social rupture between who was represented and who was doing the representing. Again, the play's ending conjures the limitations of the former by overthrowing the 'charms' of represented images of authority. Once more the trajectory is from the spell of the fiction of royalty to an awareness of the social reality of performance:

> KING Let us from point to point this story know.
>   To make the even truth in pleasure flow.
>
> [*To Diana*] If thou beest yet a fresh uncropped flower
> Choose thou thy husband and I'll pay thy dower;
> For I can guess that by thy honest aid
> Thou kept'st a wife herself, thyself a maid.
> Of that and all the progress more and less,
> Resolvedly more leisure shall express.
> All yet seems well, and if it end so meet,
> The bitter past, more welcome is the sweet.
>   *Flourish.*
>
>   [EPILOGUE]
> *The king's a beggar, now the play is done;*
> *All is well ended if this suit be won,*
> *That you express content; which we will pay*
> *With strife to please you, day exceeding day.*
> *Ours be your patience then and yours our parts;*
> *Your gentle hands lend us and take our hearts.*
>   *Exeunt omnes.*
>   (ed. G. K. Hunter, Arden)

The King of France prepares for the ending on at least two or three levels. He sets out to provide for the play's post-scriptural future a sense of pleasurable recollection of the full canvas ('from point to point') of 'this story'. But the suggested cultural uses of hindsight and insight into the play from the point of view of its dénouement are made to coalesce with the final piece of dramatic fiction. So 'the even truth' derived from recollecting 'point to point this story' combines with, even leads back to, the King's role as he (far from being a beggar yet) is paying Diana's 'dower'. Even at this moment, the boundaries of representation, and within them the form of dialogue, vanish into thin air: note (after '. . . thyself a maid') the renewed transition to the public institutionalisation of some oral uses of the play's future. But again the 'transition' is most graceful; for now the last lines in the dialogue addressed to Diana are, as it were, *cited* as some exercise in the munificent uses of 'leisure' and pastime ('*Of that* and all the progress . . .') after the play has virtually come to an end. At this point, the concluding fiction of this stage-business is already distanced through the heavily stylised effect of rhymed couplets. This is one more reason why the final metamorphosis of the last vestiges of the dramatic role of the King into the common player's performance of the epilogue does not at all come by surprise.

Even so, for George Hunter and modern editors to follow Rowe and insert EPILOGUE in brackets (because not in Folio) while at the same time retaining for it italics (which *are* in Folio) is to cope with the abruptness of the collapse of a royal role into: 'The king's a beggar.' If anywhere, here we have an element of rupture between the language of fictive representation and the actor's 'selfe-resembled' performance. Although one would wish to think so, it seems to all intents and purposes scarcely possible for the actor to make this transition 'in pleasure flow' and yet also accentuate the gulf involved in it. For the element of discontinuity appears especially pronounced after the happy fiction of 'All yet seems well' culminates in 'more welcome is the sweet'. At the frontiers of these representations of harmony in what is no happy comedy, the King abruptly renounces the signs of his royal status. As 'the play is done' and the vulnerable *locus* of royalty gives way to the *platea* occasion for audience response, the 'personator' (to use Thomas Heywood's term), performing still, steps forward from behind 'the personated'. Now the signs of signs, the symbols of status symbols surrender their little brief authority, and the feigned image of the royal crown appears, in reality, as that piece of brass on the patient actor's head. At this point the performer stands naked except for the arts of delivery from this occasion: whatever authority a performed role may have constituted in a fiction is no longer available. His true legitimation is to have pleased the audience through sustained endeavours of his art, 'day exceeding day'. For all that, the theatre's readiness 'to please' appears as no servile or passive offering: the arts of performance achieve their final authority in the division and, even, exchange of cultural labour with the audience. The performance, having outlived fictional representation, finally subsides, through an exchange of roles, in the performer's silence: 'Ours be your patience then and yours our parts.' The uses of performance have come full circle; the actors, in silent patience, confront the play's post-scriptural future. This future is thinkable as a space of mutuality only when the spectators 'express content' and perform their own 'parts' not only through their clapping hands but by rehearsing 'this story' and by remembering it 'from point to point'.

Similarly, at the end of *The Tempest*, Prospero dislodges whatever boundary there was between the represented fiction in the text of the play and the representing agent in the real world of the playhouse:

> Now my charms are all o'erthrown,
> And what strength I have's mine own,
> Which is most faint. Now 'tis true,
> I must be here confin'd by you,
> Or sent to Naples. Let me not,
> Since I have my dukedom got,
> And pardon'd the deceiver, dwell
> In this bare island by your spell;
> But release me from my bands
> With the help of your good hands.
> Gentle breath of yours my sails
> Must fill, or else my project fails,
> Which was to please. Now I want
> Spirits to enforce, art to enchant;
> And my ending is despair
> Unless I be reliev'd by prayer,
> Which pierces so that it assaults
> Mercy itself, and frees all faults.
> As you from crimes would pardon'd be,
> Let your indulgence set me free.

Having from within the role of the enlightened magician finally abjured 'this rough magic', having broken his 'staff', drowned his 'book' (V.i.50ff.), the imaginative figure of representation, called 'Prospero', collapses. But as this textual figuration is being released into the actual body of the actor, there is again, hovering over the play's ending, some precarious tension between fictional representation and true embodiment. This informs some anxious interplay between the 'bare island' (8) in the text of *The Tempest* and the 'unworthy scaffold' on which the actor is left behind, somewhat wary, lest his true 'project fails,/Which *was* to please.' Almost unnoticeably the 'charms' in the text of the fiction turn into past tense, once they are referred to the achieved cultural 'project' of dramatic entertainment, which 'was to please'. The past 'charms' of dramatic fiction are surrendered to 'the spell' which the audience has over the actor craving for applause: 'Let me not/. . . dwell/In this bare island by your spell:/But release me . . .' (5–9). Whatever authority the representation of Prospero may have enjoyed in the performed text of the play is now abdicated to that nonrepresentational realm in which the true pleasure of the audience serves as final arbiter of the fate of the drama in performance: 'But release me from my bands/With the help of your good hands' (9ff.). The renegotiation of authority is effected through the interplay between what theatrical signs imaginatively represent (what 'art' there is 'to enchant') *and* what their representing function in reality is. The underlying contradiction is between the fictional language of the text and its social history in the theatre.

Here to emphasise such interplay between language and history, text and theatre, is to suggest that dramatic representations can occupy a vulnerable space. Representational practice can be made to refer beyond itself, to the non-fictional reality of performance as this performance self-consciously articulates its own existential need for being favourably received in the clapping hands of audiences. The act of performance culminates in the awareness of its own authority when its final legitimation is negotiated (and publicly evaluated) at the point of intersection between the actual place and institution of the theatre and the fictional locality of the scene. This point of intersection is symptomatic of the difference between two types of discourse and appropriation. This difference may well have to be read in terms of some 'bifold authority' in the cultural uses of theatrical space (Weimann 1988) — uses involving discontinuity between the presence of the body of the actor and the 'absent' representation of his role, between the materiality of theatrical communication and the fictionality of textual configurations.

When at the end of several of Shakespeare's plays the subtly balanced movement from fictional text to cultural reality is, as it were, arrested, the play cancels its representational dimension by projecting itself into a non-representational social occasion. The dramatic representation, in acknowledging its own limits and finiteness, opens itself beyond its ending and confronts the precarious nature of its own limited authority, spell-bound asking for applause. If we read Prospero's 'strength' as some power or capacity for authorising his own representational strategy, then what 'strength' remains to him is situated beyond the boundaries of representation. Once his 'charms are all o'erthrown', the actor's 'strength' is to be found outside, no longer inside the representational structure of the text. As it appears, the 'I' (in 'what strength I have's mine own') is that of the representer, not the represented. The actor steps forward, relinquishing his role and whatever signs and images of fictionality were associated with his representation. What remains, after these signs of authority are all 'o'erthrown', is the actor's competence in the delivery of language and gesture. This competence needs to be endorsed according to the rules and effects of theatrical entertainment. The actor's 'strength' is 'most faint' indeed in that it is not (is no longer) enhanced by represented 'spirits to enforce', by the great images of power, the verisimilitude of rank, the book of magic, the signs of sovereignty. Rather, the actor's strength (or what authority he has) needs to be acknowledged by success in the playhouse — which is as much as to say that the authority of the actor, once it is nonrepresentational or 'signifying nothing', is not that of the text but that of the theatre itself. It is a 'strength' achieved in the provision of pleasure, an authority authorised by the success of the institution in the fulfilment of its cultural function.

While after a two- or three-hours' traffic on the stage the arts of dramatic performance could celebrate the collapse of dramatic representation as well as their own suspension in applause and memory, the question remains to what extent the act of performance itself could project some self-awareness and a sense of its own identity as distinct from the uses of dramatic representation. Even to ask this question is first of all to realise that the arts of performance and the uses of representation cannot, in fact must not, be viewed in terms of some binary relationship, as if what we are dealing with were a pair of opposites rather than a contradictory relation of complementarity. In fact, representational form in Renaissance popular drama was so viable and flexible that it could very well accommodate and, even, confine any autonomous expression of the arts and artists of performance. If we except the more sturdy sense of independence of a popular entertainer such as Will Kempe, the actors may well have been content to subsume their performing art in the overriding needs of the more nearly self-contained Renaissance play text, paying tribute to whatever 'necessary question of the play be then to be considered' (*Hamlet* III.ii.40ff.).

However, Kempe and all those in the tradition of Tarlton's clowning must have asserted the heritage of a 'selfe-resembled' style of performance that would inevitably collide with the increasingly self-contained art of dramatic writing. For them to continue to speak 'more than is set down for them' (III.ii.36) was one way of challenging the rules of dramatic representation through the sheer force of clownish performance. But at this point, as David Wiles suggests (1987, pp. 35ff.), some kind of collision must have been inevitable; the space was rapidly shrinking, as in Joseph Hall's couplet, for the headstrong popular entertainer to 'show his teeth in double rotten row/For laughter at his selfe-resembled show.'

However, Shakespeare's position *vis-à-vis* the 'selfe-resembled' arts of comic performance was more complex than his presumably quite troublesome relations with Kempe would suggest. Despite Hamlet's strictures ('there be of them that will themselves laugh, to set on some quantity of barren spectators too,' III.ii.36–7), it seemed possible for his plays to maintain some 'confidence' in the viability of the links between 'author's pen or actor's voice'. And although the Prologue to *Troilus and Cressida* (ll. 23–4) disowns such 'confidence', it must have been at least a potentiality as long as 'author's pen' could be made to retain or accommodate, by inscription, a trace of 'actor's voice', that is, a trace of extemporal language, a residue of orality, or a relic of *platea* space and audience awareness.

At this point, it seems helpful at least to glance at an early comedy where such trace of voice and embodiment persists in the clown's 'selfe-resembled' performance which, to all intents and purposes, appears strong enough to push back the frontiers of fictional representation. My text is from *The Two Gentlemen of Verona* where, astonishingly, the 'actor's voice' is inscribed by the 'author's pen' itself into a comic context of collision between the 'necessary question' of representation and some quite wilful uses of the arts of performance. This collision is amusing, because the popular performer self-mockingly reveals the limits of representation by performing a parody of it.

Launce, played — as Clifford Leech suggested in his Arden edition (p. xxvi) — in all likelihood by Kempe, enters upon the leave-taking scene of Proteus and Julia. As the gentle couple exchange their tokens and 'seal the bargain with a holy kiss', Julia's 'tide of tears' precipitates her exit in silence. Whereupon Proteus:

> What, gone without a word?
> Ay, so true love should do. It cannot speak,
> For truth hath better deeds than words to grace it.
>
> (II.ii.16–18)

Here, the problematic limits of representing 'true love', even 'truth' through the use of words, provide a cue for Launce's performance in the immediately following scene. Launce enters 'weeping', only to provide his own inversionary commentary on these romantic tears and vows. Since his version of a whole family 'weeping', 'wailing', 'crying', 'howling' is familiar enough. I would just note how Launce in his hilarious and rather obscene fashion proceeds to re-examine, in and through representation, those relations of 'truth' and 'deeds' and 'words' which are set forth in the courtly plot of romantic love:

> Why, my grandam having no eyes, look you, wept herself blind at my parting. Nay, I'll show you the manner of it. This shoe is my father. No, this left shoe is my father. No, no, this left shoe is my mother. Nay, that cannot be so, neither. Yes, it is so, it is so, it hath the worser sole. This shoe with the hole in it is my mother, and this my father. A vengeance on't, there 'tis. Now, sir, this staff is my sister, for, look you, she is as white as a lily and as small as a wand. This hat is Nan our maid. I am the dog. No, the dog is himself, and I am the dog. O, the dog is me, and I am myself. Ay, so, so. Now come I to my father. 'Father, your blessing.' Now should not the shoe speak a word for weeping. Now should I kiss my father. Well, he weeps on. Now come I to my mother. O that she could speak now, like a wood woman. Well, I kiss her. Why, there 'tis. Here's my mother's breath up and down. Now come I to my sister. Mark the moan she makes. Now the dog all this while sheds not a tear nor speaks a word. But see how I lay the dust with my tears.

> (II.iii.12–32)

Here, it is not good enough to say that the player's performance involves the parody of dramatic representations of romantic tears and vows. For what an actor, whose 'art is rooted in minstrelsy' (Wiles 1987, p. 74), says and does can no longer be comprehended as part of that part which a character named Launce represents in the play at large. While re-enacting his own burlesque version of weeping, the actor so distances the fiction of leave-taking that, on some *platea*-like space, he can interrogate the representational use of the signs of the signs of parting. What this interrogation reveals is that someone who, like Julia, has no eyes to see can weep 'herself blind' at parting. And in order to show 'the manner of it', the clown shows up the relations between what is represented and what is representing in their tenuousness and arbitrariness. The 'shoe', which serves as a sign, 'is my father.' But what 'This shoe' signifies is extremely unstable; in fact, the process of representation is so unsettling and, as it were, so destabilising, that the order of signs and their meanings is turned upside down no less than five times. And so it goes, until Launce provides a thoroughly comic version of that equivocation which can be traced in a divided dramaturgy where a character is and is not a character because the represented role can implicate the representing actor. This is especially so when discontinuity of role and actor involves the rupture between a signified woman and a signifying boy actor, as when Troilus is facing the 'bifold authority' of the platform state on which 'a thing inseparate/Divides more wider than the sky and earth,' so that he can mingle the representation of his despair with some representing consciousness, and say, 'This is, and is not, Cressid' (V.ii.144/146ff.). But the equivocating effect is drastically comic when Launce says: 'I am the dog. No, the dog is himself, and I am the dog. O, the dog is me, and I am myself. Ay, so, so.' Here Launce turns a creature into a sign that itself calls for a sign to be signified according to the clownish rules of representing representation. The confusion is complete when the clown is the dog and when 'the dog is me, and I am myself.' The actor is made to speak true *sermo humilis*; but the knowledge of his humble station, even the ridiculousness of this topsy-turvydom of signs, the sheer vulgarity of shoe and sole (and hole), the obscene self-deflating reference to the organs of sexuality cannot humiliate the actor. His, indeed, is — in Hegel's terms — 'the blessed ease of a subjectivity which, as it is sure of itself, can bear the dissolution of its own ends and means'. Only (and this has less to do with the assertion of subjectivity than with the indefatigable presence of the comic player), the entertaining body of the well-known actor, almost certainly that of vigorous Will Kempe, remains impervious to the rules of representation and the rhetoric of synecdoche. For, finally, when all is said and done, when the signifiers that are representing and the signifieds that are represented have come full swing in the order of their confusion, one thing remains: the self-embodied identity of the comic actor himself: 'O, the dog is me, and I am myself. Ay, so, so.' It is the actor, who, although he plays a part, yet remains himself. Just as the boy actor in front of Calchas' tent 'is and is not Cressid,' so Launce is the *dog*, the laughable underdog, and yet is himself, but not in the role of Lance but in the part, presumably, of William Kempe.

Finally and quite summarily, these readings suggest a number of practical and theoretical desiderata, including the need for further studies in the arts of performance. Here there is room briefly to formulate (not necessarily to answer) three main questions only.

First, the interaction between fictional representation and its actual reception in the theatre is mediated by performance; but this performance, as part of a pleasurable occasion, involves such contingency as can gracefully be intercepted by the epilogue. The epilogue is designed so as to 'release' or 'set . . . free' the actor(s) from both representational closure and the anxiety about the performed play's success. Hence, the play's post-scriptural future (including its renewed performance) cannot safely be taken for granted. The agents of performance serve more than just the cause of concurrence between text and audience. As the actors release themselves in the movement from fictional representation to cultural reality, such release may be 'conjured' but is not actually effected by benign gestures of compliance. Rather, what the epilogue cannot help addressing itself to is a divided mode of authorisation, what in a reading of the Prologue to *Henry V* I have called 'bifold authority'. As exposed to the divided authorities of *locus* and 'place' (and as confronted with the bifold convention of empathy and distance), the audience in its expectations could easily be thwarted or confused. Further studies in the plays' cultural future would have to address this question much more sharply than the present essay has been able to do.

Second, the cultural uses of the performed text are not of course confined to the oral cultivation of collective memory. The Shakespearian play, as George Hunter (1978, p. 30) notes about *Othello*, 'allows the audience its prejudice and then inverts it'. Impossible to define these uses of drama in terms of the modernist practice of disrupting the audience's horizon of expectation. Rather, in order to establish the full register of Elizabethan strategies of reception we need to historicise the theatrical transaction more incisively and in a larger context. As Marvin Carlson (1985, p. 5) notes, 'the text-performance-audience interaction should not be considered in a vacuum, but rather as an event embedded in a complex matrix of social concerns and actions, all of which "communicate" or contribute to giving the theatre experience its particular "meaning" to its participants.' Again in this wider field, as Richard Schechner (1988, p. 161) suggests, the theatre is 'but one of a complex of performance activities' (including all kinds of social rituals, sport, dance, and music). But even when a 'poetics of performance' is defined in narrower terms than a poetics of culture, there is a need for intertwining the uses of dramatic language with those of 'visual signals' (Hunter, 1980), with the dramaturgy of theatrical space (Styan, 1989), and the semiotics of theatre architecture (Carlson, 1989), each in their respective historical, anthropological and technological dimensions.

Finally, how can performance criticism come to terms with the heterogeneous uses of representational form and localised space, especially as the latter easily overlaps with the *platea* tradition of open dramaturgy? This question needs to be given more space than this essay allows for; for while the representation of dramatic fiction collapses in the language of the epilogue, the emerging 'voice' of its speaker cannot elude a different, non-fictional framework of representational activities. In the first place, this voice follows a prescribed text and, within the limit of its textual inscription, is representative of the theatre's institutionalised practices, fears and interests. Such 'representativity' in the language of the epilogue is nothing feigned; it does not constitute a *locus* of verisimilitude, even when, as in *The Tempest*, the play metaphor artfully sustains the collapse of representational form into the self-embodied language of the theatre's sense of its own fragility. From the point of view of performance criticism, it seems essential to be aware of 'the spacious breadth of this division' (*Troilus and Cressida* V.ii.150) in the uses of representation and performance. In order to be fully aware of either side of a divided order of representation, the authority of the stage itself should not be viewed as in a lapsed relation to the authority of the literary text. Once we avoid privileging textual over nontextual significations (and vice versa), the path is free for us to *negotiate* the claims of textual authority as against stage authority and to contextualise and historicise the two at their point of intersection.

I wish to thank Ann Whitaker (Cornell University) for kindly reading and perceptively commenting on this essay in manuscript.

References

Quotations from Shakespeare, unless otherwise noted, are from *The Complete Works*, ed. Peter Alexander (London and Glasgow: Collins, 1951).

Berger, Harry, Jr. (1989) *Imaginary Audition: Shakespeare on Stage and Page*, Berkeley and Los Angeles: University of California Press.

Carlson, Marvin (1989) *Places of Performance: The Semiotics of Theatre Architecture*, Ithaca and London: Cornell University Press.

Elam, Keir (1980) *The Semiotics of Theatre and Drama*, London: Methuen.

Hornby, Richard (1987) *Script into Performance: A Structuralist Approach*, New York: Paragon House Publishers.

Howard, Jean E. (1988) 'Crossdressing, The Theatre, and Gender Struggle in Early Modern England', *Shakespeare Quarterly*, 39 (Winter 1988), pp. 418–40.

Hunter, G. K. (1978) 'Seneca and English Tragedy', in Hunter, *Dramatic Identities and Cultural Tradition: Studies in Shakespeare and his Contemporaries*, Liverpool: Liverpool University Press, pp. 174–213.

Hunter, G. K. (1980) 'Flatcaps and Bluecoats: Visual Signals on the Elizabethan Stage', *Essays and Studies*, n.s., 33.

Schechner, Richard (1988) *Performance Theory*, rev. and exp. edn., New York and London: Routledge.

Styan, J. L. (1989) 'Stage Space and the Shakespeare Experience', in Thompson, M. and R. (eds.) *Shakespeare and the Sense of Performance: Essays in the Tradition of Performance Criticism in Honor of Bernard Beckerman*, London and Toronto: Associated University Presses, pp. 195–209.

Thompson, Marvin and Ruth (1989) 'Performance Criticism: From Granville-Barker to Bernard Beckerman and Beyond', in Thompson, M. and R. (eds.) *Shakespeare and the Sense of Performance: Essays in the Tradition of Performance Criticism in Honor of Bernard Beckerman*, London and Toronto: Associated University Presses, pp. 13–23.

Weimann, Robert (1985) 'Mimesis in *Hamlet*', in Parker, P. and Hartman, G. (eds.) *Shakespeare and the Question of Theory*, London and New York: Methuen, pp. 275–91.

Weimann, Robert (1988) 'Bifold Authority in Shakespeare's Theater', *Shakespeare Quarterly*, 39 (Winter 1988), pp. 401–17.

Wiles, David (1987) *Shakespeare's Clown: Actor and Text in the Elizabethan Playhouse*, Cambridge: Cambridge University Press.

Worthen, W. B. (1989) 'Deeper Meanings and Theatrical Technique: The Rhetoric of Performance Criticism', *Shakespeare Quarterly*, 40 (Winter 1989), pp. 441–55.

Lois Potter

SEEING AND BELIEVING

The blind Earl of Gloucester describes the morally insensitive man as one who 'will not see/Because he does not feel' (*King Lear*, IV.i.62–3).[1] Yet everyday experience — for instance, the response to television programmes about atrocities and disasters — seems to indicate that, on the contrary, many people do not feel *until* they see: it is the sight of human suffering that induces a feeling for the sufferer. Gloucester's words, however, are particularly apposite in the context of the theatre. As he speaks, for example, he is asking the audience to believe not only that he is blind but that his face is that of a man whose eyes have been brutally stamped out only a short time ago. Even if the actor is wearing heavy make-up, his appearance is unlikely to present anything which a doctor would recognise as the result of such an experience. In most productions, his blindness is to some extent stylised, even hidden. The spectators' response is based, not on what is literally in front of them, but on their translation of that sight. A spectator who has already been moved by the scene of Gloucester's blinding will collude in a prolongation of the emotional experience, seeing the character through Edgar's eyes. A theatrically sophisticated spectator may also recognise that the visual representation of blindness is in keeping with the style of the production generally, and thus accept even a patently unrealistic depiction. These two responses are not incompatible. In both cases, the spectator is applying a theatrical code in order to 'see' in a particular way.

But spectators are not always willing or able to apply such a code. Confronted with an unfamiliar verbal language and with a visual language that is not directly mimetic, they focus on the one language they do understand: that which the actor speaks involuntarily when his or her human identity shows through the superimposed code of the performance. Thus, in the famous episode in *Tom Jones* (Book XVI, Ch. 5), where Tom and Partridge attend a performance of *Hamlet*, Fielding makes comic capital out of Partridge's inability to ignore the evidence of his senses. Partridge is comic when he sees Hamlet merely as 'the little man', but Tom's superiority to him derives simply from the fact that he knows that Hamlet is being played by the great David Garrick, and thus suppresses his perception of the actor's unimpressive physique. With no such reason to be tolerant of Mr Wopsle and his fellow-actors, Pip in *Great Expectations* (Ch. XXXI) joins the rest of the audience in noticing that the Ghost not only has a cough but is prompting himself from a badly concealed script.

It is precisely this 'body' language, on the other hand, that the sophisticated theatregoer takes a pride in ignoring. Though Renaissance scholars are often notoriously bad audiences for Renaissance plays, it is noticeable that in even their most theatrically orientated readings they generally avert their eyes from the embarrassing physical reality of the actors. Discussing a play in terms of its hypothetical performance means discussing, not an individual event, but a platonic ideal of a production, abstracted from all the accidental and irrelevant factors which result from the non-ideal nature of the human beings involved in it. Yet — as is indicated by the fictional examples I have just mentioned — these apparent irrelevancies are precisely what make the greatest impact on the average spectator. What will concern me in this chapter, therefore, are some moments in Renaissance, mainly Shakespearian, drama when, because of the real conditions of the actor and the stage, the contrast between what we see and what we are apparently meant to see becomes so acute as to stretch the theatrical illusion to breaking-point.

When Ben Jonson compared the relation of the intellectual and sensual elements in the masque to that of the soul and the body,[2] it gave him a good deal of satisfaction to think that, however much the latter might dominate during the performance, only the former would ultimately survive. While a good deal of evidence of theatre history *has* survived, in the form of painting, photography, and videotapes, his point remains substantially correct. We cannot 'see' the actors of the past with the same eyes as their original audience: Garrick and Pritchard, as Macbeth and Lady Macbeth, seem only a henpecked husband and bossy wife; Isabella Glyn's monumental Victorian Cleopatra looks like an advertisement for corsets. It is possible that we are more demanding in this respect than the contemporaries of Garrick and Glyn. It is easy to ridicule the Victorian theatre for its elaborate attempts at scenic illusion, but what we demand, and sometimes almost get, is no less extravagant: a perfect visual likeness between the living actor and our ideal image of the role.

References to the physical appearance of characters in Renaissance drama have been scoured for evidence about the possible appearance of the actors who played them. It is chiefly in comedy that one can find

such exploitation of the physical and idiosyncratic. In Jonson's Induction
to *Cynthia's Revels*, in which three children squabble over who will
speak the prologue, the smallest boy (he later draws the short straw,
saying, 'The shortest is come to the shortest' [l. 24]) suggests that they
let the audience vote on it — to which another boy replies, 'Oh no, sir
gallant; you presume to have the start of us there' (l. 12).[3] Clearly, we
have here a joke about the rivalry among these little child stars, and it is
the audience's pet who is allowed to talk about his own appearance,
much as a comedian talks about his fatness or funny walk. It is possible
that the reference to Hamlet as 'fat and scant of breath' is a similar
reflection of the confidence in audience affection for the entire physical
reality of a favourite performer. Most of the physical characteristics
required of a role, however, could easily be superimposed on almost any
actor: Richard III's hump, Orlando's chestnut hair, even Falstaff's bulk.
Like Laurence Olivier's self-confessed taste for false noses, these
excrescences may protect the actor from the sense of self-exposure; they
may also, however, be a response to anti-theatrical polemicists, who, as
Peter Stallybrass has noted, 'insistently dwell upon the theatre as a
spectacle of the body and of clothes'.[4] As if to deny the vulnerable and
provocative qualities of the living actor, or the individual traits which
might allow him to become independent of the character he played, the
dramatic language often seems eager to transform him, verbally, into a
picture, a statue, or, as in Menaphon's description of Tamburlaine, a
colossal emblem:

>   'twixt his manly pitch
> A pearl more worth than all the world is placed,
> Wherein by curious sovereignty of art
> Are fixed his piercing instruments of sight,
> Whose fiery circles bear encompassed
> A heaven of heavenly bodies in their spheres
> That guides his steps and actions to the throne
> Where honour sits invested royally.
> Pale of complexion — wrought in him with passion,
> Thirsting with sovereignty, with love of arms;
> His lofty brows in folds do figure death,
> And in their smoothness amity and life;
> About them hangs a knot of amber hair
> Wrapped in curls, as fierce Achilles' was,
> On which the breath of heaven delights to play,

Making it dance with wanton majesty;
His arms and fingers long and sinewy,
Betokening valour and excess of strength:
In every part proportioned like the man
Should make the world subdued to Tamburlaine.

(*Part One*, II.i.11–30)

One can only agree with Cosroe's response:

Well hast thou portrayed in thy terms of life
The face and personage of a wondrous man.   (31–2)

Edward Alleyn, as Tamburlaine, would have left the stage only six lines
before Menaphon's speech; he never looked like this description, and
neither did anybody else. As J. S. Cunningham and others point out in
their notes on this passage, many of its details are based on epic
descriptions.[5] It is a direct challenge to the senses, an example of the
myth-making power of words.

A still greater challenge, because it describes something which the
audience can see for itself, is the scene (*Merchant of Venice*, III.ii) in
which Bassanio makes his choice among the three caskets. At this
comparatively static moment one's gaze is focused on the speakers and
the objects of their attention: first Portia speaks, while Bassanio reads
the three inscriptions to himself; then Bassanio meditates aloud on the
meaning of the inscriptions, opens the leaden casket, finds Portia's
picture, and talks about it. The director sometimes inserts various kinds
of business here: Gratiano and Nerissa may carry on their courtship in
dumb show; Bassanio may seem on the point of opening the wrong
casket and Portia may react accordingly. But on the whole the scene is
decorated not with action but with elaborate imagery. Portia describes
Bassanio as a Hercules about to save her from a sea-monster: the
audience knows that he is virtually bankrupt and that, if anything, it is
she who will be saving him. Whether we respond ironically to the
contrast between the elaborate Renaissance painting evoked by her
words and the evidence of our own eyes, or enter into her subjective
experience of the situation, the important thing is that the contrast
exists:

                    Now he goes,
With no less presence but with much more love
Than young Alcides when he did redeem
The virgin tribute paid by howling Troy
To the sea-monster. I stand for sacrifice.

> The rest aloof are the Dardanian wives,
> With blearèd visages come forth to view
> The issue of th' exploit. Go, Hercules.   (*MV* III.ii.53–60)

Still more striking is the double vision required by Bassanio's speech. As he looks at the caskets, he hears the song 'Tell me where is fancy bred', and deduces, rightly, that it is a warning not to pay too much attention to 'outward shows' (73). He rejects the golden casket because it reminds him of other kinds of beauty which often turn out to be false. One of these, rather surprisingly, is the 'gold' of women's hair. Like the 'amber' of Tamburlaine's, it is both a colour (and thus capable of being light enough to wave in the wind) and a solid, elaborately carved artefact. But it is also, potentially, something else:

> So are those crispèd, snaky, golden locks
> Which make such wanton gambols with the wind
> Upon supposèd fairness, often known
> To be the dowry of a second head,
> The skull that bred them in the sepulchre.   (*MV* III.ii.92–6)

Perhaps the image of golden hairs cut off from a dead body to make a wig for someone else reflects an awareness (ours, not Bassanio's) of the skull within the golden casket. Portia's own hair, as seen on the portrait in the leaden casket, inspires another comparison, both complimentary and sinister:

> Here in her hairs
> The painter plays the spider, and hath woven
> A golden mesh t'entrap the hearts of men
> Faster than gnats in cobwebs.   (*MV* III.ii.120–3)

Why should Bassanio talk about the painted hair on the painted woman, when the real woman is standing before him? Perhaps to keep us from making too direct a comparison between Bassanio's description and the 'real' Portia — who, whether played by a boy or an actress, is probably wearing a wig similar to the one described in the first part of Bassanio's speech. Yet the lines, far from trying to distract us from the resemblance between the 'golden mesh' and the 'golden locks', seem to invite us to contemplate it. Bassanio's speech, culminating as it does in a contrast between the painted and the real woman, intensifies our awareness that the latter is as much a work of art as the former.

In Shakespeare's Sonnet 21 the beauty of the man to whom the poem is addressed is significantly contrasted with the 'painted beauty' of

women. Annette Drew-Bear, pointing out that some kinds of make-up
were literally poison, has provided a good deal of evidence for the use of
face-painting in tragedies to indicate spiritual corruption or disease.[6]
Thus, an obviously made-up face — 'The harlot's cheek, beautied with
plastering art' — signified prostitution. It is not surprising, then, that
there are so many references to the blushing of both male and female
characters. But, here again, the comparisons move back and forth,
denying at one moment what they affirm at another. The statue of
Hermione, which is really Hermione herself, is described as if it were
painted:

> The ruddiness upon her lip is wet.
> You'll mar it if you kiss it, stain your own
> With oily painting.   (*Winter's Tale*, V.iii.81–3)

This is a comment on an un-made-up actor, pretending to have been
painted by an artist whose skill has exactly captured an un-made-up
complexion. But Leontes also protests,

> But yet, Paulina,
> Hermione was not so much wrinkled, nothing
> So agèd as this seems.   (*Winter's Tale*, V.iii.27–9)

If these wrinkles are visible to the audience as they are to Leontes, then
they must have been painted on Hermione's face; her 'natural'
complexion is a work of art after all.

Othello's blackness, likewise, is described in language that makes it
seem artificially created. Not only does Brabantio speak of his 'sooty
bosom' (I.ii.71), but the Moor himself uses the comparison 'begrimed
and black/As mine own face' (*Othello*, III.iii.392–3). Thomas Rymer
protested that for a black man to speak this way was illogical: 'The
Indians do as they ought in painting the devil white'.[7] It is as if Othello
had internalised the racist assumption that a black man is really a dirty
white man. Yet Othello's face is literally 'begrimed', as generations of
actors had reason to know: the difficulty, first, of creating an effective
make-up, and then of keeping it off Desdemona's clothes and skin, was
one of their chief preoccupations. Ellen Terry was impressed by Edwin
Booth's thoughtful decision to hold a fold of his robe in his hand
whenever he had to touch her; when she played opposite Henry Irving,
she commented, 'Before he had done with me, I was nearly as black as
he.'[8] It was this awareness that the character was not 'really' black at all,
an awareness that was more acute on stage than in the reading, that
made it possible for *Othello* to be so popular even in the ante-bellum

American south.[9] Real prejudice towards the performance, as opposed to the play, surfaced only when genuinely black actors began to play the part.

Othello's colour may be compared with Coriolanus' blood. Unlike the other figures mentioned so far, whose physicality is static and statuesque, Coriolanus is not only described as taking part in violent action, he is required to demonstrate it on stage. Courage is the one quality with which even his enemies credit him; if he is not credibly courageous, the play is meaningless. Yet he himself ironically suggests that the whole thing is a theatrical illusion: 'For that I have not washed my nose that bled' (I.x.47). It was Falstaff who supposedly told his followers at Gadshill how to simulate the results of heroic conflict: 'to tickle our noses with spear-grass to make them bleed; and then to beslubber our garments with it' (*1 Henry IV*, II.v.312–14). Caius Martius also refers to his blood as 'this painting/Wherein you see me smeared' (*Coriolanus* I.vii.68–9), and he later completes the painting-bleeding-blushing configuration by announcing:

> I will go wash,
> And when my face is fair you shall perceive
> Whether I blush or no.   (*Coriolanus* I.x.67–9)

It is as if he had been reading Jonson's prologue to the revised *Every Man in His Humour*, which ridicules the would-be illusionistic treatment of battles and the wounds turned into scars in the tiring house. Dressed in his own blood as in a costume, he does not show his wounds to the audience any more than to the Roman populace, and, in this double-bluff, it is his refusal to show them that makes them real.

One cannot be sure how far the theatrical treatment of battle scenes created the kind of illusion which Martius' lines seem designed to destroy. Alan C. Dessen, who has argued the need for greater stylisation in many aspects of the production of Renaissance plays, suggests that stage fights, in particular, should be seen as 'patterned action' rather than 'psychological realism'.[10] Certainly, this might help the director who, Dessen found, had to avoid swordplay to avoid getting unwanted laughs. But realism need not work against the symbolic effect. Jean-Louis Barrault writes interestingly of his reaction to Olivier's Lear, who played the Dover scene with blood on his bare feet:

> Looking at them, I suddenly realized that the blood on the feet made it possible for Olivier to forget about trying to show that his feet were bruised and sore and on the contrary to concentrate all his energy in rendering the sublime and serene poetry of Lear.

Realism, pushed to its extreme limit, frees poetry. In France King
Lear would have had no blood on his feet, and the actor playing this
part would have been compelled to show that this part of his
anatomy was troubling him; this would have been a kind of
stylization which would have detracted from his concentration on
rendering the turmoil of his mind and soul.[11]

It has been argued that the theatre differs from the circus in that one
is 'a spectacle of illusion' and the other 'a spectacle of actuality'.[12] In
fact, there are many moments in the theatre which offer both kinds of
spectacle. While it is recognised that an actor who fights or dances
onstage is performing these acts 'in character', there is always an
irreducible element in them which is recognised as part of his own skill.
This element of the real is one of the reasons why a stage fight is
exciting to watch; even though the spectators know that it has been
learned, it is also potentially real. The physical reality of the actor, in all
his fallibility and frailty, is most evident at the moments when, as so
often happens in Renaissance tragedy, it is asked to impersonate suffering
and death. The legends of actors genuinely dying during a performance,
and the weird fascination of the story of Molière's death, a few hours
after his pretended one in *Le Malade Imaginaire*, may well reflect a
superstitious distrust of any playacting of serious events (in *The White
Devil*, Webster 'punishes' Flamineo for his elaborately faked death by
making him die in earnest immediately after it). Such legends are
perhaps the inevitable result of the intense effort of imagination by
which the audience brings itself to believe in the reality of stage deaths
in the first place. There is something very revealing, and perhaps
slightly sinister, in what Kenneth Tynan wrote in his review of Laurence
Olivier's *Macbeth*: 'We wanted to see how he would die, and it was not
he but Shakespeare who let us down.'[13] Tynan did not mean simply that
he wanted to know how Olivier would play the death scene that
Shakespeare had failed to write. What lies behind his words is a
passionate desire not only to *see* but also to believe in the complex
experience of a death which is both fictitious and real, both Macbeth's
and Olivier's.

Glimpses of the theatrical machinery need not be damaging.
Recognition of the illusory, 'constructed' nature of Portia's beauty and
Othello's blackness is part of a general recognition of the theatre as an
image for the deceptiveness and transitoriness of all earthly appearances.
Vindice in *The Revenger's Tragedy* forces the same kind of awareness
on audiences by the visual trick of dressing a skull in '[at]tires'. By
drawing on comparisons with the dramaturgy of the moral allegorical

drama, Dessen has shown how often the ability to see is an indication of moral awareness. Thus, when Hamlet asks his mother, 'Ha, have you eyes?' (III.iv.66), and later tries to make her see her husband's ghost, he is appealing to both literal and spiritual vision.[14] But, as Fielding's account of Partridge's response makes clear, our own ability to believe in the ghost follows from our ability to believe in Hamlet himself. This means, among other things, believing in Hamlet when he insists that he has 'that within that passeth show' (I.ii.85) — that which is just as invisible as the ghost, or as the visage which Desdemona says she saw in Othello's mind. 'Is man no more than this?' asks Lear, looking at the 'poor, bare forked animal' that Edgar represents (III.iv.96–7). Tragedy notoriously demands that man *should* be more. But, as my examples have been showing, the very nature of the stage, and the problematic nature of its illusions, call into question the existence of anything beyond the material. Charles Lamb's complaint is well known: at even the best performance 'we find that instead of realizing an idea we have only brought down a fine vision to the standard of flesh and blood.'[15] He would have agreed with Jonson's division, already quoted, between soul and body, words and performance.

Did Shakespeare agree with it as well? Ernst Honigmann has suggested that Ben Jonson's attacks on unclassical dramatic practices were a constant influence on Shakespeare's writing.[16] The submerged theatrical references I have been noting can be seen as a response to Jonson's location of the comic in the mechanical and physical qualities of the theatre that he identified with soullessness because they were also the qualities that escaped his own authorial control. But there also seems to be an equal awareness of the dangers of the opposite extreme: the over-reliance on authorial power, the temerity, even unnaturalness, involved in the staging of the unstageable. The Marlovian atmosphere of the staging of the French wars in *1 Henry VI* results from the fact that, as in *Faustus*, the play condemns and punishes black magic (in the form of Joan of Arc), yet makes full use of its own magic effects — cannons, sieges of the tiring-house, alarms and excursions — to give the illusion of reality. The Prologue to *Tamburlaine* promises that the audience will *see* the hero's great feats as well as hear his stunning language; the passage I quoted earlier is an example of Marlowe's confidence that his words could simply *replace* whatever the actor had embodied. By contrast, the opening Chorus to *Henry V* is a virtual exorcism of theatrical black magic. Gary Taylor has suggested plausibly that 'O for a Muse of Fire' reflects Shakespeare's recent reading of Chapman's *Iliad* and his sense of the difference between the stage and the epic poem.[17] It also reminds us, I think, of the more presumptuous dramatist who had tried to abolish this difference. The *Henry V* Chorus, wishing that it could give us 'the warlike Harry, like himself' on a stage where princes would act and monarchs behold, is acknowledging its inability to emulate Faustus' black arts, which had raised the spirit of Alexander the Great to delight the German emperor. Unlike the spectacular 'shows' of *Faustus*, those of *Henry V* will be performed by 'flat unraised spirits' with no magic at their disposal. They are, nevertheless, spirits. The plays, then, recognise the reality of the 'fine vision' to which Lamb referred, even while recognising that its stage incarnation might be only 'flesh and blood'. The very qualities in the theatre which make it — literally — disillusioning also reinstate the theatrical illusion in another form. What is real in all acting is the need for courage.

Notes

1 Shakespeare quotations are taken from *The Complete Works*, ed. S. Wells and G. Taylor, Oxford: Oxford University Press, 1986. Quotations from *King Lear* are from the Folio text, here called *The Tragedy of King Lear*.

2 *Hymeneai, or the Solemnities of Masque and Barriers at a Marriage*, in Ben Jonson, *The Complete Masques*, ed. Stephen Orgel, The Yale Ben Jonson, New Haven and London: Yale University Press, 1969, p. 75.

3 *The Complete Plays of Ben Jonson*, ed. G. A. Wilkes, based on the edition of C. H. Herford and Percy and Evelyn Simpson, vol. II.

4 'Reading the Body: *The Revenger's Tragedy* and the Jacobean Theatre of Consumption', *Renaissance Drama*, n.s. XVIII (1987), 121–48, p. 125.

5 Christopher Marlowe, *Tamburlaine the Great*, ed. J. S. Cunningham, Revels Plays, Manchester: Manchester University Press, 1981, Part One, 2.1.

6 'Face-Painting in Renaissance Tragedy', *Renaissance Drama*, N.S. XII, 1981, pp. 71–93.

7 *The Critical Works of Thomas Rymer*, ed. Curt A. Zimansky, New Haven: Yale University Press, 1956, p. 152.

8 Ellen Terry, *The Story of My Life*, London: Hutchinson, 1908, p. 204.

9 See Charles B. Lower, 'Othello as Black on Southern Stages, Then and Now', in Philip C. Kolin, ed., *Shakespeare in the South*, Jackson, Miss.: University Press of Mississippi, 1983, pp. 199–228.

10 Alan C. Dessen, *Elizabethan Stage Conventions and Modern Interpreters*, Cambridge: Cambridge University Press, 1984, p. 21,

and 'Modern Productions and the Elizabethan Scholar', *Renaissance Drama*, XVIII (1987), pp. 205–223.

11 'Shakespeare and the French', translated from *A Propos de Shakespeare et du Théâtre* (Editions de la Parade, 1949), p. 39, and reprinted in *Shakespeare in Europe*, ed. Oswald LeWinter, World Publishing, USA, 1963, Penguin Shakespeare Library, Harmondsworth, 1970, p. 358.

12 A. D. Hippisley Coxe (1980) 'Equestrian Drama and the Circus', in *Performance and Politics in Popular Drama*, ed. D. Bradby, L. James, and B. Sharratt, Cambridge: Cambridge University Press, 1980, p. 109.

13 K. Tynan, *A View of the English Stage 1900–1964*, London: Davis-Poynter, 1950 [1975], p. 118.

14 Dessen, *Elizabethan Stage Conventions*, pp. 130–55.

15 'On the Tragedies of Shakespeare, Considered with Reference to their Fitness for Stage Representation', *Life, Letters and Writings of Charles Lamb*, ed. Percy Fitzgerald, 6 vols, London: Enfield Ed., vol. IV, p. 191.

16 *Shakespeare's Impact on His Contemporaries*, London: Macmillan, 1982, pp. 109–20.

17 Note to 1.2 in *Henry V*, ed. Gary Taylor, Oxford Shakespeare, Oxford: Oxford University Press, 1984.

Marion Trousdale

CORIOLANUS
AND THE PLAYGOER IN 1609

In 'Flatcaps and Bluecoats: Visual Signals on the Elizabethan Stage', an essay that appeared in *Essays and Studies 1980*, George Hunter argued that on the Elizabethan stage 'the individual is given full meaning only when caught up into his social role' (p. 26) and that 'all the characters are understood first in terms of rank and function'. I do not so much disagree with this observation as wish to complicate it. Character as it relates to dress I wish to examine not only as it appears on the stage in what I am positing as the first production of *Coriolanus* in 1609,[1] but as we can imagine it appeared in the audience that attended that first performance at the Globe. My argument is that performance as a means of projecting character as a field of force, as Hunter describes it, is as characteristic of the society that frequented the theatre as it is of the actors who showed that society on stage. That suggests that the hierarchy we take for granted in Elizabethan society and which Hunter himself refers to as part of his argument is not hierarchy as we imagine it retrospectively — a received and inflexible structure within which social identity is a given and violence is cloaked with the acceptable garb of validating ceremony. Rather the markings of rank, like the topics of argument, were material and occasional. They could be assembled and were assembled in the society, as on the stage, to enable the performer in both instances by means of visible signs to present a persuasive show. Thus acting as successful performance not only put in question established degree, as others have pointed out; it also drew upon and validated deeply held social practices that themselves subverted established social position.

What then can we tell about the seventeenth-century audience at the Globe? Were we to imagine attending the Globe in 1609 for the first night, or rather the first afternoon, of *Coriolanus*, we would know, from Andrew Gurr's painstaking reconstruction in *Playgoing in Shakespeare's London*, to expect a mixed audience, and it would appear that all of the theatres were both crowded and noisy. Drayton describing the Rose, which we now know to have been quite small, mentions the 'thronged Theatre' and the 'Showts and Claps at ev'ry little pawse' (Gurr, 1987, 45, 215). We know that at the Fortune, as well as at other theatres, the audience hissed to express their disapproval. 'Clapping or hissing is the onely meane,' William Fennor notes in 1616, 'That tries and searches out a well writ Sceane' (Gurr, 1987, 230), and Dekker in the Prooemium to *The Gvls Horne-booke* tells his readers that he sings like the cuckoo in June, 'hisse or giue plaudities, I care not a nut-shell which of either' (B1).

Obviously whoever was in that first audience, they actively participated in the action on the stage. The extent of that participation is indicated not only by the descriptions we have of the onstage audience rejecting the play the company has chosen to present as in *The Knight of the Burning Pestle*, but by the suggestion in the same play and earlier, in the performance of William Gager's *Ulysses Redux* at Christ Church, Oxford, that members of the audience felt important enough to consider themselves part of the action on the stage. Theatre, as Bruce Smith has remarked, is people talking to people, and as Gurr amply illustrates, in 1609 the talking went both ways. Whether standing in the pit, sitting in the lords' room, or sharing the platform with the actors, for the auditors at the Globe, going to the theatre was as active and public a performance as acting on the stage.

The response of a disappointed audience at the Hope Theatre on 17 October 1614 gives us some idea as to just how active an audience might be. The audience is described in some detail by John Taylor, the water poet, in *Taylor's Revenge*. He was to have had a rhyming contest with William Fennor who failed to appear. Taylor says that he personally stepped out on the stage to appease the crowd: 'But they all raging, like tempestuous Seas:/Cry'd out, their expectations were defeated/And how they all were cony-catch'd and cheated:/Some laught, some swore, some star'd & stamp'd and curst. . . . One sweares and stormes, another laughs & smiles,/Another madly would pluck off the tiles,/Some runne to th'doore to get againe their coyne.' But their response was not only vocal: 'For now the stinkards, in their irefull wraths,/Bepelted me with Lome, with Stones, and Laths,/One madly sits like bottle-Ale, and hisses,/Another throwes a stone, and 'cause he misses,/He yawnes and bawles, and cryes Away, away:/Another cryes out, Iohn, begin the Play/. . . .' One from the audience, he reports, 'valiantly stept out vpon the Stage,/And would teare downe the hangings in his rage.' Their active response Taylor sums up as the 'clapping, hissing, swearing, stamping, smiling,/Applauding, scorning, liking, and reviling' of what he calls the 'Hydra-headed multitude'. In desperation Taylor himself begins to act (145).

It is obvious that the stinkards, as Dekker among others described the lowest of these playgoers, felt as entitled to judge and be listened to as the gallant in the sixpenny box. It had been just such a presumption of privilege as playgoer that had led the Merchant Taylors' school to cease performances in 1573. 'Whereas at our Common Playes . . .', they stated, 'everye lewd persone thinketh himselfe (for his penny) worthye of the chiefe and most commodious place withoute respecte of any other, either for age or estimacion in the comon weale, whiche bringeth the youthe to such an impudente famyliaritie with theire betters that often tymes greite contempte of Maisters, Parents, and Magistrats followeth thereof' (Harbage, 1941, p. 13); and Dekker in 1609 suggests that the sense of shared privilege among the public theatre audience had become even more widespread. 'Sithence then the place,' he writes in *The Gvls Horne-booke* in 1609, 'is so free in entertainment, allowing a stoole as well to the Farmers sonne as to your Templer: that your Stinckard has the selfe-same libertie to be there in his Tobacco-Fumes, which your sweet Courtier hath: and that your Car-man and Tinker claime as strong a voice in their suffrage, and sit to giue iudgement on the plaies life and death, as well as the prowdest Momus among the tribe of Critick' (Harbage, 1941, p. 13).

Coriolanus then, one might say, puts on stage the stinkards who frequent the public theatres and puts them on stage in much the same dress as they appeared in the audience at the Globe. They are aproned men with caps who, in the words of the Merchant Taylors, thought themselves 'worthye of the chiefe and most commodious place withoute respecte of any other'. A company of mutinous citizens, according to the Folio stage direction, begins the play, and Martius in his first appearance characterises them in words reminiscent of Marullus in *Julius Caesar*. Their opinion, in Martius' view, is worth no more than their social position. 'Rubbing the poor itch of your opinion,' he tells them, 'you make yourselves scabs' (Riverside Edn., I.i.165). It is a remark that carries the same social judgement as Dekker's. Like Jonson, Martius characterises the commoners as deficient in judgement while assertive of their status. When stopped by the Tribunes in Act III when the crowd has turned against him, Martius calls it 'a purpos'd thing . . . To curb the will of the nobility . . . with such as cannot rule,/Nor ever will be ruled' (III.i.38–41), and when they banish him, Martius curses them as 'You common cry of curs! whose breath I hate,/As reek a'th'rotten fens, whose loves I prize/As the dead carcasses of unburied men/That do corrupt my air' (III.iii.120–3). It would appear to be such commoners thronging the theatres that made the city fathers worry about playhouses as places of public disturbance. If we ask what the first

audience of *Coriolanus* saw, we might say that what that part of the
audience saw when they watched *Coriolanus* was, throughout all of the
play, an unsympathetic if commonplace image of themselves.

But the audience was not made up only or even chiefly of aproned
men, and although assertive of their own importance, it does not seem
to have been principally aproned men who had the means to refashion
themselves through dress. Told by Master Probee that he and Master
Damplay have been sent 'unto you, indeed, from the people,' the Boy in
The Magnetic Lady asks 'which side of the people' and is told 'Not the
Faeces, or grounds of your people, that sit in the oblique caves and
wedges of your house, your sinfull sixe-penny Mechanicks' (sixpence
being the minimum price of admission to the Blackfriars Theatre); to
which Damplay adds, '. . . the better, and braver sort of your people!
Plush and Velvet-outsides! that stick your house round like so many
eminences' ['Induction or Chorus'].

From the correspondence of Philip Gawdy it would appear that some
of these people along with less distinguished members of the multitude
were caught up in the impressment carried out in the playhouses by the
city authorities in 1602 (Gurr, 1987, p. 66), and to judge from other
letters he wrote to his family, these people came to the theatre as they
went to Court, to show themselves in velvet and plush. Dekker advises
his gallant that if he wishes to be taken for a gentleman, he should sit on
the stage and 'talk loudly' to publish his 'temperance to the world' that
he might appear 'as a gentleman to spend a foolish hour or two'. One
must imagine that like such a gentleman as Philip Gawdy, Dekker's
gallant was concerned as well with his dress. And that dress is assembled
in imitation of betters. Whether the visible trappings Gawdy purchases
are a saddle for his father, hose for his brother or a dress for his sister,
the models are the accoutrements of those with power and place. 'For I
can assure yow that bothe the quene, and all the gentlewomen at the
courte weare the uery fashion of your tuff taffata gowne with an open
wired sleve and suche a cutt, and it is now the newest fashion,' he writes
to his sister Anne in December 1587 (Gawdy, 28). In December 1593,
he writes to his brother: 'I have boughte the a sadle with the furniture
coryspondente no other then my L. of Essex, Sr. Charles Blunt, Sr
Roger Williams and such other cavilleros at this hower do vse. The
footclothe bought of a clothe dyed out of a blewe blankett, which neuer
will change coller for any weather garded not after the old fashion but
the newest in request and most profitable, for lace therwith is alderman
lyke and suche as will hange vppon euery taynter' (Gawdy, 77). He
makes a similar observation about the hose he has bought. 'Thy hose I

haue bought of the mallard coller. It will holde well a perfecte wynter coller, paved and rowled just according to the fashion. I will not saye that very greate men I tooke the pattern from them [*sic*].' Even in Redenhall near Halston in Norfolk, Gawdy's family seat, the great men in the court are the arbiters of fashion, and as Gawdy copied Cecil or Essex or Blunt, so the lesser gentry and indeed those who were not gentry copied such gentry as Gawdy.

George Hunter, in the essay I mentioned earlier, points out in a different context that clothes, in a way in which we are unaccustomed to marking, were the means by which the society and the individual constituted themselves. Using the example of the apprentice Quicksilver in *Eastward Ho*, Hunter shows the extent to which clothes, as they say, make the man. Quicksilver, who claims to be of gentle parentage, keeps a chest of clothes with the usurer Security, and in Act II, using what he calls his finery, he changes his appearance from that of an apprentice, charged by statute to wear only the appropriate clothes provided by his master, into that of a nobleman. Hunter sees in this change 'a breach with social reality . . . an outside without an inside' (31). Losing his clothes in a shipwreck when escaping to Virginia, he is press-ganged for the army and subsequently ends up in gaol. His return at the end to a proper sense of clothing Hunter sees as the 'visual sign of social self-knowledge and mental balance'. But identity as we have examined it so far does not appear to be that stable, and although one can argue that Quicksilver's sense of self is represented by his awareness of the importance of how he is dressed, his attitude toward that dress and toward the social codes such dress embodies reveals not only the extent to which dress is felt to determine identity but the ways in which social rank in the period is attached to what one wears. Gawdy is a gentleman by birth. That does not keep him from associating status with fashion. Rather, like the actors that dressed up in expensive garments in order to draw the crowds to the theatre, Gawdy sees clothes as a means of social identity and seeks for himself and his family through fashionable dress a position enhanced by its exterior association with the powerful men at court.

To judge from such pamphleteers as Philip Stubbes and Stephen Gosson, and the repeated proclamations enforcing the sumptuary laws, Quicksilver's attraction to finery in the way of dress was characteristic of the society at large. 'How often', Stephen Gosson asks in *The School of Abuse* in 1579, 'hath her majesty, with the grave advice of her honorable councell, sette down the limits of apparell to every degree, and how soone againe hath that pride of our harts overflowen the channel?'; and he observes that 'overlashing in apparel is so common a fault, that the very hyerlings of some of our players, which stand at reversion of vi.s by the weeke, jet under gentlemens noses in sutes of silke' (p. 39). The decree of 1582 ordering people of all degrees to obey the sumptuary regulations which specified what each was entitled to wear, observes that the luxury of the times had 'greatly prevailed among people of all degrees in their apparel' (Baldwin, 231). The decree issued in 1588 observes that no reformation in dress had followed the earlier decrees (Baldwin, 226). Francis Baldwin, after looking closely at all of the sumptuary proclamations, remarks that 'even the queen's high indignation was not sufficient to terrify offenders against the sumptuary laws' (226). The sumptuary decrees show us what Quicksilver shows us. If it is felt that how you dress is meant to tell us who you are, then changing clothes can change status. This is the double bind of the fact that how you dress tells us who you are.

We can see the kind of social dilemma this creates in the remarks of Philip Stubbes. He is at once fascinated with dress — he describes it in minute detail — and offended by it. His descriptions of what he identifies as abuses are the descriptions of someone who could not tear his eyes away from the magnificence of what he saw. Of the notorious ruffs he remarks that they 'are eyther clogged with golde, siluer, or silke lace of stately price, wrought all ouer with needle work, speckled and sparkled here and there with the Sonne, the Moone, the starres and many other Antiques straunge to beholde. Some garments are wrought with open worke downe to the midst of the ruffe and further . . . some with purled lace so cloyd, and other gewgawes so pestred. . . . Sometimes, they are pinned vp to their eares, sometimes they are suffered to hang ouer their shoulders, like flagges or Windmill sayles fluttering in the wind, and thus euery one pleaseth her selfe in her foolish deuices' (43). Of their doublets he observes: 'The women also there haue Doublets and Jerkins as men haue here, buttoned vp the breast, and made with wings, weltes and pinions on the shoulder pointes, as mans apparel is in all respectes' (44). His admiration for what he is ostensibly condemning can be seen in the detailed way in which the clothes are described. 'If the whole gowne be not Silke or Velvet, then the same must be layd with lace, two or three fingers broad all ouer the gowne, or els the most part. Or if not so . . . then it must be garded with great gardes of Veluet, euery garde foure or sixe fingers broad at the least, and edged with costly lace' (45). The ambivalence of Stubbes' attitude toward the extravagant dress he condemns in such loving detail can be seen even more clearly in the way in which the sheer magnificence of the garments he describes is itself, to him, a source of national pride:

> 'But I haue heard them say, that other nations passe them for
> exquisite finenesse and brauery in apparell: as the Italians, the
> Athenians, the Spaniards, the Chaldeans, Helvetians, Zuitzers,
> Venetians, Muscouians, and suchlike: . . . The Muscouians,
> Athenians, Italians, Brasilians, Affricanes, Asians, Cantabrians,
> Hungarians, Ethiopians, Dutch, French, or els what nations soeuer
> vnder the Sunne, are so farre behinde the people of England in
> exquisitnesse of apparell, as in effect, they esteeme it little or
> nothing at all . . . for it is manifest that all other nations vnder the
> Sunne, how strange, how new, how fine, or how comely soeuer
> they thinke their fashions to be, when they bee compared with the
> diuers fashions, and sundry formes of apparel in England, are most
> unhandsome, brutish and monstrous. And hereby it apeareth, that
> no people in the worlde are so curious in newfangles, as they of
> England be' (9–10).[2]

Other documents confirm Stubbes' boast. It would appear from a
complaint of one Thomas Gylles against the Yeoman of the Revels
in 1572 that even earlier the demand for extravagant clothes was
such that both independent tradesmen and the Yeoman of the Revels
had clothes for hire. The garments for hire by the Yeoman of the
Revels were garments that belonged to the Queen. Gylles' complaint
states:

> 'Wheras the yeman of the quenes Magestyes revelles dothe vsuallye
> lett to hyer her sayde hyghnes maskes to the grett hurt spoylle &
> dyscredyt of the same to all sort of parsons that wyll hyer the same
> by reson of wyche comen vsage the glosse & bewtye of the same
> garmentes ys lost & canott sowell serve to be often allteryde & to be
> shewyde before hyr hyghnes . . . for ytt takythe more harme by
> ounce werynge Into the cytye or contre where yt ys often vsyd then
> by many tymes werynge In the cowrt by the grett presse of peple &
> fowlnes bothe of the weye & wether & soyll of the wereres who for
> the most part be of the meanest sort of mene to the grett dyscredytt
> of the same aparell which afterwards ys to be shewyd before her
> heyghnes & to be worne by theme of grett callynge.'

He had complained before with no results 'by reson that the sayd
yeman havynge alloen the costodye of the garmentes dothe lend the
same at hys plesuer ffor remedy heroff . . . And your orator shall praye
vnto allmyghty gode for your honores longe lyffe & prossperytye for
your orator ys grettlye hynderyde of hys lyvynge herbye who havynge
aparel to lett & canott so cheplye lett the same as hyr hyghnes maskes

be lett as knowytt god who ever preserv you In honor & felycytye'
(Feuillerat, 409).

It is interesting to put beside the preoccupations of Stubbes the
accounts in Henslowe's diary which show how important dress was to
the actors on the stage. The list of playing apparel written in the hand of
Edward Alleyn (291–4) includes a scarlet cloak with gold laces and gold
buttons down the side, a scarlet cloak with silver lace and silver buttons,
a short velvet cloak embroidered with gold and gold spangles, a damask
cloak with velvet, a scarlet [cloak?] with buttons of gold faced with blue
velvet, a black velvet gown with white fur, a crimson robe stripped with
gold faced with ermine, a coat of crimson velvet cut in panes and
embroidered in gold, a carnation velvet jerkin laced with silver. Like the
members of the audience who by acquiring the right clothes could
acquire at the same time a social identity, the actors on the stage
projected the character they wished to represent by means of elaborate
dress. And Alleyn's list, like Stubbes's description, reveals a similar
ambiguity in its definitions of that social identity. 'Daniels gowne' like
'will somers cote' at least suggests the possibility of character established
by recognisable dress, and we know from other inventories (317, 321)
that at least some well-known stage personalities (Tamburlaine, Henry
V) have particular garments associated with the part. Thus the expensive
clothes in Alleyn's wardrobe could project character, suggesting self-
fashioning. At the same time established characters are imagined as
fixed. Tamburlaine is not so much created as recognised by means of
what he wears.

What would such an audience see as they watched *Coriolanus* on the
stage? They would see in the first instance a Roman who questioned the
belief that dress could be the means of giving or assuming a local
habitation and a name. Coriolanus changes clothes three times during
the course of the play. During most of his time on stage he is the Roman
warrior who safeguards the city from the Volscians. Wearing the short
Roman kirtle and using what was taken to be Roman armour,[3] the actor
playing the character of Coriolanus paradoxically is playing a man for
whom identity is not something one can put off with one's clothes. This
can be seen very clearly when he wears the toga of humility in order to
win the necessary voices. 'May I change these garments?' he asks
Sicinius after pleading for the plebeians' voices, and told that he may,
remarks that he'll 'straight do; and knowing myself again,/Repair to the
senate-house' (II.iii.144). Like the ideal posited by the sumptuary laws,
Coriolanus' continuing sense of himself is of one whom clothes cannot
change. Even when returning to Rome as the hero of the Volsces and

presumably dressed like a Volsce, Coriolanus in the presence of his kindred and at the intercession of his wife and mother allies himself with Rome. He is the citizen Hunter describes, the one for whom clothing is the visual sign of social self-knowledge. Change in Coriolanus' eyes is a sign of weakness. It is the fact that the crowd can be wooed as well as the fact that they are cowardly that makes him have no respect for the crowd. This is then a man who, we might imagine, represents on stage an Elizabethan ideal. He is unfailingly courageous, and in his death, as Cavell remarks, the city loses the best hero it ever had. Like Jonson's his standards never vary. As the best of the playwrights, he refuses to appease the hydra-headed multitude.

Yet fame for a playwright or a soldier, like the status of a citizen, exists only when publicly inscribed. Like the clothes for which the populace hungered and which consumed the wealth they were meant to display, Coriolanus' constancy consumes him. His inability to woo the mob means that he fails to gain that fame he hungers for, for that only the mob can bestow. Stubbes reports that

> 'So farre hath this cancker of pride eaten into the body of the common welth, that euery poore yeoman his Daughter, euery Husband man his daughter, and euery Cottager his Daughter will not spare to flaunt it out, in suche gownes, petticots, and kirtles, as these. And notwithstanding that their Parents owe a brase of hundredpounds more than they are worth, yet will they haue it. . . . For they are so impudent, that all be it, their poore Parents haue but one cow, horse, or sheep, they will neuer let them rest, til they be sould, to maintain them in their braueries' (46).

Although with more cause because of greater public worth, Coriolanus is similarly impudent, and similarly imprudent. Unable to fashion himself as both auditory and actors did, unable to indulge a love of finery, or even to understand it, unable in a consciously histrionic society to play more than one part, Coriolanus is destroyed. More accurately, like Narcissus whom he resembles in self-love, Coriolanus destroys himself.[4]

I draw several conclusions from this. *Coriolanus* on the stage in 1609 affronts the audience on whom its popularity depends. But a closer look suggests a deeper sympathy with an auditory that expected to be known by their clothes. In addition to wearing a Roman kirtle, Coriolanus it would appear has a beard and wears a hat. This makes him not only a Roman but an Elizabethan Roman, one for whom the ability to act a part with the props at hand was as important as being able to sway a mob.

My concern in this essay has been with what the audience saw in

1609, if the play did have an audience in that year. And I have confined my attention to the ways in which a deep and abiding concern with dress might be thought to tell us something about the contemporary reception of the play. But dress as we see it used in *Coriolanus* and in Stubbes attaches itself to a broader spectrum of values, one in which the honor and integrity of the military man can only be compromised in a society in which the values and the voices of the common man have a commanding say. Dress in this context coexists with ideas of valour, and some idea of at least one man's perception of that valour is described by Edward Grimstone, once secretary to Sir Edward Stafford, the English ambassador in Paris.

Grimstone dedicates his *Generall Historie of the Netherlands* to Robert Cecil and prefaces what he excuses as a translation with observations about the relationship between a country and its sovereign. 'The one is when as the prince seekes to haue a full subiection and obedience of the people, and the people contrariwise require, that the prince shold maintaine them in their freedoms and liberties, which he hath promised and sworn solemnly vnto them, before his reception to the principalitie' (781). He mentions Philip II in this regard, but as the history continues, it is the Earl of Leicester as governor of the Netherlands who objects to the traditionally democratic rule. Leicester complains that all instructions from the Council of Estates 'were no other in effect, then limitations of his commission. . . . In the end (to content his Excelency) the deputies of the states sayd, that hee should not bee bound to those instructions, but that they were made for the Councell of Estate, and that his Excelency was not to bee bound to conclude, any matter of importance by plurality of voices.' Grimstone reports that 'To this resolution the Estates were hardly to bee drawne, as well foreseeing, that hee not beeing tide to any instructions might easily bee seduced by bad Counsell' (911).

Coriolanus too refuses to be bound by voices, and to give public acknowledgement to the estates on whom his office depends. Like Essex who followed in the footsteps of Leicester, he sought the sole distinction of military glory. What the histrionic inscribes as a social norm is a questioning of such traditionally noble values as givens and prescribed. The classical prototype Grimstone mentions is not the story of Coriolanus but that of Lucrece. Tarquin's banishment, he points out, brings the republic into being. We might see in the 1609 performance of *Coriolanus* at the Globe an affirmation of the social code of Quicksilver and his clothes.

Notes

1 1609 is an arbitrary date. Philip Brockbank in the Arden edition places the play's composition between 1605 and 1610. Plague occurs in each of those years. Brian Parker who is editing the play for Oxford believes it might have been performed originally at Blackfriars. The argument of this essay assumes a performance at the Globe.
2 Frank Whigham makes a similar point in his discussion of sumptuary legislation and the social attitudes toward dress. See *Ambition and Privilege: The Social Tropes of Elizabethan Courtesy Theory*, Berkeley: University of California Press, 1984, pp. 154–69.
3 See Moelwyn Merchant, 'Classical Costume in Shakespearian Productions', *Shakespeare Survey*, 10, 1957, pp. 71–6.
4 This is documented in the excellent essay by Stanley Cavell, '*Coriolanus* and Interpretations of Politics', *Themes out of School: Effects and Causes*, Chicago: University of Chicago Press, 1988, pp. 60–96.

References

Baldwin, Francis Elizabeth (1926) 'Sumptuary Legislation and Personal Regulation in England', *Johns Hopkins University Studies in Historical and Political Science*, 44, Baltimore: Johns Hopkins Press, pp. 1–282.
Dekker, Thomas (1609) *The Gvls Horne-book*, London.
Feuillerat, Albert (1908) *Documents Relating to the Office of the Revels in the Time of Queen Elizabeth*, London: David Nutt.
Letters of Philip Gawdy, ed. Isaac Herbert Jeayes (1906) London: J. B. Nichols & Sons.
Gosson, Stephen (1579) *The School of Abuse*, London.
Grimstone, Ed[ward] (1608) *A Generall Historie of the Netherlands . . . Continued vnto this present yeare . . . 1608*, London.
Gurr, Andrew (1987) *Playgoing in Shakespeare's London*, Cambridge: Cambridge University Press.
Harbage, Alfred (1961) *Shakespeare's Audience*, New York: Columbia University Press.
Henslowe's Diary, ed. R. A. Foakes and R. T. Rickert (1961) Cambridge: Cambridge University Press.
Herford, C. H. and Simpson, Percy and Evelyn (1938) *Ben Jonson*, vol. VI, Oxford: Oxford University Press.
Hunter, G. K. (1980) 'Flatcaps and Bluecoats: Visual Signals on the Elizabethan Stage', *Essays and Studies*, ed. Inga-Stina Ewbank, London: John Murray, pp. 16–47.
Shakespeare, Riverside edition (1974) Boston: Houghton Mifflin.
Smith, Bruce R. (1988) *Ancient Scripts and Modern Experience on the English Stage 1500–1700*, Princeton: Princeton University Press.
Stubbes, Philip (1595) *Anatomie of Abuses*, London.
Taylor, John (1868) *Works Reprinted from the Folio Edition of 1630; Part II*, printed for the Spenser Society.

'JACK AND JILL':

A CONSIDERATION OF *LOVE'S LABOUR'S LOST*

AND *A MIDSUMMER NIGHT'S DREAM*

FROM THE POINT OF VIEW OF ACTOR AND DIRECTOR

It might be thought that one amateur and five professional encounters with *Love's Labour's Lost*, and only three professional with *A Midsummer Night's Dream*, is an odd balance for a twentieth-century theatre man. *A Midsummer Night's Dream* is probably the most performed of all Shakespeare's plays, given its simple language and instant availability for open-air (often amateur) productions. *Love's Labour's Lost*, on the other hand, with a woefully peculiar and controversial text, had little or no performance history until Peter Brook's 1946 Stratford production (with a twenty-eight-year-old Paul Scofield as Don Armado) followed by Hugh Hunt's 1949 Old Vic creation starring Michael Redgrave as Berowne. This rang all the bells, and inspired Peter Hall to embrace the play, first at Cambridge in 1953, then at Stratford in 1956. I saw none of these until 1956, but was inspired by Hall's memory of the 1949 one, and his own skill in our production at Cambridge in 1953.

It was love at first sight. The strange alchemy of wit, romance, pedantry, fantastication, and melancholy haunted generations of Cambridge actors and directors: David Jones directed it in 1973 at Stratford in between two productions by John Barton, one in 1965 and one in 1978. On leaving Cambridge, Ian McKellen, Corin Redgrave, Derek Jacobi and others performed at the Lyric, Hammersmith, in 1959 a Victorian musical version of the play, calling it *Love's Labours.* My memories of that include a musical version of 'Honorificabilitudin-itatibus' which *declined*, and the butler at the end bringing a newspaper called the *Mercury* on a silver salver, announcing the death of Queen Victoria to the assembled young people, who included four ladies from the Apollo Theatre. 'The words of the Mercury are sad after the songs from the Apollo,' said Armado, the old actor, as the curtain fell.

Oddly enough, in Victoria's time, the play was unknown, although the Act V scene with the Muscovites (and material surrounding it) was used for many years as part of the libretto for *Cosi Fan Tutte*, the Da Ponte script being considered too indecent for performance. I am sure, however, that nobody at that time would have accepted the dialogue at

the end of IV.i of *Love's Labour's Lost* if it *had* been produced: Boyet,
Rosaline, Maria and Costard have here perhaps the most explicit sexual
wordplay in Shakespeare.

I was greatly entertained to discover that an audience of 2,500
schoolchildren (age 14–16) understood the *double entendres* immediately
at a matinée given by the RSC in Omaha, Nebraska, in 1975 — and
even more surprisingly, so did an audience of 250 largely illiterate
Greeks in the village of Hortos in 1986, watching my production with
students of the Guildhall School. In fact, all the word games (and whole
sections of the play are seemingly little else) succeed much more in
action with audiences, than a mere reading of the text would suggest. I
have long been of the opinion that rhythm alone accounts for much of
this. The opposite is demonstrably true — actors who cannot sense the
tight cueing of line upon line, who do not sense the antiphonal charm of
the couplets, soon find the play drifting away from them.

The most striking aspect of *Love's Labour's Lost* is the maturity
which underlies so much of the courtly dance of the couplets, and the
pedantry and fantastication of the prose, in what seems to have been an
early play. It is full of muddles in the script available to us — perhaps
the most extreme being the evidence that the ladies in III.i are masked
on their arrival (no one of Shakespeare's skill could have intentionally
retained that idea after thinking up the masking in Act V). Throughout
the play, however, the psychology rings true. The men are inexperienced,
extreme, but narrow in their dedication to philosophy, wildly over the
top in their love once it is declared, puzzled by female directness,
defeated by female wit, and only at the very end beginning to understand
the true feelings that lead the girls to test their new vows of love to the
utterance. It is a poignant rite of passage because the girls have also
been cruel in their apparent certainty.

Each time I have been involved in the play, its deeper tones seem to
appear earlier in performance, justifying anew the volte-face after
Mercadé's entrance, making it more and more inevitable, although
brilliantly concealed from the audience until it occurs. The end of Act
IV — naturally the interval in a modern two-part version — is on
Berowne's lines:

> Light wenches may prove plagues to men forsworn.
> If so, our copper buys no better treasure.   (ll. 361–2)

Superficially read, that means 'look out for trouble', but the
implications are wider. Berowne still thinks of the girls as light — giddy
at least, if not sexually unfaithful. He has no real evidence for this belief

— it is a carry-over from his soliloquy about loving the worst of all ('A whitely wanton with a velvet brow') and it shows him still incapable of love combined with respect, blaming female sensuality for yet another Fall of Man. There is more to be cured here than the upset of the Muscovite charade can achieve.

Much turns on the solemnity of the vow. It is difficult for modern directors and actors to convince audiences of how much that matters. In Santa Cruz, I set the play in 1905, USA — the last age of American idealism, as well as of imperial elegance, when a gentleman's word was still supposed at least to be his bond. We made it very clear that the knowledgeable Berowne signed the schedule against his better judgement, out of friendship for the King, that when he broke the vow his concern was that it made him ridiculous, not that it made him forsworn — and his wondrous Jesuitical speech in justification ('Have at you then, affection's men at arms') convinced the others against *their* better judgement. Convinced, they never recognise their fault again, and blame the collapse of the oath on the ladies' beauty:

'Rebuke me not for that which you provoke,' says the King in Act V; Berowne, likewise:

> Therefore, ladies,
> Our love being yours, the error that love makes
> Is likewise yours.   (ll. 763–5)

It will not do, of course — the real lightness, flightiness, and superficial sensuality is shown in the play to be male, not female. To judge from audiences leaving the show in Santa Cruz, the quarrel continued on the way home, the men attacking the gravity of the tasks set for their counterparts in the play ('The girls had damaged their confidence enough already'), the women defending the Princess and her team ('That's just the point: you men never understand — the boys were awful in their confidence that the girls would give in in the end.').

The oathbreaking is only half the story. Shamed by that, the girls' destruction of their charade, and the deception with the masks, the men lash out unmercifully at their social inferiors, Sir Nathaniel, Holofernes, and their mental inferior Don Armado. However we may think that pedantry deserves a come-uppance in the play, the behaviour of Dumaine, Longueville and Berowne (and the only man in the ladies' group, Boyet), is unforgivable. The Princess does say, 'That sport best pleases that doth best know how,' but the men interpret that as a licence to heckle and bully the honest, if unfortunate performers. One notable sequence rings the tocsin of warning for those that can hear: 'Jud-Ass, away!' scream the men at Holofernes/Maccabeus, to which he replies, 'This is not generous, not gentle, not humble.' Simple, unpedantic and devastating; the actor takes off his silly helmet, looks them straight in the face, says the lines simply, and exits. The first inescapable shiver of reality. Then, Armado responds to an endless list of second-rate one-liners, culminating in 'Hector's a greyhound,' with the unforgettable epitaph:

The sweet war-man is dead and rotten. Sweet chucks, beat not the bones of the buried. When he breathed he was a man. (*LLL* V.ii.654–6)

Finally, a piece of business that seems inherent in the text, has found favour with many directors, at least since the 1960s: Armado's substitute for a hair-shirt, Jaquenetta's dishcloth, is pulled from beneath his jacket and thrown about the stage from courtier to courtier as he vainly tries to snatch it back, only to land at the feet (or sometimes, in the face) of Mercadé as he enters with the bad news.

In Santa Cruz, I followed Barton's 1978 Stratford rearrangement of the text in Act V, placing the Princess's and King's lines 343–56 just before Costard enters, on Berowne's line (485), 'Welcome pure wit, thou part'st a fair fray.' There is no scholarly justification for this whatsoever, but theatrically it makes great sense. The quarrel between Boyet and Berowne is ultimately lighthearted, Berowne ending it by saying, 'Peace, I have done.' The royal quarrel over the oath-breaking is deadly serious, and coming after the apparent relaxation, just before the Nine Worthies' pageant, we remember it much more clearly. It also explains the King's reluctance to see the pageant.

Another hint, early on in the play, that all is not jolly, is the Princess's concern with killing the deer. It is only the Princess who expresses this view, no one else even comments on her remarks — unlike the situation Shakespeare exploits later in *As You Like It*, when first the duke, then the first lord reporting Jaques' speech, then Jaques with the hunters, all express an attitude of regret, much in tune with modern thinking. The Princess, from her first entrance onward, has — it seems to me — the conscience of the play in her keeping. She demands respect for her father, she teases the King's forester, but listens to what he says and rewards him, she organises the downfall of the Muscovites. She walks through a minefield of emotions and responsibilities at the end of Act V, as an orphaned child, newly-made queen, and recipient of a love suit, not just from an attractive young man, but from a neighbouring king, with all the attendant dynastic problems. This speech is a masterpiece of judgement, beautifully constructed, but full of delicate spontaneity

— a daunting challenge, but a great gift to a fine actress. Mercadé's entrance breaks the apparent mood of the play, but the Princess effects the changes. The progress of these last lines of the play depends on her, and I have been most fortunate with both my actresses. My mind returns, however, to the transformation of Geraldine McEwan in Stratford in 1956. Hitherto known only as a sprightly, eccentric, squeaky-voiced West End comedienne, she surprised everyone with her maturity at this moment. I seem to remember a definite lowering of the pitch of her voice, the result of shock.

Almost at the end, Berowne says, 'Our wooing doth not end like an old play — Jack hath not Jill.' The lovers' quarrel in *A Midsummer Night's Dream*, however, ends before the last scene, when Puck reunites the correct pairs with the words, 'Jack shall have Jill, naught shall go ill.' It seems to be conventional wisdom that *Love's Labour's Lost* is the earlier play of the two — many of the conceits are too obscure for performance, there are few passages of comedy equal to the Mechanicals' scenes in naturalness, and the blank verse passages are fewer and less notable than those in *A Midsummer Night's Dream*. But, and it is a big but, the ending of *Love's Labour's Lost* is much more extraordinary in its stagecraft than anything in *A Midsummer Night's Dream*, and is about newly discovered feelings and responsibilities. 'Jack hath not Jill' has much greater meaning to an audience that has heard Puck say 'Jack shall have Jill,' — although it is possible to argue the opposite.

One of the strangest areas of *Love's Labour's Lost* has always been, for me, the Don Armado plot. Strange, because many lines in his second scene (III.i) are so obscure that they are normally cut. I refer to those involving the Ape and the Humble Bee. I certainly cut them from both my productions, and they were cut by David Jones in the 1973/5 RSC production in which I first played Armado — to my great relief. Armado lives in a world of fantasy and is initially connected to us only through his relationship with Moth. Here he has two scenes dominated by his infatuation with the country girl Jaquenetta, which not only breaks his oath to the King but dishonours him as a soldier. Yet in Act V, until Costard reveals the pregnancy at the end of the Nine Worthies' pageant, Jaquenetta is not mentioned, and Armado ignores Moth almost entirely. In V.i, he is just a very pompous royal ambassador — very funny, but without charm or melancholy. His glory comes at the end: the majesty of his ripostes to the courtiers is surpassed by the humility of: 'I have seen the day of wrong through the little hole of discretion, and I will right myself like a soldier.' These lines set the balance of the last scene most judiciously.

By comparison, *A Midsummer Night's Dream* seems the easier play to direct, and its acting roles simpler. Like *The Tempest*, it depends on an atmosphere of magic that is an open invitation to brilliant designing. A recent edition of *American Theatre* magazine reviewed four major United States productions, all with extraordinary concepts of direction and design, and significantly failed to discuss a single acting performance.

In my time I have acted Quince for Peter Hall in the 1962 Stratford production, and Theseus for Robin Phillips in Exeter in 1968 (the latter having Victorian costume, hobby-horses for the hunting scene, and a pond for wetting everyone in the forest), but did not have the opportunity to direct the play until 1989, with the graduating class of the Denver National Theatre Conservatory. My actors were able, unlike so many in the United States, to speak with their own voices when acting in Shakespeare, not with that travesty of language, Standard Stage Speech, but I was terrified to discover that the budget for the production was to all intents and purposes, nil. The theatre had some spare metal piping and an oddly random collection of costumes from previous shows. There was no costume designer, so, in order to impose some unity, I pulled out everything on the racks that was white or off-white. Puck wore white cut-off trousers, Oberon the same with a shot silk cloak, Titania in white pants with a white robe; all three were barefoot and basically lived in the lighting gallery above the thrust stage, descending by the three metal pipes. The mortals were basically turn-of-the-century: Bottom and his friends wore early industrial bib-overalls. There was some spectacular doubling to cover the play with thirteen people — Titania ran very fast to couple Starveling, Oberon played Flute, Puck was Philostrate (Peter Brook's double, and easy to accomplish) and, riskiest of all, Theseus and Hippolyta donned Bunraku-black to work minute stick puppets as flying fairies (and to provide them with a variety of voices).

The result was fast and delicate, leaving large areas to the imagination. Speaking was light, accurate and American without much nasal twang, rhetorically well-structured but without affectation. Music was taken from recordings of wooden flute music of the Andes, the sounds, in fact, of the rain forests, quirky and mysterious. I am certain that necessity drove me to a Shakespearian conclusion, and now even the very witty RSC 1989 production, with the forest as a Never Never Land and Puck as a twisted Peter Pan, seems an imposition on a play that speaks so clearly for itself.

It is undeniably true that given more rehearsal time (my cast were also playing in *King Lear*) Shakespeare's acute perception of sexual role-playing could have been made clearer. My experience of playing Theseus in 1968 introduced me to his need to compete with Hippolyta in every way. Directing the play, I became more aware of how well she scores against him — better than Titania against Oberon in the forest. When Theseus says (I.i.122), 'What cheer, my love?' he indicates clearly how eloquent is Hippolyta's silence — the laws of Athens condemning a maiden to death for disobedience to her father are not for her. Theseus has to have the better hounds in the hunting scene — the immortal description of Hippolyta's pack ('So musical a discord, such sweet thunder') is not allowed to stand unchallenged — but when it comes to assessing the previous night's experience, Hippolyta is the more instinctive. It is a fascinating exchange, because Theseus' analysis of the imagination has become famous as an extract. In context, his cool Renaissance mind despises imagination and its tricks, whereas Hippolyta allows for the growth of 'great constancy, but howsomever strange and admirable'. Yet in another context (V.i.209–15), Theseus defends theatrical imagination against her:

> HIPPOLYTA This is the silliest stuff that ever I heard.
> THESEUS The best in this kind are but shadows, and the worst are
>   no worse if imagination amend them.
> HIPPOLYTA It must be your imagination, then, and not theirs.
> THESEUS If we imagine no worse of them than they of themselves,
>   they may pass for excellent men.

She does say, 'Well shone, Moon. Truly, the moon shines with a good grace,' and 'Beshrew my heart, but I pity the man,' about Pyramus, but her last lines are both practical and impatient: 'How chance Moonshine is gone before Thisbe comes back and finds her lover?' 'Methinks she should not use a long one [passion] for such a Pyramus. I hope she will be brief.' In contrast, Titania is totally reconciled, in love and spirit, with Oberon after her experience (or, as she thinks, dream), of loving an ass.

This, and other major differences, have led me to suspect the validity of the Oberon/Theseus, Titania/Hippolyta doubling, first employed by Frank Dunlop in his Edinburgh International Festival production (Titania/Hippolyta was Cleo Laine) then, famously, in 1970 by Peter Brook, and now fashionable everywhere. I simply could not use it: Oberon/Theseus became a part so much larger than the others that it would have been unfair in a student production. In practice I found the play stronger in its original form. The double *explains* the play in the same way that doubling Cordelia and the Fool explains 'And my poor fool is hanged,' in the last scene of *King Lear*. I have seen my daughter play that double, and despite all my paternal prejudice in favour, I know it to be wrong. The echoes are mysterious and should remain so. Why spend so much time, as we all do now, defending the imaginative process of theatre against scenic elaboration, literalism, and conceptual hyperbole — and they try to dot every 'i' and cross every 't' because we trust so little in our audience?

Another problem all directors and actors face is the relentless pressure to be funny far too early in the plays. This again could well be the result of overfamiliarity — my production of *Love's Labour's Lost* was compared by a San Francisco critic to three others he had seen, in California alone, in the previous year. It is, to defend my colleagues, more likely to be the fear that if an audience does not laugh at what is termed a 'comedy', then it does not understand. In fact, an audience does not laugh *until* it understands — or rather does not laugh at the *play*. Comic entrances (Dull on a bicycle, Armado with a butterfly net to catch Moths, Bottom and his companions encumbered with professional equipment, fairies trying on their wings, Titania in a flying bubble like the Good Witch of the North) are all very well but, it seems to me, Shakespeare is very careful not to make his characters overly comic in their first scenes — he draws the audience into an understanding of who these people are, how they work, what are their problems, and how they relate to each other. Of course it is comical to see Berowne upturn the expectations of the King and his friends, then to wrong-foot the King with the Princess's arrival, then to accept the oath — but the genuine concern of all to try to live a better life, and Berowne's detailed explanations of its difficulties, are the true seedbed for the growth of deep and fully engaged laughter later on. Theseus' support for the ancient law, and Hermia's attempt to rebel against it, are serious matters. Adolescent suffering may be over-illustrated with classical examples, but we must believe in its power. When Quince and his men attempt to put together their production, we must see how genuinely difficult these literal-minded artisans find the process. Bottom's unquenchable optimism, and experience, is a matter of wonder to his companions. The beautiful sadness of their penultimate scene, with Flute's threnody on the sixpence a day Bottom would have earned (and the fact that had their sport gone forward, they would all have been Made Men) will work only if we have believed in them in I.ii. I can remember a relentlessly funny first scene at the Schiller Theatre, Berlin, in 1964 that left the audience quite drained of laughter (because drained of care) by Act V.

In the extraordinary play-within-the-play scenes, greater temptation

beckons, and it is a rare production that does not make Sir Nathaniel
lose his text more times than Shakespeare indicates, that does not
require more laughter from wobbling ladders (Guthrie's *A Midsummer
Night's Dream* at the Old Vic in the 1950s), deflating hobby-horses
(Barton's *Love's Labour's Lost*, 1980), misplacing the heart that hops,
etc., than from the miraculously touching attempts by professional men
(carpenter, bellows-mender, joiner, weaver, tailor, tinker, curate,
schoolmaster, policeman, soldier of fortune) who are amateurs when it
comes to the theatre. The people on stage who make fun of these
amateurs are professional at nothing. Even Theseus, who speaks like a
rational moderate before, shows little tact and a rather patronising
attitude to the players once Pyramus and Thisbe is over ('If he that writ
it had played Pyramus, and hanged himself in Thisbe's garter, it would
have been a fine tragedy'), so we wonder how good a duke he is by
Shakespeare's exacting standards.

The two events have great similarities, but they are also very different.
One is a play, fully cast, and, were it not for Puck's intervention, quite
well rehearsed by the standards of the time. It is a simple, effective
story, and although Quince's text is bathetic, I have seen audiences
moved by Flute's final speech as Thisbe. Peter Brook said that we laugh
at the idea of 'His eyes were green as leeks' at our peril — Flute and
Quince may well have been as proud of the colour of the leeks they grew
as North-of-England gardeners are of the size of their marrows — and
Shakespeare makes Pistol suffer tortures for mocking a leek in *Henry V*.

The pageant of the Nine Worthies is a duller prospect to us, merely
speeches introducing the characters, with all their actions in the past.
Apart from Moth who does not speak (Holofernes describes him) but
kills dogs and wrestles with serpents, Costard/Pompey, the first Worthy,
is the only one allowed to finish.

We never know what Alexander or Judas did, or what Hector's gift
was: the aristocrats destroy everything once Costard lays down his arms
— and even he is successful only because of his invincible optimism ('I
hope I was perfect, I made a little fault in "great"'). The absurdity lies in
the contrast between the greatness of the heroes and the village nobodies
who play them — but we find as the show proceeds that the players are
truer to their roles than the aristocrats are to theirs. The purpose of this
pageant (the third, at least, in the play, if you think of the Oathbreakers
at the end of Act IV, and the Muscovites earlier in Act V) is instructive.
Had Theseus been present ('The best in this kind are but shadows, . . .')
the story would have been different; here even the King can only
remain silent — he never rebukes his unruly courtiers.

We will not follow Shakespeare's intentions, I am convinced, if we do not care for, and relish, the village characters, and Don Armado. We must be amazed by Holofernes' dexterity with words, astonished by the complexity of the 'pricket' improvisation, we must recognise the true obsessional, the manic teacher we laughed at behind his back in our youth, but whose enthusiasm was infectious. The gentleness of Sir Nathaniel and his wonder at Holofernes, the slow but certain tread of Dull's logic, the joy of Armado at Moth's precocious skills, his determination to 'turn sonnet', his passionate devotion to the idea of the moment (once it was honour, then it was melancholy, now it is love) — these characters and their characteristics must engage us to the full. Then we can laugh with joy, and not because buttons are pushed.

The lovers in both plays present technical problems. Sharp definition of verbal styles, immaculate cueing and almost no pauses at all are mandatory in the Act IV quartet of the Oathbreakers (*Love's Labour's Lost*) and the III.ii quartet of lovers in *A Midsummer Night's Dream*. The *Love's Labour's Lost* scene is more formal — it is not until Berowne's great speech of justification that blank verse, with all its natural richness, is heard, whereas it is the ruling method in the lovers' quarrel, enabling much greater variety of pace and style. Mechanically, however, the *Love's Labour's Lost* scene is funnier. Berowne up the tree is a wonderful device, his descent to castigate the King ('Now step I forth to whip hypocrisy') a delight, and the entrance of Costard and Jaquenetta to blow away *his* hypocrisy provokes the joy only great comic plotting can achieve. The audience has been waiting in delicious expectation for this, from the moment that Costard delivers the wrong letters in the earlier scene.

The comedy in *A Midsummer Night's Dream* is gentler. The girls have a much fuller text than the boys — there is nothing in the boys' parts to equal the exquisite recollection of:

> The sisters' vows, the hours that we have spent
> When we have chid the hasty-footed time
> For parting us, . . .   (*MND*, III.ii.199–201)

Both actresses can recreate here with real intensity the joys of past friendship; Helena has most of the lines, but in performance, Hermia's unspoken response should prove equally effective. Tracing the emotional graph of the scene: Demetrius' sudden awakening to passionate declaration, Helena refusing the advances of both lovers, Hermia's progress from incomprehension to rage, the battle between 'puppet' and 'maypole', the fight in the fog, leading to final exhaustion and sleep —

this whole sequence is a test of actor and director on almost every level. The text must dance with absolute precision, the moves and physical business must mirror the emotional development, as always, but must never break the structure and flow of the text. Hermia's verbal attack on Helena always becomes physical, but the golden rule must be adhered to: no sudden lunges, jumps, turns or falls except on line endings or full stops.

I have found that Shakespeare's thrust stage, with its focal points at the diagonals as well as the centre, proves a much easier space than a proscenium theatre in which to choreograph this scene. The patterns of movement can readily combine dynamic action with formality, the audience can be involved in turn with each of the four protagonists as the focus shifts across the space they and the audience inhabit, and what is in fact a delicate contrivance looks natural and spontaneous.

In England, the actors' current fashion (supported by some of the better critics) is to deride overemphatic and elaborate design or direction. One of the problems confronting interpreters of Shakespeare in his original language, however, is the excitement created amongst critics (and audiences) by productions from Japan, Georgia, Poland, Italy, etc. in recent years, brilliant productions that would make little or no sense if an English text acceptable to actors and scholars were used. I except from this statement Terry Hands's extraordinary Comédie-Française production of *Richard III*, where a new French translation by Jean-Louis Curtis raided the street argot of many cities, thus finding a vocabulary wide enough to encompass Shakespeare's kaleidoscopic method. The Georgian Rustaveli Theatre production of the same play was a great experience, but was, by contrast, oversimplified. Fortunately, the comedies remain, so far, an English possession. *A Midsummer Night's Dream* that truly follows Jan Kott's 'Titania and the Ass's Head' to its logical conclusion has not yet proved the sensation of the London International Festival of Theatre. A *Love's Labour's Lost* that substitutes an Ashram in Poona for the Academe of Navarre has not yet been invited to be India's main contribution to the Edinburgh or Los Angeles Festivals — but neither experience may be far away. What survives of the original in these translations? Often, a gallery of high-voltage characters, and an over-emphatic plot line, in which Shakespeare's undertones become overtones, but rarely anything to do with his imagery. It is good to be reminded of the strength of the plots — the old canard still survives that only his verbal music matters — but it is our duty, I think, to attempt the Everest of Shakespeare's entire vision every time we start a production in English.

Of course, we fail. We are delighted, but confused by the range of Shakespeare's references, by the inherent contradictions in his characterisations, by the prismatic quality of his images, reflecting different lights and shapes every time we experience them. The choices every actor or director *has* to make become more difficult at each new encounter. It takes great courage, and great patience, to allow the colours to go on changing throughout the rehearsal process, to discourage actors from casting their early discoveries in concrete, but if I have learnt anything from acting in and directing these plays it is to wait, and wait, and listen and then listen again.

Kenneth Muir

CHARACTERISATION IN ELIZABETHAN DRAMA
AND ITS IMPLICATIONS FOR THE MODERN STAGE

Since I had the chance of reviewing Fineman's admirable edition of
Maurice Morgann's Shakespearian criticism,[1] I have tried to elaborate
on Morgann's theory that the sense we have of the reality of
Shakespeare's characters is due largely to the conflicting impressions
we are given of them. I touched on this in my address to the Congress of
the International Shakespeare Association in Washington in 1979, and
in greater detail in a paper read at a later Stratford conference, entitled
'Shakespeare's Open Secret'.[2] In both of these I tended to assume that
Shakespeare was unique in this respect, at least among British
dramatists; but it may be worth while to consider briefly in what ways,
and to what extent, his contemporaries made use of his methods, either
because these were derived naturally from Elizabethan stage conditions,
or because some of his contemporaries were influenced by his plays,
and, secondly, to discuss what effect Shakespeare's method of
characterisation has, or should have, on performances of his plays in the
present century.

I argued that the conflicting — the 'secret' — impressions were caused
not merely by the divergent views expressed by characters about each
other and by unexpected words and actions, but by a number of other
factors. These included Shakespeare's deliberate deviation from well-
known sources, which would upset the expectations of the audience;
the use of imagery to modify or contradict the views we should derive
from a paraphrase of a speech, as in Macbeth's soliloquy in the last
scene of Act I, where a prose version would completely conceal the
horror he feels, and ascribe his reluctance to murder Duncan to self-
interest; the basing of characters on stage types — Falstaff is more
complex than a Miles Gloriosus or Riot, though he may remind us of
both; the influence of Morality plays, enabling Shakespeare to suggest a
metaphysical conflict between good and evil, and thus modifying
psychological motives — Iago emerges as a demi-devil, ensnaring the
soul of Othello, as well as a soldier disappointed of promotion, an
imaginary cuckold, and a zealous racist. Then Shakespeare uses some
characters as choric commentators in ways which cause us to modify

our opinion of them; and, lastly, Shakespeare appears to identify with some characters more than with others, so that we may discern the poet of the Sonnets behind the mask of Hamlet, or the expert playwright at work when Iago and Vincentio hatch their plots.

The first dramatist to be considered is Christopher Marlowe. Born in the same year, Shakespeare and Marlowe clearly influenced each other, though Marlowe's early death prevented him from being influenced by the secret impressions Morgann found in Shakespeare. One of his sources, Holinshed's *Chronicles*, he shared with Shakespeare, and he made the same kind of alterations in dramatising the reign of Edward II as any competent dramatist would be bound to make. He kept reasonably close to the source of *Faustus*, and few members of his audience would be acquainted with the sources of *Tamburlaine*. In any case, he was not re-dramatising stories which were already popular on the Elizabethan stage, as Shakespeare was to do with *Hamlet* and *King Lear*, so that Marlowe's deviations were less likely to be noticed.

Most of Marlowe's characters are portrayed unambiguously; the audience is not provided with conflicting impressions. Perhaps he has not been given sufficient credit for showing the development of characters: we see the effect of persecution on Barabas, the gradual deterioration of Isabel and, most strikingly, the way in which Edward's favourites begin as careerists and end up as loyal and loving.

It has often been said, even in his own day, that Marlowe identified with his tragic heroes; and it was natural, therefore, that he should sometimes speak directly through their mouths. Perhaps his own disillusionment with the university curriculum is reflected in the first scene of *Dr Faustus*. Certainly the ecstatic address to the bogus Helen bears witness to his own love of the classics. In both these cases the sentiments are appropriate to the speaker. Some members of Marlowe's original audience would doubtless assume that to have sexual intercourse with a devil ensured the hero's damnation, while others would partially excuse him because of his worship of beauty.

In *Tamburlaine* there is a less successful intrusion of the poet. We can believe that the cruel and barbarous hero can become enamoured of Zenocrate, and she of him. Power is a potent aphrodisiac, we are often told. But it is more difficult to accept that Tamburlaine would proceed to speak of

> Our souls, whose faculties can comprehend
> The wondrous architecture of the world,
> And measure every wand'ring planet's course,

> Still climbing after knowledge infinite,
> And always moving as the restless spheres:[3]

or that in another famous speech he should indulge in a Shelleyan lament that the mind in creation is a fading coal:

> If all the heavenly quintessence they still
> From their immortal flowers of poesy,
> Wherein as in a mirror we perceive
> The highest reaches of a human wit:
> If these had made one poem's period,
> And all combin'd in beauty's worthiness,
> Yet should there hover in their restless heads
> One thought, one grace, one wonder, at the least,
> Which into words no virtue can digest.[4]

Marlowe realised that these lines are out of character, for he makes Tamburlaine apologise for harbouring effeminate thoughts. He may have intended to suggest that his hero was not merely a ruthless adventurer, but one with the instincts of a poet. There were Elizabethans who were cruel, as well as good poets: Marlowe himself was so reputed.[5] Nevertheless, in this case we feel the intrusion of Tamburlaine's creator, whereas this difficulty does not trouble us with Hamlet when he echoes his creator's complaints about the miseries of existence.

Webster's attitude to his characters is initially unambiguous. It is difficult to suppose that the original audience agreed with Ferdinand's hysterical denunciation of his sister's lust:[6] for Webster first establishes that Antonio is a good man and a shrewd judge of character, demonstrating this by giving us portraits of Bosola, the Cardinal and Ferdinand, and, finally, of the Duchess. Bosola is employed to spy on the Duchess, the two brothers use extraordinary threats, and her proposal to Antonio gives us a favourable impression of her delicacy, determination and charm. Nevertheless we are given conflicting impressions of the main characters. The primary objection of the brothers to the remarriage of their sister is their inordinate pride of birth; but, after her murder, Ferdinand confesses that he hoped to inherit her great wealth. As this ignores the existence of a son by her first marriage, mentioned not long before,[7] we are bound to suspect, not carelessness on the part of the author, but that Ferdinand's concealed motive is sexual jealousy, and that he cannot bear to think of his sister in the arms of another. Audiences were accustomed to incestuous motivation in the plays of

the period. The Cardinal displays the hypocrisy, lechery and unscrupulous-
ness we have been led to expect; but he too surprises us in Act V when
he is concerned theologically in a question about hell. Bosola, a
malcontent, who agrees to perform damnable actions for money,
nevertheless pities his victims. The motive for his changing sides is
partly Ferdinand's refusal to reward him, yet it is clear that his mental
torture of the Duchess is designed to prepare her to face death, neither
in despair, nor in fear, but in a state of Christian resignation. Even the
devil is constrained to serve divine purposes.

In *The White Devil*, written earlier, Webster does not use such
conflicting impressions, except in a rudimentary way, as when the
ambassadors variously express disapproval of Vittoria's sinfulness and
admiration for her spirited defence. The trial was apparently Webster's
invention; but as Professor Boklund showed in his perceptive
examination of the possible sources of the play,[8] we cannot always be
certain that he deliberately departed from historical facts. Isabella was a
gay person, indifferent to her husband, and she took at least one lover.
She was murdered by her husband, in revenge for her adultery, some
years before he met the White Devil. She was quite unlike the saintly
martyr depicted in the play, but Webster may have been unaware of her
real character. In any case he wished to contrast the good woman who
pretends to be unpleasant in order to excuse her husband's behaviour,
with an evil woman, Vittoria, whose wickedness is masked by her
external beauty. The historical Bracciano died a natural death: Webster's
protagonist is poisoned. Here and elsewhere Webster improves on
history by intensifying the guilt of the evil characters, ensuring that
they meet their deserts.

Thomas Middleton experimented in a wider range of genres than any
of his contemporaries. What may be true of his citizen comedies is
largely inapplicable to his later tragedies, to the brilliant political satire,
A Game at Chess, or to the middle masterpieces, such as *More
Dissemblers Besides Women*. If we are to believe the editors of the
Oxford Shakespeare,[9] who sometimes seem to go beyond the evidence,
Middleton collaborated with Shakespeare in two or three plays; or, as
others think, he altered the original scripts of *Macbeth* and *Timon of
Athens*. Yet he seems to have absorbed little of Shakespeare's
characteristic methods. His witches, as many have recognised, contrast
with Shakespeare's Weird Sisters; and his possible contributions to
Timon of Athens — for example, nearly all Act III — are not easily
compatible with the great diatribes of the disillusioned hero.

Middleton's sources were less well known than Shakespeare's, so that his deviations from them would not have been observed by most of his audience. Few of them would have been acquainted with *La Sorella* and have noticed that the scenes derived from that play in *No Wit, No Help like a Woman's* were totally different in tone.

Middleton was a persistent collaborator. One play which he wrote on his own is *Women Beware Women*. At first sight it might seem that Middleton was giving us conflicting impressions of his characters. Bianca is first presented as a woman who cheerfully marries for love, accepting without complaint a much lower standard of living than that to which she has been accustomed. Later in the play she is portrayed as a murderer. The relationship between Isabella and her uncle is at first described as a marriage of true minds:

> Those two are nev'r asunder: they've been heard
> In argument at midnight: moonshine nights
> Are noondays with them; they walk out their sleeps;
> Or rather, at those hours appear like those
> That walk in 'em, for so they did to me . . .
>   O affinity,
> What piece of excellent workmanship art thou!
> 'Tis work clean wrought, for there's no lust, but love in't,
> And that abundantly.[10]

Later in the same scene Hippolito confesses his incestuous feelings. Isabella is tricked into believing that Hippolito is no relation, and when Livia reveals the truth Isabella plots to murder her. But in neither case is the audience left with conflicting impressions. The point is that Middleton is displaying the rapid deterioration of most of the characters. Bianca begins by being contentedly poor. After being raped by the Duke, she is tempted by luxury and power, incites the murder of her husband, and attempts the murder of the Cardinal for his initial objection to her marriage. Leantio, at first a sympathetic character, is later seduced by Livia and boasts of being her gigolo. Before the end of the play, Guardiano, the ward, Isabella, Livia, Hippolito and Bianca have all become murderers. Not one of these characters is depicted ambiguously. Although at his best Middleton could justifiably be regarded as the most impressive of Shakespeare's heirs, replacing Fletcher in that role, his method of characterisation owes nothing to his great collaborator.

We may turn lastly, and still more briefly, to the work of John Ford, in which the influence of Shakespeare is generally acknowledged. In *'Tis Pity She's a Whore*, for example, there are obvious resemblances to Shakespeare's portrait of a more innocent love. Putana performs the function of Juliet's Nurse, and Bonaventura that of Friar Lawrence. There are more significant resemblances between *The Lover's Melancholy* and *King Lear*. Meleander's madness has several echoes of the scene in which Cordelia assists at her father's recovery, and his satirical strokes recall Lear's exposure of the great image of authority. Moreover, the recognition of Parthenophil as the lost Eroclea is based closely on the recognition of Marina by her father, the culmination in both cases being the mention of the girl's name. T. S. Eliot complained that Ford used the situation 'on a level hardly higher than that of the device of twins in comedy'.[11] Ford 'had no conception of what [Shakespeare] was trying to do'; his characters 'speak another and cruder language . . . there is no symbolic value'. This is surely unfair to Ford.[12] Although he could not have written Eliot's own *Marina*, he was the only one of Shakespeare's successors who understood what his master was doing, and the verse, which Eliot praises, is evidence, I believe, that Ford was not unaware of the symbolic value of the Shakespearian parts of *Pericles*. Yet his method of characterisation is unlike Shakespeare's. There are, it is true, conflicting impressions of Perkin Warbeck, but in the end the audience is left in no doubt that he was a sincere self-deceiver, identifying himself with the role he has been playing. Many of Ford's characters illustrate the case-histories of Burton, and they tend to be as constricted as characters in modern plays who conform too closely to Freud's theories. It is instructive to contrast Shakespeare's use of Timothy Bright, which was undeniable, but does not get us very far in unravelling the complexity of Prince Hamlet.

These examples of Shakespeare's contemporaries are enough to support the view that his method was more complex than any of theirs. Other examples — Fletcher, Jonson, Massinger, Marston, Chapman — would lead to the same conclusion. Only Webster and Ford appear to have been aware of, and used, some of Shakespeare's methods. Coleridge, in a letter to William Sotheby, testified to the uniqueness of Shakespeare's method of characterisation, although he ascribed that uniqueness to a single ability:

> It is easy to cloathe Imaginary Beings with our own Thoughts and Feelings; but to send ourselves out of ourselves, to *think* ourselves in to the Thoughts and Feelings of Beings in circumstances wholly and strangely different from our own: *hoc labor, hoc opus*: and who has achieved it? Perhaps only Shakespeare.[13]

Each new critical movement or fashion is liable to have theatrical repercussions. When it was maintained that Shakespeare was our contemporary, few directors could resist the temptation to stress the contemporary relevance of the plays. When Brecht was in the ascendant, no history play at Stratford was complete without the appearance of Mother Courage's cart. When the Theatre of Cruelty was the rage, it was not difficult to show that *Titus Andronicus* was a true forerunner, and that *King Lear* belonged to the Theatre of the Absurd. In the age of Sartre, we were treated to existentialist versions of several of Shakespeare's plays. When critics revealed the significance of imagery, it was rumoured that actors had been instructed to italicise iterative images.[14] One is therefore somewhat apprehensive at the possible impact of a 'Morgannatic' Shakespeare on theatrical practice.

Yet we are protected to a large extent by two opposing principles already operating. Each new production of a well-known play at the National Theatre or at Stratford-upon-Avon is naturally an attempt to be different, different especially from its immediate predecessors. This often means that directors will discard or blur words or deeds which conflict with their chosen interpretation. Such selective scripts will forfeit a good deal of the complexity we have been analysing. But here the opposing principle comes to the rescue: all good directors and actors quarry in the text for the sub-text, so that on occasion we are driven to ask 'Handy-dandy, which is the text and which the sub-text?'

There are some fundamental differences between Shakespeare's original audiences and those of the present century. One of the most significant is that nearly everyone at a modern performance, even in the days when one gained entry to the Old Vic for 5d, has studied one or more of Shakespeare's plays at school, and four out of five members of a Stratford audience are not merely educated, but *in* education as teachers or pupils. Elizabethan spectators, on the other hand, were primarily listeners, and even the comparatively illiterate enjoyed listening to poetic dramas. Shakespeare's contemporaries would see his plays performed by a single company in which Burbage invariably played the main tragic heroes. The contrast with today's conditions is startling. Any lover of drama now has numerous opportunities of seeing Elizabethan plays performed, and of comparing one performance with another. A personal experience will illustrate this point. Although I have lived for sixty years in the North of England, far from London and Stratford and Bristol, I have seen a dozen or more performances of many of Shakespeare's plays, some in York, Leeds, Manchester and Liverpool, but mostly in London and Stratford. In writing stage histories of two of Shakespeare's plays — *Troilus and Cressida* and *Richard II* — I found, to my surprise, that I had seen most productions of these plays during the last sixty years. One even has numerous opportunities of seeing several productions of the major plays of Marlowe, Jonson, Webster and Middleton. This means that each new performance competes in our minds with others we have seen. Those who watched Ian Charleson's performance of Hamlet a few weeks before his premature death would have compared it to those of Rees and Pennington in the 1980s, of Kingsley and Howard in the 1970s, of Warner and Bannen in the 1960s, of Redgrave in the 1950s, of Helpmann, Evans, Olivier and Gielgud in earlier years, and of Ernest Milton and Ion Swinley in the 1920s — I mention only a selection of those I have witnessed. Each new Hamlet is haunted by his predecessors, and not merely by the good ones. Actors incorporate into their performances fragments of earlier interpretations, handed down, perhaps, by Irving, Macready, Garrick, or even Betterton. Most performances we see we shall doubtless regard as unsatisfactory in one way or another, but remember them gratefully for the delivery of a single speech, even a single line or phrase —

> Why would'st thou be a breeder of sinners? . . .
> Absent thee from felicity awhile . . .

Our conception of Hamlet, our acceptance of his 'reality', is enriched by diverse performances, so that we can pronounce confidently that this or that was out of keeping with the real Hamlet.

But if the secret impressions provided by diverse performances give us something unknown to Shakespeare's original audiences, the proliferation of criticism not only influences directors and actors, it also complicates the reactions of audiences. Many members of an audience at *Othello* will have come across the controversy, either at first hand, or discussed in editions, between Eliot's accusation of Bovaryism and Helen Gardner's defence of the noble Moor, between Leavis's derogatory essay and the testimony of Iago to Othello's goodness. All Shakespeare's greatest plays have aroused the same controversies. Is *Antony and Cleopatra* 'all for love' or 'all for lust'? Is *Measure for Measure* a 'Christian' play, or a satire on the belief that the world is providentially governed? Does Lear deserve all he gets?

Hamlet is the play that has aroused the greatest disagreements. The hero is condemned as a neurotic, an egotist, as a scoundrel, as immature. His delay is ascribed, by those who believe he did delay, to Oedipus complex, to world-weariness, to doubt about the morality of revenge, to the impossibility of killing Claudius without harming Gertrude, and to many other reasons. Marxists and Fabians stress the power struggle in the play, which they regard as essentially political. Some critics maintain that the Ghost is a devil, tempting Hamlet to commit mortal sin; others believe that he is exhorting his son to perform a sacred duty. There appear to have been no violent differences between the critics before the nineteenth century about the play: now the character of Hamlet is the chief Shakespearian enigma. We discuss him, foolishly, as though he were a real person. A good case can be made out for many of the rival interpretations, but, as I have argued elsewhere,[15] partial interpretations are false.

Notes

1 Maurice Morgann, *Shakespearian Criticism* (ed. Daniel A. Fineman, Oxford, 1972). Reviewed *TLS*, 1972, p. 867.

2 These articles are reprinted in Kenneth Muir, *The Singularity of Shakespeare* (Liverpool, 1977), and Kenneth Muir, *Shakespeare: Contrasts and Controversies* (Brighton: Harvester Press, 1985).

3 1 *Tamburlaine*, II.vii.21–5, in *The Plays of Christopher Marlowe*, ed. Roma Gill (Oxford, 1971).

4 1 *Tamburlaine*, V.i.165–73, in edition cited in n. 3.

5 It was Thomas Kyd who claimed that Marlowe was 'intemperate and of cruel heart'. See Frederick S. Boas, *Christopher Marlowe* (Oxford: Clarendon Press, 1940), p. 242.

6 Lisa Jardine, however, in *More Harping on Daughters* (Harvester Press, 1983), Ch. 3, argues that most members of a Jacobean audience would agree with Ferdinand.

7 *The Duchess of Malfi*, ed. F. L. Lucas (London: Chatto & Windus, 1958), III.iii.82.

8 G. Boklund, *The Sources of* The White Devil (Upsala, 1957).

9 William Shakespeare, *The Complete Works*, ed. Stanley Wells, Gary Taylor *et al* (Oxford, 1986), p. 997.

10 Thomas Middleton, *Women Beware Women* I.ii.63–7, 69–72, in *Three Plays*, ed. Kenneth Muir (London, 1975).

11 T. S. Eliot, *Selected Essays* (London, 1932), pp. 195–6.

12 Cf. Muir, *Shakespeare: Contrasts and Controversies*, pp. 162–3.

13 S. T. Coleridge, *Letters*, 13 July 1802.

14 Cf. Muir, *The Singularity of Shakespeare*, pp. 198–211.

15 Cf. Muir, 'Hamlet among the Idealogues', *Aligarh Journal of English Studies*, XIII (1988), pp. 67–71.

Inga-Stina Ewbank

THE MIDDLE OF MIDDLETON

The middle plays of Middleton have been something of an embarrassment to critics. Wedged between the early, satirical comedies and the
two great tragedies, they seem to suggest 'the absence of a clear pattern
of development in Middleton's dramaturgy' (Mulryne, 1975). Largely
unedited and unperformed, with a few notable exceptions,[1] they have
remained elusive in the midst of the re-discovery of minor Jacobean
drama in recent decades. Margot Heinemann (1980) has written
illuminatingly on their relation to the political and religious climate of
the period; and Anne Lancashire (1983) has argued convincingly that,
when Middleton in a dedication to the manuscript of *The Witch*
describes the play as 'ill-fated', this need not mean that it had been a
theatrical flop but could refer to the dangerous closeness — deliberate
or not — of the play's intrigues and witchery to real-life events: to the
Frances Howard/Earl of Essex divorce hearings in 1613 and the trial of
the same Frances and Robert Carr for the Overbury murder in 1615–16.
But on the whole criticism would seem to agree with Dorothy Farr's
(1973) description of Middleton's middle career as 'a series of flat
levels, probably determined as much by the situation in the theatre as by
any clearly defined artistic purpose'.

And of course these, like most plays of the age (indeed, of any age),
were determined by the situation in the theatre. If they were intended to
cater for the taste for tragicomedy, then — and this is my argument in
this essay — this intention is not so much *opposed* to an artistic purpose
as part of it. Within a year or two (roughly 1615–17, although the date of
The Witch remains in dispute[2]) Middleton wrote, with Rowley, *A Fair
Quarrel* for Prince Charles' Company and, unaided, *The Witch* and
More Dissemblers Besides Women for the King's Men: three quite
different plays, none of which is a masterpiece, but all of which
manifest particular forms of theatrical energy. The source of that
energy, I would argue, is a peculiarly Middletonian version of scepticism:
scepticism, that is, applied to the substance of human affairs as well as
to theatrical forms and conventions, to human nature as well as to the
mirror held up to it by the arts of performance.

The scepticism, then, of these plays raises questions of intertextuality.

(156)

It has often been pointed out by editors and other critics[3] that Middleton drew heavily on existing texts, dramatic and narrative, piecing together 'borrowings' as he needed them. But in the theatre, and particularly in the repertory theatres of Jacobean London, three decades or more into a period of unequalled theatrical activity, intertextuality has to be understood in terms beyond the purely textual. It may involve actors who, when the play and its 'source' text belong to the same company, perform in both. Regular play-goers in modern repertory theatres, let along movie-goers, know that parts cling to actors and that their present performances may, willy-nilly, activate audience memories of past roles. How much of the Rainman is there in Dustin Hoffman's Willy Loman, or vice versa, and how much of both was there in his Shylock? Burbage, who went on acting until his death in 1619, presumably had major parts in *The Witch* and *More Dissemblers*. If, as seems likely, he was still alive when Middleton (if we trust the Oxford editors) adapted *Macbeth*, inserting among other things two songs and a dance from *The Witch*, then he and the rest of the company will have had an acute — but probably not untypical — exercise in intertextuality. And — as Middleton must have known — the effect on an audience of the tragi-comedy of *The Witch* would be conditioned by the fact that, in the same playhouse and with the same cast, they had seen the tragedy of *Macbeth*.

For playhouse intertextuality also involves audiences among whom a fair number can be depended on to recognise the 'source' of a passage or an episode or a whole plot. We can only speculate about the effect of such recognition — of, for example, seeing *The Winter's Tale* for the first time and finding that Hermione, unlike her prototype in *Pandosto*, was alive and that Shakespeare's play, unlike Greene's popular romance, had no need to have the erring husband/father commit suicide in order to 'close up the comedy with a tragical stratagem' (Greene, 1907, p. 85). Middleton seems to use the sounding-board of a well-known source in a number of ways. It can be a short-hand device, as when in *A Fair Quarrel* the Colonel suddenly decides that his sister is 'the fairest restitution' his life could yield Captain Ager and she is accepted by the Captain, unblinkingly: 'Worthy Colonel,/H'as such a conquering way i'th'blessed things!' (IV.ii.99 and IV.iii.124–5). This way to a happy ending is at once so blatantly contrived and so clearly derived from a familiar source — the subplot of Heywood's *A Woman Kill'd with Kindness* — that it looks as if Middleton is signalling a self-conscious version of 'the danger not the death',[4] and possibly with his tongue in his cheek, too.

But such intertextuality does not have to equal parody. When the

King's Men put on *The Witch*, whether or not this was prompted by a wish to re-use at Blackfriars the witches' antimasque in Jonson's *Masque of Queens*,[5] the witch scenes did not mock *Macbeth*. They obviously presented a spectacular contrast: the songs, 'The Witches' Dance' (V.ii), the descent of 'A Spirit like a Cat' and Hecate herself 'going up' on the song 'Now I go, now I fly' (III.v). But the contrast could be used to complement *Macbeth*, for possibly all of these elements, if we accept the 'reconstruction' in the Oxford *Complete Works of Shakespeare* (1986), and certainly some, as recorded in the First Folio, were grafted on to the text of *Macbeth* to make that play more of a show. The contrast must also have been one of tone: the world of Middleton's Hecate is so much less eerie and more domesticated than that of Shakespeare's weird sisters. Compared to Macbeth's visit to the 'secret, black, and midnight hags', Almachildes' is social, not to say sociable. He comes bringing Hecate a somewhat soggy 'toad in marchpane', wrapped up in a handkerchief with some other goodies for her son; and before he collects his love charm, he settles down to supper with her — a real human one, not the ethnic meal that he refuses even to contemplate: 'dost think I'll eat fried rats/And pickled spiders?' (I.ii.224–5).

Middleton's witch scenes also contain explicit self-parody in the shape of Hecate's son, Firestone, whose malapropisms undercut the sinister lists of contents in the witch-brew and who generally acts as a clown, debunking the black magic of his mother's world. Witchcraft was a serious and even topical subject in the reign of James VI & I; and there is plenty of the horrific in *The Witch*. But Middleton's witches are not part of a vision of cosmic evil. Rather than parodying Shakespeare's play, *The Witch* provides its audience with an alternative: a world in which the words of 'these juggling fiends' can be laughed at, and where there is always a way out for the human characters. The supernatural witches have no part in the dénouement: there the human 'witches'[6] have their sexual intrigues disentangled by twists so sudden as to draw attention to their own artifice. The Duke who has insisted on drinking toasts to his Duchess out of her father's skull — while she retaliates by bedtricking Almachildes in order to blackmail him into killing the Duke — rises, a *dux ex machina*, from the couch where he lies supposedly dead, to declare all evils null and void and, apparently without irony, to thank heaven for such a wife.

> Who, though her intent sinn'd, yet she makes amends
> With grief and honour, virtue's noblest ends.   (V.iii.129–30)

Against the perfunctoriness of this Fletcherian ducal world, that of the less exalted characters is more fully realised — not so much because characters' motives are explored but because it is documented on stage as a solid bourgeois world of food and drink and domestic life. Though theoretically Ravenna, the setting is here in practice the London of *A Chaste Maid in Cheapside*. Sebastian comes back from three years in the wars to find that Isabella, pre-contracted to him, has that very day been married to Antonio. The new husband's impotence — brought about by a charm which Sebastian acquires from Hecate — is dramatised through his attempts to recover manhood via a concoction of 'two cocks boil'd to jelly' with half an ounce of pearl. Francisca, Antonio's sister, is pregnant by the rake Aberzanes; and the arrangements for her secret lying-in, and for the disposal of the baby, are given us with as much circumstantial detail as if her name had been Moll Flanders or Roxana. To a modern audience, the dramatic interest of the play would lie in confrontations such as those between the two sisters-in-law. Francisca comes back, pale and 'a little sharp i'th'nose' after childbirth, and Isabella, who has discovered the truth of her sister-in-law's supposed travels, turns on her in a speech of reproach:

> 'Twas ill done to abuse yourself and us,
> To wrong so good a brother and the thoughts
> That we both held of you. I did doubt you much
> Before our marriage-day; but then my strangeness
> And better hope still kept me off from speaking.
> (III.ii.97–101)

The haunting cadences of this less-than-sincerity (for we know just how 'good' Isabella finds her husband, and how little the two form a 'we both') look forward to Middleton's tragedies.

It is also out of this world that one good deed, enabling the turn to tragicomedy, springs. Sebastian (in disguise) has plotted to have Isabella at his mercy in a secluded house; but, when it comes to it, a spontaneous flicker of conscience stops him satisfying his frustrated lust: 'I cannot so deceive her, 'twere too sinful' (IV.ii.95). Yet, what ultimately makes the happy ending to this plot possible is a twist as implausible as the duke's volte-face, in that the unwanted husband is reported killed in 'a fearful unexpected accident' as he

> Blinded with wrath, and jealousy, which scorn guides,
> From a false trap-door fell into a depth
> Exceeds a temple's height.
> (V.iii.29–31)

The elaboration of Antonio's fall, continuing down 'the dungeon, that falls threescore fathom/Under the castle', no doubt gives it a hellish, retributive dimension. But it is retribution which strikes very selectively. Unlike the convenient self-execution of D'Amville at the end of *The Atheist's Tragedy*, to which it has been compared (George 1967), this one death in *The Witch* draws more attention to itself as plot convenience than as a moral *exemplum*. Similarly Sebastian's is the single good deed shining in a naughty world. Middleton is not making genuine growth in moral awareness the philosophic justification of a tragicomic formula.[7] Rather, he is playing with plots — with putting in practice that wishful 'if' which, in a notable scene in *The Duchess of Malfi* (a play which Middleton much admired),[8] makes Ferdinand, through his dazzled eyes, envisage the happy ending which might have been, *if* Bosola had 'oppos'd [himself]/. . . Between her innocence and my revenge' (IV.ii.276). The world of Webster's play does not allow the movement from tragedy to tragicomedy on an easy 'if', any more than Lear can be allowed to see Cordelia revive — 'This feather stirs; she lives. If it be so . . .' — or Macbeth to retrace his steps by addressing his wife as the duke does in *The Witch*: 'Vanish all wrongs: thy former practice dies' (V.iv.126). In the end the interconnections between *The Witch* and *Macbeth* illuminate a scepticism directed not at Shakespeare's tragedy but, self-reflexively, at the sheer fragility of the enacted 'if' which underpins the tragicomic form Middleton is using, and at the belief in human perfectibility which alone could underpin a truly moral tragicomedy. He *uses* the gap between form and morality, with implications that are both philosophic and artistic.

In Middleton's comedies repentance and retribution are kept to a minimum. The audience is left in no doubt about the corruptness of the world they are watching, but most of the inhabitants of that world are allowed to go unpunished. Marriage or money, or both, crowns their sexual and financial transgressions. The audience know their immorality, but the characters know what works. Thus at the end of *A Chaste Maid in Cheapside*, when Maudlin Yellowhammer tells her son to use his university logic to prove his Welsh whore honest, that gentlewoman herself wraps up Maudlin's cynicism and Tim's naïve logic ('*Uxor non est meretrix, ergo falacis*') and tempers them both into a comfortable pragmatism:

> Sir, if your logic cannot prove me honest,
> There's a thing called marriage, and that makes me honest.
>
> (V.iv.115–16)

In the tragicomedies under discussion, similarly, potential tragedy is averted not so much by awakened consciences as by a general reasonableness and readiness to take a relative view of social and moral issues. In *A Fair Quarrel* the reconciliation of Captain Ager and the Colonel is bound to appear fragile and hysterical at the side of the Russell plot, where Jane — who has had a baby out of wedlock — turns on her would-be blackmailer with her own version of 'publish and be damned':

> Poison thyself, thou foul empoisoner;
> Of thine own practice drink the theory.   (III.ii.135–6)

Her reasonableness receives support, social as well as moral, from the female loyalty of the blackmailer's sister: 'One fault heaven soon forgives, and 'tis on earth forgot' (III.ii.174–5); and in the dénouement Russell, departing from the conventional absolutism of stage fathers, confirms this argument: 'One spot a father's love will soon wipe off' (V.i.232).

The lines and the plot just quoted may be written by Rowley, but similar attitudes dominate the happy ending of *More Dissemblers Besides Women* which is entirely by Middleton. In Act I of this play the Duchess is driven by her passion for Andrugio to abandon her seven-year seclusion in widowed chastity, and she spends the subsequent Acts dissembling and scheming to marry him. But he is in love with Aurelia, and in the final scene the Duchess proves to have access to the kind of common sense alien to, say, Leonora in Webster's *The Devil's Law-Case*: she accepts that Andrugio has chosen someone 'younger, fairer' than herself (V.ii.128). Privately — in an aside — she admits that she has only what she deserves (V.ii.131–3), and as a public gesture she makes the kneeling pair of lovers rise and receive her blessing. At this point the reasonableness passes over to the relationship between Andrugio and Aurelia. This girl has all along been in love with Lactantio (whom we know all along to be a male dissembler) and has been merely using Andrugio to escape from the fort where her father has imprisoned her, and from the Governor of the fort whom her father is pressing her to marry. As she and Andrugio are being blessed by the Duchess, Lactantio enters, and she is ready to rush into his arms. He, thinking that he is sure to marry the Duchess (who has been dissembling love for him in order to catch Andrugio), rejects her. Rather than dying broken-hearted, Aurelia takes stock of her situation, much like an early Moll Flanders, counting first her mistakes —

> I have undone myself
> Two ways at once; lost a great deal of time,
> And now I'm like to lose more. O my fortune!
> I was nineteen yesterday, and partly vow'd
> To have a child by twenty, if not twain: —   (V.ii.153-7)

and then her blessings. So she throws herself on Andrugio with the argument that experience is better than innocence:

> Have you forgiveness in you? there's more hope of me
> Than of a maid that never yet offended.   (V.ii.160-1)

Luckily for her, this logic works with him. No absolutist, Andrugio can forgive, not like the Duke in *The Witch*, by saying 'Vanish all wrongs', but because he has a practical, almost quantitative, view of love: 'I have a love/That covers all thy faults'. Doubt and belief are balanced into a way of life as he fetches for reasons for doing what he obviously wants to do:

> I'll once believe a woman, be't but to strengthen
> Weak faith in other men.   (V.ii.169-70)

On the whole, at the end of this play where nearly everybody dissembles, there is very little reason to 'believe' in the truth of either men or women, or to accept Andrugio as a Mirror for Married Men. But the final stance of the play is not just an exposure of self-deceit and hypocrisy; it is that of a scepticism which admits that sometimes belief is necessary for survival. Survival may be more important than spotlessness, and the last twist in the dénouement deals with Lactantio who — like Lucio in *Measure for Measure*, but taking his fate in far better spirit — has to marry his cast-off mistress. She has followed him throughout, disguised as a page and pregnant, until she falls spectacularly into labour in the midst of a dancing lesson; and his last thought in the play, effectively deglamorising the convention of the transvestite heroine, is for the rescue of the page's breeches: 'we shall have need of them shortly, and we get children so fast. . . . My son and heir need not scorn to wear what his mother has left off' (V.ii.249ff.). The Duchess affirms this stance in the closing speech of the play:

> We all have faults; look not so much on his:
> Who lives i'th'world that never did amiss?   (V.ii.259-60)

If the Duchess's rhetorical question were all, these plays would be rather smug. They are not, mainly because they also grapple with scepticism in other ways. Scepticism as a doctrine — 'that little or nothing is known or rationally believed or the object of justified belief' — is not only, as N. M. L. Nathan declares disarmingly at the beginning of his book, *Evidence and Assurance* (1982), 'boring enough'. It is also fairly self-defeating as a dramatic subject. But this is not true for the 'quite different sceptical doctrine' which Nathan proceeds to discuss, namely 'that for much of what we believe an infinite regress of justification is both necessary and impossible'. In a very small way Andrugio at the end of *More Dissemblers* is pursuing such a justification, felt as both necessary and impossible. Other characters in Middletonian tragicomedy are far more fully and, in terms of each play's structure, centrally engaged on a search for what Nathan (p. 2) defines as 'radical assurance': 'the species of justified believing power to gain which we are I think liable so often to want in vain'. Foremost of these is Captain Ager in *A Fair Quarrel*:

> Could but my soul resolve my cause were just,
> . . . .
> But as it is, it fears me.   (II.i.20–4)

Fighting a duel in an unjust cause meant damnation, as Fredson Bowers long since pointed out (Bowers, 1937); so attention must be paid to Ager's search for radical assurance that he is not what the Colonel has called him: 'the son of a whore'. The question is what kind of attention. Because his search for evidence comes to turn on his mother's chastity, modern critics have wanted to see in Captain Ager 'a further, darker motive — a subconscious Oedipean obsession' (Holdsworth 1974, p. xxv). And because Ager's strange doubts are not accounted for, Middleton has been credited with 'an almost Freudian awareness of how characters may disintegrate before the implacable demands of sexuality' (Schoenbaum 1956–7, p. 17). At this point we may need to remind ourselves that it is Middleton's Captain we are dealing with, not Strindberg's (in *The Father*); and that the long soliloquy which dramatises his state of doubting at the opening of II.i is more Puritan (Heinemann, p. 115) than Freudian, and most of all like a *psychomachia* where 'fear' and 'assurance' fight for domination in his soul. While tragically intense, this speech is also presented as notably futile. It does not progress, because by definition it cannot; it can only go on in circles, re-phrasing the same dilemma. He doubts because he doubts. Though he has been compared to Hamlet, he is exactly not like Hamlet in lacking any evidence, such as Gertrude's 'o'erhasty' re-marriage.

Against his practical knowledge of his mother's honesty Ager can only marshal the theoretical knowledge of conventional misogynist 'truths':

> My good opinion of her life and virtues
> Bids me go on, and fain would I be ruled by't;
> But when my judgement tells me she's but a woman,
> Whose frailty let in death to all mankind,
> My valour shrinks at that.   (II.i.26–30)

Besides, Ager's delight when, later in the scene, his mother assures him of her honesty is entirely directed towards the duel; and when, to save his life, she withdraws that assurance, slandering herself, it is not her moral corruption he laments but his own loss of 'the joys of a just cause' (II.i.199) — further reason for suspecting oedipal readings of this character.

So, if Captain Ager's dilemma as the sceptic in search of justification which is 'both necessary and impossible' must command some respect, it is also clear that Middleton has presented it so as to emphasise its absurdity. Out of texts borrowed from himself and others (Holdsworth, pp. xvi–xvii) he has constructed a search for truth which leads only to a lie. As mother and son confront each other, the more they question the less they know each other. Within a minute or two of rejoicing at her passionate speech of self-justification, he is just as ready to believe his mother's self-slandering lie, seeing her alleged adultery from his own myopic viewpoint:

> Had you but thought
> On such a noble quarrel, you'd ha' died
> Ere you'd ha' yielded.   (II.i.199–201)

His honour rescued by the Colonel calling him a 'coward', he can resume his 'noble quarrel'; and the irony is underlined when, after wounding the Colonel, he congratulates himself: 'Truth never fails her servant, sir' (III.i.165). This is indeed a strange Triumph of Truth.

If then the Ager scenes in *A Fair Quarrel* dramatise the absurdity of man's search for truth, his inability to find it even in actual experience and the personal trust that should be based on it, then *More Dissemblers Besides Women* bases its whole structure on the exploration of such absurdity. The play is so explicit and elaborate about letting characters first construct and then deconstruct their moral and philosophical position, that one can only assume that Middleton must have expected his audience to be entertained by the kind of sophistry with which the

Cardinal, in III.i, hypocritically persuades the all-too-willing lords to re-interpret what he has written about the Duchess:

> The books that I have publish'd in her praise
> Commend her constancy, and that's fame-worthy;
> But if you read me o'er with eyes of enemies,
> You cannot justly and with honour tax me
> That I dissuade her life from marriage there:
> Now heaven and fruitfulness forbid, not I!
> She may be constant there, and the hard war
> Of chastity is held a virtuous strife,
> As rare in marriage as in single life;
> Nay, by some writers rarer; hear their reasons . . .
> (III.i.263-72)

Reading the Duchess is the main theme of the play, as her self-knowledge and others' knowledge of her are tested.

The play opens with a '*Song within*' celebrating the Duchess's chastity and exhorting listeners to 'come and read her life and praise'. In these early scenes she is allegorised: the Cardinal repeatedly refers to her as 'my triumph', and even 'my religious triumph', and she presents herself as a moral pageant:

> I'll come forth
> And show myself to all; the world shall witness,
> That, like the sun, my constancy can look
> On earth's corruptions, and shine clear itself.
> (I.iii.54-7)

Cocooned from life, in the maintenance of her vow never to marry again, she is indeed in the position of Integrity in the Lord Mayor's pageant which Middleton wrote in 1623, entitled *The Triumphs of Integrity*: enclosed within her 'crystal sanctuary'. Such a position is tenable only by separating abstract ideas from actual life, which is precisely what the Duchess does (I.iii.22-5). At the same time, dramatic logic is preparing her fall. She asks the Cardinal a rhetorical question:

> Can you believe that any sight of man,
> Held he the worth of millions in one spirit,
> Had power to alter me?
> (I.iii.49-51)

In the next moment she has sight, not of any man but of Andrugio, and her crystal walls collapse at once.

The scene of her fall has been constructed so as to deconstruct the idea of 'victory': to highlight the ironies of collapsed faith and the fragility of constancy. It works by emblematic patternings rather than psychological motivation. In the opening lines of the play we heard how the Duchess had 'kept the fort' of her chastity 'most valiantly'; suddenly this fort is conquered by Andrugio, the victorious general returning from the war, without his seeing her or uttering a word in the entire scene. Andrugio's martial victory is being celebrated with a masque of Cupid, the 'little conqueror', which he does not watch, as he spends the time reading a letter where he learns that his beloved Aurelia (who we know is not very chaste) has been incarcerated in a (real) fort. The Duchess watches him and we watch them both, noting the aptness of the ironic patterns, neatly tied together in the Duchess's exit line: 'O hard spite,/To lose my seven years' victory at one sight!' (I.iii.128). The fall, her language emphasises, is not so much of a woman as of a principle: 'My faith is gone forever;/My reputation with the Cardinal' (I.iii.124–5).

The Cardinal, as we have already seen, has literally translated the Duchess into texts:

> I make her constancy
> The holy mistress of my contemplation;
> Whole volumes have I writ in zealous praise
> Of her eternal vow.   (I.ii.4–7)

To him she is 'grace confirm'd', the very proof of faith: 'He kills my hopes of woman that doubts her' (I.ii.67). The absoluteness of the Cardinal's assurance is in itself a warning signal, and this is immediately confirmed as he turns to praise the chastity of his nephew, Lactantio, whom we already suspect as a dissembler and who is about to be the centre of an involvement with two women, one of them pregnant by him. Lactantio is a practised hypocrite who informs us, in an aside, that the Cardinal's texts are unreliable: 'I'm writ chaste/In my grave uncle's thoughts, and honest meanings/Think all men's like their own' (I.ii.141–3).

However, once he has absorbed the shock of the Duchess's changed attitude, the Cardinal can turn hypocrite, too. He is given a whole scene of soliloquy — II.ii — in which he reconstructs his text and his faith. Thinking that the Duchess (who learnt to dissemble as soon as she fell in love) has a passion for Lactantio, he first proceeds to persuade his supposedly celibate nephew to marry — a scene which is like a bizarre take-off on the first group of Shakespeare's Sonnets, and which Lactantio, who sees only his own hypocrisy, sums up more accurately than he knows, as 'the reward/Of neat'st hypocrisy that ever book'd it' (III.i.215–16). Secondly he takes on the lords, in the scene I have already referred to, teaching them to re-read the Duchess so that what was formerly 'virtue', 'triumph', etc., now comes to mean the opposite:

> She cannot truly be call'd constant now,
> If she persever, rather obstinate,
> . . . . the grace and triumph
> Of all her victories are but idle glories,
> She wilful, and we enemies to succession.   (III.i.301–6)

This, in turn, leads to the ironic scene (IV.ii) in which disingenuousness meets disingenuousness, as the Cardinal and the lords come to convince the Duchess that she should marry. Even the conventional imagery of love and war can be constructed to serve a new purpose: 'The war . . . so just and honourable/As marriage is' (IV.ii.21–2). At the climax of this charade the Duchess fakes anguish — 'O, what have you done, my lord!' — and in reply the Cardinal fakes a high philosophical aim: 'Laid the way plain/To knowledge of yourself and your creation' (IV.ii.35–7). The Duchess is left alone on stage to soliloquise, drawing attention to the Cardinal's 'religious cunning' and the double-crossing she is herself engaged in. We are presented not so much with a mirror held up to nature as with a series of reflecting mirrors — or, to put the same point differently, with the question, 'What price knowledge and self-knowledge now?'

More Dissemblers Besides Women, in the way it re-writes the text of the Duchess as the figure of chastity and constancy, and so questions the very notion of self-knowledge, also contains interesting aspects of theatrical technique which return us to Middleton's sceptical use of conventional dramatic structures. Questions of intertextuality have been woven into the discussion of Middleton's scepticism: how far, for example, is the precariousness of the resolution of the Ager plot in *A Fair Quarrel* foregrounded by the play's dialogue with *Hamlet* — as if Gertrude had really been chaste and Laertes and Hamlet had both survived their duel, the latter to marry the former's sister? The outstanding example of such intertextuality in *More Dissemblers* is the scene in which the Duchess announces to the Cardinal that she is in love. She chooses to do so by staging a repeat of the scene, seven years earlier, of her husband's death, 'That I may think awhile I stand in presence/Of my departing husband' (II.i.38–9). She prevails upon the Cardinal to speak her husband's part, which he does with apparently perfect recall, while she, also with total recall, speaks her own. The effect is a unique kind of play-within-the play which serves both as a flashback and a step forward, not to say a *peripeteia*. For, on the point of repeating her former vow of perpetual chastity, she suddenly stops and 'can go no further'. It is as if she, single-handed, was trying to enact the very principle of tragicomedy: undoing the potentially tragic past, getting out of the bind (which was to undo Middleton's tragic heroines) of being 'the deed's creature'. Technically it is like a kind of Jacobean *Krapp's Last Tape* where the replay is intended to wipe out the old tape and replace it with a new version.

This strange ritual, set off from the rest of the text by a heavier rhythm and occasional rhymes, cannot be justified simply in plot terms — although it gives proof of the jealousy which drove the dying duke to press for the vow, and it brings into theatrical prominence his search for assurance and the Duchess's readiness, at the time, to comply. As she rehearses her former speech —

> My lov'd lord,
> Let your confirm'd opinion of my life,
> My love, my faithful love, seal an assurance
> Of quiet to your spirit, that no forgetfulness
> Can cast a sleep so deadly on my senses,
> To draw my affections to a second liking —   (II.i.69–74)

it is as though Gertrude were to have staged 'The Mouse-Trap'. Positions in *Hamlet* are strangely reversed. It is the Cardinal, speaking the duke's part, who has the lines against second marriage: it 'shows desire in flesh;/Thence lust and heat, and common custom grows;/But she's part virgin who but one man knows' (ll. 79–81). It is the Duchess's inability to repeat her vow that enacts the Player King's sceptical lines about the instability of human purpose and the frailty of good intentions ('Our thoughts are ours, their ends none of our own': *Hamlet* III.ii.208). And it is we, the audience, who are made to say that the Duchess, speaking her lines of seven years ago, 'doth protest too much'.

The device draws attention to itself — and, I would suggest, draws attention to its use and abuse of *Hamlet*. It is as if a less culpable Gertrude should have explained to Hamlet — who, like the Cardinal, bases his world picture on a woman's chastity and constancy — that she cannot keep her vow, and as if Hamlet would then have been able to rationalise and accept the new state of affairs. If Burbage played the Cardinal, the audience might have had a peculiarly direct sense of a tragicomic alternative to the Shakespearian tragedy. In any case, in a play so much concerned with the re-writing of texts, this scene would stand out as a self-conscious piece of theatre, sceptically echoing a text extremely familiar to audiences at the Globe or Blackfriars.

More generally, *More Dissemblers* also suggests a scepticism about Romance conventions: one which is to be carried into Middleton's tragedies. *Women Beware Women* begins where a romantic comedy might have ended, with the elopement and marriage of Leantio and Bianca; and *The Changeling* explores the tragedy of love at first sight. In *More Dissemblers Besides Women* the first scene introduces a young pair of lovers suffering under parental, and avuncular, oppression. To escape this, Lactantio persuades Aurelia to disguise as a boy; and an uninitiated spectator would have every expectation that this device would be sustained throughout the play, to a happy ending. But Aurelia no sooner appears, in the next scene, in male disguise than the plot reaches an anticlimax and the device is quite literally deconstructed. Besides, Aurelia's transvestite entry comes immediately upon the exit of the presumed Page, who has just told Lactantio of her pregnancy, so the romantic glow is already much dimmed. Much is made of Aurelia's disguise. First, in a brief exchange, she dupes the gullible Cardinal; then, in a passage which inverts Cleopatra's attempt to help arm Antony,[9] Lactantio disarms Aurelia:

> I arrest thee
> In Cupid's name; deliver up your weapon,
> > [*Takes her sword*]
> It is not for your wearing, Venus knows it:
> Here's a fit thing indeed! nay, hangers and all;
> Away with 'em, out upon 'em! things of trouble,
> And out of use with you.   (I.ii.172–7)

As we have seen, the play is permeated with imagery of love and war, used with deepening irony. Here a Petrarchan conceit is put, as it were, live on stage, and at the same time it is subverted with phallic innuendo. More drastically still, in the next moment Aurelia's father and the Governor enter — representatives of the crabbed old whom romantic lovers conventionally manage to outwit — and the father subverts a sacred Elizabethan stage convention by seeing at once straight through Aurelia's disguise. The discovery is made very funny, as the lovers attempt to put up a verbal smoke-screen. To prove that the girl is a gentleman stranger, they speak a home-made foreign language, only to have it immediately deconstructed by the father:

Nay, and that be the language, we can speak it too:
Strumpettikin, bold harlottum, queaninisma, whoremongeria!
(II.i.201–2)

Which, translated out of honesty into English, becomes: 'Shame to thy
sex, and sorrow to thy father!' (l. 203). So Aurelia is carried off to be
incarcerated in the fort, and Lactantio is left to lament the anticlimax,
cynically:

If I can 'scape this climacterical year,
Women ne'er trust me, though you hear me swear. (II.i.237–8)

Not to trust — whether it be words or deeds, texts or dramatic
conventions, including the form of tragicomedy itself — is perhaps in
the end what we learn from Middleton's tragicomic mirror. He draws
on 'the situation in the theatre', not as a passive imitator, nor as a
simple parodist, but as engaging actors and audiences in a dialogue with
a whole body of Jacobean drama. In so doing, these plays offer enough
peaks — as well as troughs — seriously to challenge the mapping of the
middle of Middleton as 'a series of flat levels'.

Notes

1 R. V. Holdsworth's edition of *A Fair Quarrel* (1974) is an exception,
  and so was the 1979 National Theatre production of the same play,
  directed by William Gaskill. Costumed in the puff breeches of the 1617
  Quarto title-page's illustration, and moving stiffly on the plain stage of
  this 'straight' production, the actors created a world pretty unsure about
  its values and clumsy in its efforts to define them — leaving us with a
  vigorously mixed emotional impact.
2 Dates from 1609 to 1615–16 have been suggested, but the later date is
  generally seen as most likely. 1609–10 would suit the idea that Middleton
  was re-using the antimasque from *The Masque of Queens* (see note 5,
  below), but this is long before Middleton's known connection with the
  King's Men, and before any of his other tragicomedies. See Lancashire
  (1983), *passim*, for the bearing of the events in the life of Frances
  Howard on the dating and the reception of the play, and pp. 176–7, note
  23, for a bibliography of discussions of the dating.
3 See, e.g., Holdsworth (1974), pp. xv–xviii; McElroy (1972) finds
  instances of literary parody throughout Middleton's career; and Rowe
  (1979) sees in Middleton's subversion of the New Comedy tradition the
  key to his comic *and* tragic vision. Rowe's interest is thematic rather
  than theatrical: *The Witch* is barely mentioned, and *More Dissemblers*
  'explores the less attractive and, at times, frightening aspects of the love

and renewal celebrated by traditional comedy' (p. 175). Howard Barker's version of *Women Beware Women*, performed at the Royal Court Theatre in 1986, is an extreme example of intertextuality: the first half retains substantial sections of the first three and a half Acts of Middleton's text, while in the second half, as the blurb to the playscript has it, 'Middleton's characters speak Barker's language and enact Barker's plot'.

4 The phrase is originally Guarini's, made familiar by Philip Edwards' by now classic essay on Fletcher's tragicomedies (1961).

5 Jonson's *Masque of Queens* was performed at Whitehall on 2 February 1609; and the Malone Society editors of *The Witch* (1950) cite (p. vi), with some reservations, the suggestions made by W. J. Lawrence (1928) and others, that 'the King's players, desiring to use for their own theatre the antimasque of twelve witches which had been their share in the Court performance, employed Middleton to write a play in which it could be repeated'.

6 Lancashire (1983) rightly points out that *'The Witch* shares with Middleton's *The Changeling* a type of title thematically connecting, on a moral level, the various plots', so that 'the witch' is not only Hecate 'but also the various characters in all plots who sexually enchant one another by fair means or foul' (p. 173).

7 See Fletcher's well-known definition of that formula in his address 'To the Reader' in *The Faithful Shepherdess*. The genre is explored fully in the essays edited by Nancy Klein Maguire (1987). Lancashire (1983) argues interestingly that, with its use of song, dance and spectacle, and with its (probable) reference to real court figures, *The Witch* should be approached as related generically to the court masque rather than to Fletcherian tragicomedy. Middleton 'deliberately uses in *The Witch*, for moral point, the basic masque techniques of metamorphosis or revelation' (p. 171). The problem with this reading, it seems to me, is that the moral metamorphoses happen *not* in theatrical moments of spectacle, song or dance, but in plot twists: masque and Fletcherian tragicomedy, if anything, subvert each other.

8 See his poem 'In the just worth of that well deserver, Mr John Webster, and upon this masterpiece of tragedy' prefixed to the 1623 Quarto of *The Duchess of Malfi*.

9 *Antony and Cleopatra* IV.ii.5–15. As Stanley Wells pointed out when I read a version of this paper at the Shakespeare Institute, Stratford-upon-Avon, in November 1989, *if* Middleton's scene contains a memory of a performance of Shakespeare's, then it also provides evidence, otherwise strangely lacking, that *Antony and Cleopatra* was actually performed on the Jacobean stage.

References

Note: Quotations from Middleton are from *The Works of Thomas Middleton*, ed. A. H. Bullen, 8 vols. (London, 1885–6), with the following exceptions: *A Fair Quarrel* is quoted from the edition by R. V. Holdsworth (London, 1974), *The Witch* from Peter Corbin and Douglas Sedge's edition of *Three Jacobean Witchcraft Plays* (Manchester, 1986) and *A Chaste Maid in Cheapside* from the edition by Alan Brissenden (London,

1968). The Malone Society reprint of *The Witch*, edited by W. W. Greg
and F. P. Wilson (Oxford 1950 [for 1948]) is referred to, as is R. Mulryne's
edition of *Women Beware Women* (London, 1975).

Barker, Howard (and Thomas Middleton) (1986) *Women Beware Women*,
London.

Bowers, Fredson (1937) 'Middleton's *Fair Quarrel* and the Duelling Code',
JEGP, 36, pp. 40–65.

Edwards, Philip (1961) 'The Danger Not the Death: The Art of John
Fletcher', in *Jacobean Theatre*: Stratford-upon-Avon Studies 1, ed. J. R.
Brown and B. Harris, London.

Farr, Dorothy M. (1973) *Thomas Middleton and the Drama of Realism: A
Study of Some Representative Plays*, Edinburgh.

George, David (1967) 'The Problem of Middleton's *The Witch* and its
Sources', *N&Q*, 212 [N.S. 14] pp. 209–11.

Greene, Robert (1907) *Pandosto*, ed. P. G. Thomas, London.

Heinemann, Margot (1980) *Puritanism and Theatre: Thomas Middleton
and Opposition Drama under the Early Stuarts*, Cambridge.

Lancashire, Anne (1983) '*The Witch*: Stage Flop or Political Mistake?' in
'*Accompaninge the players': Essays Celebrating Thomas Middleton,
1580–1980*, ed. Kenneth Friedenreich, New York.

Lawrence, W. J. (1928) *Shakespeare's Workshop*, Oxford.

McElroy, John F. (1972) *Parody and Burlesque in the Tragicomedies of
Thomas Middleton*: Jacobean Drama Studies, 19, Salzburg.

Maguire, Nancy Klein, ed. (1987) *Renaissance Tragicomedy: Explorations
in Genre and Politics*, New York.

Nathan, N. M. L. (1982) *Evidence and Assurance*, London.

Rowe, George E. Jr. (1979) *Thomas Middleton and the New Comedy
Tradition*, Lincoln, Nebraska.

Schoenbaum, S. (1956–7) 'Middleton's Tragicomedies', *MP*, 54, pp. 7–19.

Shakespeare, William (1986) *The Complete Works*, General Editors Stanley
Wells and Gary Taylor, Oxford.

Ernst Honigmann

TEN PROBLEMS IN *DR FAUSTUS*

(1) The master-problem that has kept awake many students of *Dr Faustus*, when they might have been better employed saying their prayers, is a textual problem. Should we put our trust in the so-called A-text, first published in 1604, eleven years after Marlowe's death, or in the B-text, first published in 1616? The A-text, only 1517 lines long, 600 lines shorter than the B-text, was for many years regarded as the inferior version — a view that some editors would now like to reverse. Six hundred lines — or 40 per cent of the shorter text, nearly 30 per cent of the longer one — are worth arguing about, but, as the devil said to Faustus, side-tracking him with frivolities, all in good time. The problems that I wish to discuss are largely theatre-problems; while we cannot avoid referring back now and then to the textual evidence, my frivolous questions are concerned with the play in performance, from general conception to minutest detail, even non-verbal detail. For instance, how should Faustus die at the end? And: how does Mephostophilis react when Faustus dies? And: should Helen of Troy have a part in the death-scene?

(2) I begin with the 'general conception' of the play and a point of theology. When, precisely, is it too late for Faustus to repent? He himself, the Good and Bad Angel and others comment repeatedly on this crucial issue. Repeatedly and confusingly — so what are we to think? In a famous essay W. W. Greg explained that the turning-point comes when Faustus kisses Helen of Troy. Signing his pact with the devil, Faustus became a spirit and, said Greg, took on the 'infernal nature, although it is made clear throughout that he still retains his human soul'.[1] When Faustus makes Helen his paramour, however, he commits 'the sin of demoniality, that is, bodily intercourse with demons,' and the 'implication of Faustus' action is made plain in the comments of the Old Man and the Angels'. After the kiss Faustus is lost for ever.

    The Old Man, who has witnessed the meeting [with Helen] (according to the 1604 version), recognises the inevitable:

> Accursèd Faustus, miserable man,
> That from thy soul exclud'st the grace of heaven
> And fliest the throne of his tribunal-seat!

The Good Angel does no less:

> O Faustus, if thou hadst given ear to me
> Innumerable joys had followed thee . . .
> Oh, thou hast lost celestial happiness . . .[2]

Greg failed to mention that neither of these seemingly decisive statements occurs in both texts. The Old Man's summing-up comes from the A-text, the Good Angel's from the B-text. For whatever reason,[3] each of the two texts is less emphatic about Faustus' unavoidable fate than modern texts that print both passages.

Greg's much-quoted essay may serve as an example of a critical tendency to which I shall return — the tendency to overexplain. Literary critics like to explain everything, especially if a text seems to be dark or difficult; dramatists often choose to be dark or difficult, for their own very good reasons, and, if so, may look upon the critic as a meddling nuisance. As Wordsworth put it:

> One impulse from a vernal wood
>   May teach you more of man,
> Of moral evil and of good
>   Than all the sages can.
>
> Sweet is the lore which Nature brings;
>   Our meddling intellect
> Misshapes the beauteous forms of things:
>   We murder to dissect.

The Helen of Troy episode in *Dr Faustus* is clearly important, though not necessarily as explained in Greg's 'theological' analysis. Those who have not consulted learned books on demonology — or, as I would guess, the large majority of the play's spectators — might well wonder why kissing a spirit should be a more heinous offence than signing a pact with the devil in one's own blood.

In a valuable edition of the A-text, David Ormerod and Christopher Wortham recently called upon theology to 'overexplain' other mysteries. The pact with the devil, they claimed, 'is illegal and void. In English law and even more so in the Roman law which Renaissance humanists so much admired . . . immoral contracts are not binding . . . Faustus has not the power to "give both body and soul to Lucifer" (A 550), as he purports to do'; 'Lucifer cannot change Faustus into a spirit.' Also, 'a pact with the devil can be repudiated without harmful effects', and 'the repentant witch will always be forgiven', according to writers on witchcraft.[4] If correct, Ormerod and Wortham have disposed of Greg's explanation, which saw the pact with the devil and the kissing of Helen of Troy as decisive turning-points. I would say, however, that they have simply replaced one set of 'certainties' with another. Like Greg, they sought to explain — or 'overexplain' — a theatrical problem, how we react to Faustus' wish to repent, by appealing to theological and legal authorities who are not actually a part of the play.

Now it is true that we often bring to a play our knowledge of our own world, when this is required of us. We judge the domestic and social relationships in a play such as *Hamlet* by our own experience, both personal and literary — though not all the relationships here are equally transparent. A shouting-match between a mother and son — yes, we think we know where we are. A king who has married his 'sometime sister', the 'imperial jointress of this warlike state' (*Hamlet* I.ii.8) — that's unusual (what exactly is an 'imperial jointress'?).[5] A man instructed to revenge a murder by a ghost — that has happened to very few of us; even if we have encountered such a situation in literature, or in the theatre, we react more tentatively, we suspend judgement. In other words, sometimes we feel at home in the play-world, sometimes not — and it goes without saying that 'our knowledge of our own world' gives us little firm guidance when we meet a ghost, a spirit or a devil.

The audience's uncertainty can have an important function in a play. Marlowe, like Shakespeare, knew it, and developed the 'technique of uncertainty', with which he had already experimented in *Tamburlaine*. We are attracted *and* repelled by Tamburlaine; Dr Faustus, as a dramatic hero, is equally ambivalent — and his intellectual slithering, and the presence of angels, devils and spirits, hugely add to our difficulties. It may be, then, that we are meant to be less decisive in our judgements than are some of the play's editors; rather, that we should admit to being as confused as Faustus:

> I do repent, and yet I do despair:
> Hell strives with grace for conquest in my breast.   (A 1330)[6]

Instead of the certainty of the editors, who assure us that, after kissing Helen of Troy, Faustus is lost — or, contrarily, that a pact with the devil is void and that Faustus, if repentant, will be forgiven — the play, I think, offers us a 'technique of uncertainty', both in the advice given to Faustus by others and in his own indecisiveness. This uncertainty is heightened by the excellent team-work of the devils; whereas the Good Angel alone represents heaven, as a supernatural spokesman, the devils act together and always appear to win the upper hand. Indeed, whenever the Good and Evil Angel compete the Evil Angel always has the last word, with one exception, and on this occasion Lucifer, Beelzebub and Mephostophilis rush in and appear to win again.

> *Enter Good Angel and Evil.*
> EVIL ANGEL Too late.
> GOOD ANGEL Never too late, if Faustus can repent.
> EVIL ANGEL If thou repent, devils shall tear thee in pieces.
> GOOD ANGEL Repent, and they shall never raze thy skin.   (A 706)

For once the Good Angel does not give up first, and Faustus cries

> FAUSTUS Ah Christ, my Saviour
>   [Help] to save distressed Faustus' soul.

The devils react immediately, and Christ seems strangely passive.

> *Enter Lucifer, Beelzebub, and Mephostophilis.*
> LUCIFER Christ cannot save thy soul, for he is just,
>   There's none but I have interest in the same.
> FAUSTUS O who art thou that lookst so terrible?

Lucifer intimidates him, Faustus feels overpowered and promises, henceforth, 'never to look to heaven' (A 725).

Christ, I said, seems strangely passive, and this is another source of uncertainty. When Faustus calls on Mephostophilis, and even when Wagner and the clowns summon him, he appears; when Faustus calls on Christ, there is no response. Whether Faustus implores Christ to save him or blasphemes against Christ or God, heaven remains silent. In other plays heaven's aloofness seems less surprising; Barabas or Richard III may blaspheme and get away with it — in *Dr Faustus* the devils respond so readily that one expects heaven to react as well. Not only when Faustus cries for help or blasphemes but also when the devils make invasive assertions, such as 'Christ cannot save thy soul, for he is just.' Uncontradicted, this statement — like so many others — creates uncertainty about heaven's power and will to win. The nearest the play comes to heavenly intervention, apart from the warnings of the Good Angel, is the miraculous inscription on Faustus' arm, after he signs the pact, and this is never explained:

> But what is this inscription on mine arm?
> *Homo fuge*: whither should I fly?   (A 517)

In *Dr Faustus* the devils seem to be so completely in charge, and heaven seems so very uninterested, that one is driven to conclude that Faustus *may* have overstepped the limits of heaven's tolerance. The Good Angel only holds out hope to Faustus on condition that he repents; bound by his pact with the devil, he declares again and again that he *cannot* repent. Do we know better, when only he knows his own spiritual state from the inside, when only he has signed a pact with Lucifer? Finding ourselves in unfamiliar spiritual territory we surely pause, and defer judgement. Theoretically he may not be beyond the reach of grace (even that is uncertain); being the man he is, however, he never really comes near to repenting, he merely wants to save his skin. Where his feeling for God and Christ seems most intense, as in the great death-speech, is that feeling genuine repentance, or simply terror of damnation?

> Ah, Faustus,
> Now hast thou but one bare hour to live
> And then thou must be damned perpetually . . .
> The stars move still, time runs, the clock will strike,
> The devil will come, and Faustus must be damned.
> O, I'll leap up to my God!   (A 1450)

Repentance, in the Christian tradition, involves two parties — the sinner and God's 'prevenient grace', reaching out and helping the sinner to repent. Milton went over this ground in *Paradise Lost*, more explicitly than Marlowe, describing Adam and Eve's repentance after the Fall:

> from the mercy-seat above
> Prevenient grace descending had removed
> The stony from their hearts, and made new flesh
> Regenerate grow instead . . .   (XI.2–5)

Marlowe, addressing a more 'popular' audience than Milton, also raised the question of God's mercy and grace, yet again without giving a clear-cut answer. In the scene before Faustus' death a scholar first advises 'Yet, Faustus, look up to heaven, remember God's mercies are infinite' (A 1400), *before* he knows what Faustus has done. After Faustus has confessed, 'Ah, gentlemen, I gave them my soul for my cunning' (A 1423), the same scholar speaks far less confidently — 'O, what may we do to save Faustus?' and 'Pray thou, and we will pray, that God may have mercy upon thee!' *May* have mercy: it is just a possibility, no more.

Nothing is gained, in my view, if an editor or critic certifies that at some point before the end Faustus is irredeemably damned, or if we are led to believe that a pact with the devil is only a piece of paper, which can be renounced at any time. *Dr Faustus* is a play about not understanding God, a play about human ignorance and uncertainty. Much will be lost if we substitute theological positiveness for Faustus' uncertainty, and for our own. In the B-text the last exchanges of the Good and Evil Angels indicate that Faustus' damnation is now unavoidable, but not specifically because of Helen of Troy. And at this point we have already reached the play's final phase, which ends our uncertainty.

(3) Next, a related problem, the role played by an invisible God. God never appears on-stage, as does Lucifer, yet this apparently absent God is also undeniably present, more so than Beckett's Godot. We are led to *expect* Godot, and we expect intervention from Faustus' God, and at the same time we feel that Faustus' God is already here, not somewhere else. Even if the devils are physically present in many scenes and the Good Angel speaks a total of only ten lines (in the A-text), God is not under-represented. He may not show himself physically yet, for all Faustus' efforts to the contrary, he seems to hide in the sinner's heart, and in that of Mephostophilis, a smouldering flicker that can suddenly flame and blaze. 'Thinkst thou', says Mephostophilis in a sudden outburst of passion —

> Thinkst thou that I, that saw the face of God
> And tasted the eternal joys of heaven,
> Am not tormented with ten thousand hells
> In being deprived of everlasting bliss?   (A 322)

The more Faustus and the devils try to suppress or by-pass God, the more real he appears to become. The very act of denying God brings him mysteriously into being, as Peter discovered before the cock-crow.

Since Marlowe wrote for a Protestant audience it is worth noting that he made use of many visible reminders of Roman Catholicism — from the second appearance of Mephostophilis as 'an old Franciscan friar' (A 269), the scenes in Rome with the Pope and cardinals, to the scenes with the Emperor Charles V, a resolute champion of Rome. The God who survives in Faustus' blaspheming heart is not harmed by the unholy antics of the play's Catholics, which confirm rather than disprove his existence. The friars chant 'Cursed be he that stole away his holiness' meat from the table: *maledicat dominus.*/Cursed be he that struck his holiness a blow on the face: *maledicat dominus*' (A 917) —

and one *feels* the disapproval of God, here and elsewhere, a very nearly physical presence, long before Faustus *sees* God's implacable frown in the death-speech:

> see where God stretcheth out his arm
> And bends his ireful brows   (A 1468)

or, as the B-text has it, 'see, a threatening arm, an angry brow' —

> Mountains and hills, come, come and fall on me
> And hide me from the heavy wrath of God! (A, B)

When Goethe came to write his more modern Faustus-play he acknowledged the problem of an invisible and seemingly indifferent God by introducing the 'Prolog im Himmel.' Here God converses with Mephistopheles, as did the Lord and Satan in the *Book of Job*, and agrees not to interfere during Faust's life-time.

> MEPH. Was wettet ihr? den sollt ihr noch verlieren
>   Wenn ihr mir die Erlaubniss gebt,
>   Ihn meine Strasse sacht zu führen.
> DER HERR So lang er auf der Erde lebt,
>   So lange sei dirs nicht verboten.
> [MEPH. What do you wager? You will lose him yet, if you give me
>   permission to lead him gently as I choose.
> THE LORD So long as he lives on earth, so long you have permission
>   to do that.]

This 'bet' helps to explain God's withdrawal — or does it 'overexplain'? I have to admit that I prefer Marlowe's less visible God, whose hidden presence broods menacingly over the play. Goethe's God speaks in a too 'personal' voice, a voice disturbingly similar at times to that of the ironical Mephistopheles:

> DER HERR Hast du mir weiter Nichts zu sagen?
>   Kommst du nur immer anzuklagen?
>   Ist auf der Erde ewig dir Nichts recht?
> [THE LORD Do you have nothing else to say to me? Do you always
>   come as an accuser? Is everything on earth wrong in
>   your eyes — for ever?]

This civilised ironical voice, like the individualised voice of the Father in *Paradise Lost*, assigns to God some of the mannerisms of the poet, and drags God down to our human level. I think that Marlowe's silent, angry God is more effective.

(4) Next, a special staging technique as theatrically potent as the felt presence of God — namely the disguisings of the devils. Marlowe also toyed with disguise in *The Jew of Malta*; Barabas, an adroit performer, as Protean as Tamburlaine had been rock-like, even dresses up as a busking musician — in a recent production by the Royal Shakespeare Company (1988) this was, rightly, a climactic scene. In *Dr Faustus* disguise becomes more pervasive, and more important, partly because the devils so often change their shapes. Mephostophilis, too ugly to attend on Faustus as a devil, is told, 'Go, and return an old Franciscan friar' (A 269). Faustus demands a wife, so 'Enter . . . a devil dressed like a woman' (A 595). Faustus feels depressed, and Beelzebub offers a 'pastime', the show of the Seven Deadly Sins, put on by devils. Later Mephostophilis brings on more 'shows' — Alexander, Darius and a Paramour; devils as soldiers; Helen of Troy. In addition Faustus and Mephostophilis disguise themselves as cardinals, and no doubt Faustus wears other appropriate robes in other scenes, as courtier, traveller, scholar — thus underlining the chameleon qualities of the man and his psychic instability.

The disguisings of the devils are particularly interesting. Mephostophilis appears in at least three different shapes — a devil, a friar and a cardinal — and probably in others, as Faustus' companion. We are meant to recognise him, whatever he happens to wear, as we recognise Faustus — and I therefore wonder whether other devils, reappearing in different shapes, should also be recognisably one and the same. Minor actors often doubled in two or more roles; in *Dr Faustus* such doubling would strengthen the play, emphasising the devil's well-known talent for surprises, even to the extent of citing 'Scripture for his purpose' (*Merchant of Venice* I.iii.99). Modern *dramatis personae* lists may have misled us, identifying the Evil Angel, for example, as someone distinct from the 'devils' that wait on Lucifer — but is this self-evidently correct? What is an evil angel if not a devil? And why should Faustus' Evil Angel *not* work hand-in-glove with Lucifer, as one of his most active assistants?

Being an old-fashioned psychomachia, like its close contemporary *The Faerie Queen, Dr Faustus* externalises internal psychic impulses — which therefore have to be seen as participating in one another's being, not as sharply separate. Sir Guyon, the Knight of Temperance, resists the vices of Fury, Immodest Mirth and of the Bower of Bliss, and all of these vices — *his* vices — although divided into separate episodes, are linked, as the viciousness or the devil within Guyon. In a play this togetherness of the vices can be physically presented by giving the same recognisable devil several disguises. Faustus says 'let me have a wife, the fairest maid in Germany, for I am wanton and lascivious and cannot live without a wife' (A 588), Mephostophilis obliges by fetching 'a wife in the devil's name' — *Enter with a devil dressed like a woman, with fire-works*. The dialogue makes it clear that the wife is a disappointment, but what exactly happens?

> MEPH. Tell, Faustus, how dost thou like thy wife?
> FAUSTUS A plague on her for a hot whore!   (A 597)

Mephostophilis presents what at first seems to be 'the fairest maid in Germany', then she pulls off her wig, or a mask, and an unmistakable devil grimaces at Faustus, switching to the body-language of a 'hot whore'. And is this the only time we see this particular devil? The boy actor who could portray 'the fairest maid in Germany' would be the ideal devil for the part of Helen of Troy — the same vice, after all, animates both episodes. Faustus does not need a wife as a companion and helpmeet, but specifically because he feels 'wanton and lascivious', and he asks for Helen of Troy not merely to see her, as did the scholars, but to enjoy her 'sweet embracings' as his paramour (A 1350).

Amongst Marlowe's most significant additions to the story of Faustus is the show of the Seven Deadly Sins. Just one of the Sins is identified as definitely female (traditionally the Sins were represented as males, as in *Piers Plowman*, Passus V, and *The Faerie Queen*, I.4). Marlowe's female Sin speaks last, climaxing the show — appropriately, given his interpretation of Faustus' character.

> FAUSTUS And what are you, Mistress Minx? the seventh and last?
> LECHERY Who — I, sir? I am one that loves an inch of raw mutton
>   better than an ell of fried stock-fish, and the first letter
>   of my name begins with lechery.   (A 790)[7]

The devil who performed Lechery could have had a major part in the play, also taking the roles of 'the fairest maid in Germany' and of Helen of Troy. As Milton showed more fully, the devil likes to play hide-and-seek with his victims.

Although the humour of the play's lechery-scenes is Marlowe's very own, the play's emphasis on Faustus' lechery derives directly and indirectly from the *Faust-book*. There Faustus not only makes a paramour of Helen of Troy, and has a son by her — he also copulates with the six wives and concubines of the Great Turk (Ch. 22), and, as the end of his twenty-four years approaches, he commands Mephostophilis 'to bring him seven of the fairest women that he had seen in all the time of his travel', and of course 'he lay with them all' (Ch. 53). In the *Faust-book* the hero calls himself 'Doctor Faustus the unsatiable speculator' (p. 35); he could just as well have claimed to be 'the insatiable copulator'.

Dr Faustus should not be understood as pure psychomachia, simply a morality-play. Like Bale's *King Johan* and some sixteenth-century successors, it mixes historical persons with personifications. Pope Adrian and Bruno, Raymond of Hungary, the Emperor Charles and others exist in their own right, side by side with devils and spirits. I am reminded of near-contemporary plays in which supernatural beings preside over the action and influence human behaviour — Revenge in *The Spanish Tragedy*, the Seven Planets in Lyly's *The Woman in the Moon*. In this last, entered in the Stationers' Register in 1595 and no doubt performed a few years earlier, Jupiter, Venus, Mars and the rest each in turn predominate, with amusing consequences for the human actors. Richard Tarlton's lost play, *The Seven Deadly Sins*, probably assigned a similar function to the Sins, if we may judge from its sequel, Part 2 of *The Seven Deadly Sins* (*c.* 1590), the plot of which has survived: here Envy, Sloth and Lechery appear to be in charge of groups of linked scenes. Many of the episodes in *Dr Faustus* are similarly connected with one or other of the Deadly Sins, who should perhaps reappear, either as bit-players in later scenes or as presiding geniuses. This would make sense of some of the least admired 'horse-play' scenes which, though now often seen as Marlowe's, not the work of a second dramatist, are still thought to be unsatisfactory. Benvolio, who strikes off Faustus' head as 'just revenge' for a pair of horns, exemplifies Wrath; the Pope, a 'proud Lucifer', Pride (B 899); Faustus asks Mephostophilis to give the cardinals their appropriate punishment ('Strike them with sloth, and drowsy idleness', B 923), and later we hear that 'the Pope will curse them for their sloth today' (B 1021). The 'great-bellied' Duchess of Anholt or Vanholt, who longs for a dish of ripe grapes out of season, exemplifies Gluttony, as does the feasting before Faustus' death 'where there's such belly-cheer/As Wagner in his life ne'er saw the like' (B 1783). While this later reactivation of the Deadly Sins would strengthen the play's otherwise loose structure, we must observe that the shorter A-text omits or condenses some of the relevant episodes, whereas the B-text more consistently threads them in. And even in the B-text they are not followed through mechanically, nor are they all given the same emphasis, as the 'planets' were in *The Woman in the Moon*. Some of the sins belong to the inner *and* outer action, some are more restricted. Faustus *covets* the power of Mephostophilis:

> Had I as many souls as there be stars
> I'd give them all for Mephostophilis   (A 347)

as Mephostophilis *covets* Faustus' soul, yet envy receives little attention (perhaps the subplot was meant to supply more envy). Some of the sins, again, are brought to notice figuratively —

> How am I glutted with conceit of this?
> Shall I make spirits fetch me what I please?   (A 110)

and again when Faustus asks for Helen as his paramour 'To glut the longing of my heart's desire' (A 1349).

At this point I have to interrupt with another remark on the play's two texts. It may seem that, unlike recent editors who prefer the A-text, I am defending the B-text, where the Seven Deadly Sins are more fully represented. Not quite: as I see it, both texts omit essential parts of Marlowe's play and both texts add post-Marlovian material. For example, the A-text refers to Dr Lopez ('Alas, alas, Doctor Fustian quotha? mass, Dr Lopez was never such a doctor', A 1176): it is generally agreed that this allusion dates from 1594, when Lopez was accused of attempting to poison the queen — one year after Marlowe's death. On the other hand, the A-text also omits passages that must be Marlowe's, such as a large chunk of the second Chorus (B 783–95). Neither of the two texts transmits the original, complete play; both texts may well transmit, in debased form, material that had a place in the lost original.

To recapitulate: it would make theatrical sense if the Deadly Sins reappear as recognisable devils in many scenes.[8] Faustus' own lechery, in particular, links several scenes that climax in the lyricism — and shamelessness — of his great speech to Helen of Troy ('Her lips suck forth my soul: see where it flies!', A 1360). Or rather, the lechery episodes reach their penultimate phase in the speech to Helen — for, if my argument holds, the same devils surely return in one more scene, a scene without dialogue, marked only by a short stage direction ('Enter devils', A; 'Thunder, and enter the devils', B).

(5) We have reached the problem of Faustus' death. In the play's source the final events of the story are told as follows:

> The students lay near unto the hall wherein Doctor Faustus lay, and they heard a mighty noise and hissing, as if the hall had been full of snakes and adders: with that the hall door flew open wherein Doctor Faustus was, then he began to cry for help, saying 'Murther, murther!', but it came forth with half a voice hollowly. Shortly

after they heard him no more. But when it was day the students . . .
found no Faustus, but all the hall lay besprinkled with blood, his
brains cleaving to the wall: for the devil had beaten him from one
wall against another, in one corner lay his eyes, in another his
teeth, a pitiful and fearful sight to behold. Then began the students
to bewail and weep for him, and sought for his body in many places.
Lastly they came into the yard where they found his body lying on
the horse-dung, most monstrously torn. . . .

The shorter A-text fails to explain exactly *how* Faustus dies, for the
hero's death-speech is succeeded immediately by the epilogue, 'Cut is
the branch that might have grown full straight. . . .' The B-text prints a
final scene that, without question, derives from Marlowe's source:

Enter the Scholars.

1 SCHOLAR Come, gentlemen, let us go visit Faustus,
For such a dreadful night was never seen
Since first the world's creation did begin.
Such fearful shrieks and cries were never heard;
Pray heaven the doctor have escaped the danger.

2 SCHOLAR O help us heaven, see, here are Faustus' limbs
All torn asunder by the hand of death.

3 SCHOLAR The devils whom Faustus served have torn him thus,
For 'twixt the hours of twelve and one, methought,
I heard him shriek and call aloud for help,
At which self time the house seemed all on fire
With dreadful horror of these damned fiends . . .

Both the *Faust-book* and Marlowe himself had pointed forward to the
dismemberment of Faustus on many occasions. The *Faust-book*
Mephostophilis threatens 'if thou keep not what thou hast promised . . .
we will tear thee in pieces like the dust under thy feet', 'I will tear thee
in thousands of pieces' (Ch. 9, 19), etc. In the play the Evil Angel
promises 'If thou repent, devils shall tear thee in pieces' (A 709), as
does Mephostophilis, 'I'll in piecemeal tear thy flesh' (A 1335). So, too,
when the horse-courser pulls off Faustus' leg — all instances taken from
the A-text — and when Benvolio and his friends strike off Faustus' head
(this occurs only in the B-text, B 1413ff.). That the dramatist was
thinking ahead to the death of Faustus while writing the Benvolio scene
is indicated, I believe, by a repeating image. Benvolio and his gang
speculate gloatingly:

MARTINO What use shall we put his beard to?
BENVOLIO We'll sell it to a chimney-sweeper: it will wear out ten
            birchen brooms, I warrant you.
FREDERICK What shall [his] eyes do?
BENVOLIO We'll put out his eyes, and they shall serve for buttons
            to his lips, to keep his tongue from catching cold.
            (B 1435)

The gruesome humour here could be Marlowe's, though the description
of Faustus' dismembered body in the source-book supplied the image:
'in one corner lay his eyes, in another his teeth'.

As a false leg and a false head had already been put to use in earlier
scenes, and Faustus had been threatened with dismemberment, I think
that he must suffer this fate on-stage, certainly in the B-version.
Otherwise the second scholar would not be able to say 'see, here are
Faustus' limbs/All torn asunder by the hand of death.' Precisely what
happens when the devils enter to collect their victim is not spelt out. I
take it as axiomatic, however, that the play's long-awaited, culminating
episode would be given its full effect in the theatre. Perhaps earlier low-
comedy pranks are now re-enacted at Faustus' expense, somewhat like
the recapitulation of the crimes of Richard III before the Battle of
Bosworth: the devils box Faustus' ears (compare A 905), beat him
(A 928), derisively offer him grapes (A 1243) and/or a crown and rich
apparel (A 525), and so on, before they finally dismember him.

Some of the devils that take part in this concluding episode must have
been identifiable — Lucifer and Mephostophilis for a start. And how
many more? Should we not bring back the Seven Deadly Sins —
Faustus' sins — and assign a prominent role to Lechery, or Helen of
Troy? She passes over the stage, a gorgeous apparition of female beauty,
then suddenly turns into a hideous devil that sits astride of the fallen
Faustus and pummels him (where?), the last glimpse we have of him
before he is torn to shreds.

Of course this sounds somewhat fanciful — but please note that *both*
texts direct that the devils enter, and they enter for a purpose. They
must do *something*: not necessarily as I have suggested, but something
along the lines previously indicated by the text. So, as elsewhere, a
performance problem connects with the problems of theology and text.
The A-text omits the final scene, in which the scholars discover the
torn limbs — could this scene be an addition to Marlowe's play? A. H.
Bullen thought the scene 'thoroughly worthy of Marlowe', and others
have agreed.[9] Ormerod and Wortham, being theologically committed,

dissented: not only are pacts with the devil void, they said, but devils 'cannot enforce the death of a human being at any moment they choose'.[10] How, then, they ask, does Faustus die? They answer that 'suicide is a possibility'. Now despair has a place in the Faustus story — yet, as I have said, the play again and again raises expectations pointing forward to the final scene of the B-text. The play *needs* the dismemberment of Faustus, at the appointed time. Like the *Faust-book*, its source, the play addresses a 'popular' audience and adopts popular attitudes, some of which may be theologically objectionable (theologians, to be sure, have been known to disagree with one another, and their views about devils were matters of opinion, not of fact). In this instance, therefore, I assume that the B-text brings us closer to Marlowe's original than A.

(6) Still in the death-scene, how does Faustus end his last speech?

> Ugly hell, gape not! come not, Lucifer!
> I'll burn my books! ah, Mephostophilis!   (A 1507)

Harry Levin commented that 'his last word is the shriek, "*Mephosto-philis*"'.[11] It could be a shriek, or it could be several other things. Once again this concentrated scene requires us to use our imagination, and to relate the detail to a larger conception. Does Faustus appeal to a trusted companion, clinging to him, hoping for help — or is his last word a shriek of pain because it falls to Mephostophilis to give him the *coup de grâce*? And if the latter, should Faustus shriek — or whisper? Here Marlowe may have anticipated Shakespeare's '*Et tu, Brute*', though other interpretations are possible.

As readers we can slide past this problem; in the theatre, in this case, we have to make a decision. Does Mephostophilis rejoice in Faustus' agony, perhaps even help to dismember him — or should he stand aside at the end, and shrug — or grieve? The 'humanity' of Mephostophilis is at issue and the relationship of the two central characters, coming to its crisis in Faustus' last word and last look.

(7) How much genuine fellow-feeling is there in this strange relationship? Quite apart from the fact that they both enjoy the same jokes, they address each other affectionately as 'my Faustus' and 'my Mephostophilis', and Mephostophilis even speaks of 'my Faustus' in the latter's absence.

> I'll wing myself and forthwith fly amain
> Unto my Faustus to the great Turk's court.   (B 1179)

If something close to tenderness seems at times to bind them together, let us remember that there is a connection between loving a person and thinking that you own him (or her). True, we note some dramatic irony as well, as when Faustus addresses 'my good Mephostophilis' (A 822); and it suits both of them to get on together, so they call each other 'sweet Mephostophilis', 'sweet friend' and the like (A 696, 1342), to oil the relationship. Yet since they also rage against each other every so often it has the dynamics of a very human relationship — including deception and (on Faustus' part) some self-deception. Mephostophilis, indeed, in so far as he was once an angel and fell with Lucifer, assumes a kind of 'older brother' stance in answering Faustus' questions about heaven and hell; he has been through it all himself, he understands Faustus' point of view — does that not beget fellow-feeling? And perhaps even affection? Ben Jonson remembered Faustus and Mephostophilis when he created Volpone and Mosca, including the delicious twist that the servant plans to outwit his master — yet Jonson's rogues strike me as a colder pair, their relationship as largely professional, whereas Faustus and Mephostophilis also interact unprofessionally. Mephostophilis risks losing Faustus' soul by speaking too honestly:

> FAUSTUS And what are you that live with Lucifer?
> MEPHOST. Unhappy spirits that live with Lucifer,
>   Conspired against our God with Lucifer,
>   And are for ever damned with Lucifer.   (A 314)

We are encouraged to think of Faustus and Mephostophilis as very close — though exactly how close remains a mystery. When they play their pranks on the Pope and others they may even hug or slap each other with delight — or, alternatively, Mephostophilis may signal to us, grimacing, that he has to humour a childish master. The *togetherness* of Faustus and Mephostophilis, in short, has been an issue throughout the play, and probably one that should not be resolved until Faustus' very last utterance, the moment of truth: 'ah, Mephostophilis!'

I must not pretend, however, that this central relationship is identical in the two texts — far from it. Two passages in the B-text, not found in A, stress the distance between the two principals, the malignancy of Mephostophilis and his delight in destroying Faustus. These passages, both placed just before the end, suggest that in the B-text Mephostophilis savours his victim's death-agony. First the devils ascend from hell to 'mark [Faustus] how he doth demean himself.' How should he, exclaims Mephostophilis —

> How should he, but in desperate lunacy?
> Fond worldling, now his heart-blood dries with grief,
> His conscience kills it, and his labouring brain
> Begets a world of idle fantasies
> To overreach the devil — but all in vain.
> His store of pleasures must be sauced with pain.   (B 1906)

All fellow-feeling has vanished. And when the scholars depart, leaving Faustus to his final meditations, Mephostophilis turns on him gleefully —

> MEPHOST. Ay, Faustus, now hast thou no hope of heaven,
>   Therefore despair, think only upon hell!
>   For that must be thy mansion, there to dwell.
> FAUSTUS O thou bewitching fiend, 'twas thy temptation
>   Hath robbed me of eternal happiness.
> MEPHOST. I do confess it, Faustus, and rejoice . . .   (B 1983)

It makes a difference, too, that in the B-text Mephostophilis remains on-stage during Faustus' interview with the scholars, and that in the B-text Mephostophilis 'brings in' Helen of Troy, the first time she appears — presumably like a ring-master or auctioneer, pointing out her special attractions. (Not so in the *Faust-book*, where Faustus tells his friends that he will 'bring her into your presence personally': ch. 45.) The Mephostophilis of the A-text has a subtler relationship with Faustus, less devilish, more human.

(8) Mephostophilis, I said, risks losing Faustus' soul by speaking too honestly. Here is another 'theological' problem, for which I see no easy solution. Many a rationalist has thought, before and after Marlowe, 'I am aware of no convincing evidence for the existence of God, therefore I shall behave as if there is no God.' Yet is it rational to go on denying God when you are talking to a self-confessed devil? And when the devil appears to be unshakeable in the conviction that God exists?

> FAUSTUS Was not that Lucifer an angel once?
> MEPHOST. Yes, Faustus, and most dearly loved of God.   (A 309)

Put the case that *one* of the supernatural beings of the Christo-Hebraic tradition incontrovertibly exists — good angel, bad angel, Lucifer — then there is an inherent likelihood that God 'exists' as well. And if a hostile witness, such as Mephostophilis, assures Faustus that God exists, how can a rational man turn his back on God? make war on the Omnipotent? and choose Hell instead? —

FAUSTUS Come, I think hell's a fable.
MEPHOST. Ay, think so still, till experience change thy mind!
(A 574)

Could it be that Faustus is a very confused doctor of divinity? or is
Marlowe a very confused dramatist? or am I guilty now of trying to
'over-explain'?

Some critics have argued that Faustus deteriorates intellectually in
the course of the play, like Milton's Satan, as witnessed by his childish
activities in the middle scenes. Alternatively, Chorus' opening statement

> So much he profits in divinity
> That shortly he was graced with doctor's name,
> Excelling all, and sweetly can dispute . . .   (B 16)

may refer to the past, not to Faustus as he now is —

> For, falling to a devilish exercise
> And glutted now with learning's golden gifts
> He surfeits upon cursed necromancy.   (B 23)

Theologians sometimes talk of a 'fall before the Fall' (Milton appears to
allude to this in Eve's dream before the Fall). Marlowe's Faustus,
perhaps, should be seen as fallen, or devil-possessed, before he signs his
formal pact — therefore intellectually impaired from the play's
beginning. I prefer this explanation because he behaves irrationally
from the beginning, already believing in spirits, and Lucifer, but not in
God. Marlowe allows us to think of Faustus as something other than
the ideal theologian by inserting implicit stage directions in the speech
in his study. 'Bid *on kai me on* farewell; Galen, come', 'Physic farewell;
where is Justinian?', 'divinity, adieu' — does Faustus simply pick up one
book after another, or should he hurl them away, frustrated, with each
sarcastic 'adieu' and 'farewell'? A frightening impulsiveness, breaking
out during this first meditation, could help to reconcile us to Faustus'
perplexing irrationality. The *Faust-book* offered this possibility: Dr
Faustus 'fell into such fantasies and deep cogitations, that . . . sometime
he would *throw the Scripture from him*' (Ch. I).

(9) We have looked at Faustus' last word — now let us take the play's
very last line, if indeed it should count as part of the play. '*Terminat
hora diem, terminat Author opus*' ('the hour ends the day, and the
author ends his work'). The origin of this so-called 'motto' has not been
traced, though the same words also occur at the end of the MS play of

Charlemagne (which is probably later than *Dr Faustus*). Greg thought it unlikely that the motto 'appeared in such a manuscript as we have assumed the copy for A to have been. It is much more likely to have been appended by the printer himself along with the publisher's device'.[12] Recent critics have come to look more favourably on the A-text, and dramatists did sometimes place a motto, or words such as *Laus deo*, at the end of a play-text — for instance, Robert Greene, who died one year before Marlowe: 'Finis Frier Bacon, made by Robert Greene, Maister of Arts. *Omne tulit punctum qui miscuit vtile dulci*'.[13] And there are grounds for thinking that Marlowe himself wrote the curious concluding line of his play, for the author finished writing at midnight and Faustus died at midnight — surely that cannot be a meaningless coincidence? Whether or nor Marlowe's audiences identified him with Faustus — and they certainly identified him with 'that atheist Tamburlaine' — he himself and his friends must have seen that he had much in common with his tragic hero, a point underscored when, Faustus' pact with the devil having ended at midnight, the author adds that the writing of his devil-pact play was also completed at midnight.

In the opening scene Marlowe often translated his Latin phrases, for the benefit of the groundlings. But not always in later scenes, where he sometimes resorted to Latin, untranslated, as a sardonic wink to the wise: '*Consummatum est*' (A 515), '*O lente, lente currite noctis equi*' (A 1459). The play's last line makes a last, cheeky point in this vein — saying in effect, 'The atheist Faustus is dead, the atheist author survives!' Though the words may not have been intended for the theatre, could anyone except Marlowe have written them?[14]

Notes

1 W. W. Greg, 'The Damnation of Faustus', *M.L.R.* (1946), XLI, pp. 97–107.

2 Greg, *op. cit.*, p. 107.

3 Michael Warren suggested, in an important article, that each of the two texts 'must be seen separately for itself', and that conflating the two texts is futile ('*Doctor Faustus*: The Old Man and the Text', *E.L.R.* (1981), XI, pp. 109–47).

4 Christopher Marlowe, *Dr Faustus: The A-text*, ed. David Ormerod and Christopher Wortham, University of Western Australia Press (1985), pp. xli–xlviii.

5 For a longer discussion of the problems in *Hamlet* see my *Myriad-Minded Shakespeare* (1989), Ch. 3.

6 I modernise the spelling and punctuation of the A and B texts. Line numbers refer to the first line quoted.

7 The A and B texts agree in the reading 'fride' (or 'fryde'). I suspect a tenth 'problem', that Marlowe wrote 'dried stock-fish'. The antithesis is not between uncooked and cooked food but between a fresh prostitute (*O.E.D.*, raw, 5; mutton, 4) and a cold, sexless person (*O.E.D.*, dry, 13; stockfish, 1c). Greg (as in note 9, p. 343) commented that 'Ward by omitting the passage showed that he understood it', but in his own 'conjectural reconstruction' (Oxford, 1950) printed 'fried'.

8 Nigel Alexander has written more fully about the Seven Deadly Sins: see 'The Performance of Christopher Marlowe's *Dr Faustus*', *Proceedings of the British Academy*, 1971, vol. LVII, pp. 331–49.

9 *Marlowe's 'Doctor Faustus' 1604–1616*, parallel texts, ed. W. W. Greg, Oxford: Oxford University Press (1950), pp. 401–2.

10 As in note 4, p. xlvi.

11 Harry Levin, *The Overreacher: A Study of Christopher Marlowe* (1954), London: Faber & Faber, p. 153.

12 As in note 9, p. 403.

13 See my *The Stability of Shakespeare's Text* (1965) for 'mottos': pp. 177–80.

14 For the tenth problem see Note 7, above.

Murray Biggs

SOME PROBLEMS OF ACTING *EDWARD II*

Anyone approaching *Edward II* for the first time is bound to notice, and may well be put off by, what seem to be abrupt and implausible shifts of attitude and behaviour among the principal figures. Literary critics have tended either to acknowledge that Marlowe had difficulty with consistency in general, or, more sympathetically, to find with F. P. Wilson[1] that the playwright was more interested in other things. Marlowe's apparently clumsy workmanship is likely to remain, however, a special problem for the modern actor trained to uncover a coherent basis for the exploration of character on stage. I propose to examine two characters in *Edward II* with this problem in mind.

First the young Mortimer. Here the question for today's actor is how to progress naturally from the bold and noble warrior of the first three Acts to the villainous schemer of Act V. The obvious answer (power corrupts), while satisfactory enough in psychological theory, must still be realised in the stage action; and it will help if we can find clues in the earlier scenes to Mortimer's later eruption.

On the face of it, Mortimer is thoroughly loyal to his country and offers his life in its defence. He honours both the kingdom and the king, so long as Edward behaves like one. He is admirable in his concern for the national exchequer, which is being frittered away on Edward's private pleasures, 'while soldiers mutiny for want of pay' (I.iv.405).[2] Money is, in fact, a key issue in the dispute between king and nobles. The Scots have captured Mortimer Senior and set his ransom at £5,000. His peers are right to expect the crown to pay off this enormous sum since Mortimer was taken prisoner in his country's cause. His nephew speaks like the paradigm of a familiar English sobriety when he condemns 'the idle triumphs, masques, lascivious shows/And prodigal gifts bestowed on Gaveston' (II.ii.157–8), as well as when he distinguishes between the 'fantastic' foreign 'liveries' affected by Gaveston and his circle at extravagant cost and the more homely attire deemed fit for the true English peerage (I.iv.406–18; cf. II.ii.183–7). It is in some sense appropriate that Mortimer later compares himself with 'a bashful Puritan' (V.iv.58). Although by then he intends the comparison as a figure of his own hypocrisy that would have

(192)

recommended itself to an Elizabethan audience, we can accept as sincere these early quarrels with a profligate royal purse.

The nobles to a man denounce the king's favourite for the baseness of his birth; and rather than dismiss their attitude as mere snobbery, we need to remember that, from their point of view, Gaveston represents a threat to the security of their class that had been wrested from the king's great-grandfather John only a hundred years earlier. Magna Carta introduced the word 'peer' to the English language; and the peers' insistence on their hard-won rights must be understood, as it would have been by a late Tudor audience, with due historical vision. Mortimer perceives that the monarch depends on the hierarchy of the feudal system, and that the hierarchy itself survives only by a symbiosis of crown and nobility:

> Thy court is naked, [he tells Edward,] being bereft of those
> That make a king seem glorious to the world,
> I mean the peers, whom thou shouldst dearly love.   (II.ii.174–6)

It perhaps indicates Mortimer's inherent respect for the throne that he delivers these and other home truths to the king when there are no inferiors within earshot: 'now you are here alone, I'll speak my mind' (II.ii.155).

All this, I submit, is to Mortimer's credit. He behaves with a public conscience, very differently from the self-seeker he will become. Yet this praiseworthy public-spiritedness is not quite our first impression of the young leader. His opening speech begins with a reminder of the noble oath he swore to the king's father; but it continues more ambiguously:

> And know, my lord, ere I will break my oath,
> This sword of mine that should offend your foes
> Shall sleep within the scabbard at thy need,
> And underneath thy banners march who will,
> For Mortimer will hang his armour up.   (I.i.84–8)

Such extreme resolution sounds less than wholly patriotic. The note of petulance returns later in the Act: 'My lords, now let us all be resolute,/ And either have our wills, or lose our lives' (I.iv.45–6).

Three times in Act I Mortimer suggests that he is seeking a legal pretext to revolt from the king (I.ii.73; I.iv.54–5; I.iv.279); and we may wonder if his motives are entirely unmixed. It seems clear that he cannot stomach Edward personally when he 'walks aside' from the reconciliations between the king and the other nobles (I.iv.352). This 'written-in' stage direction is an unmistakable hint to the actor, who can show Mortimer as barely getting through the two-line acceptance speech that the text and perhaps public decorum require of him. The character says nothing for the rest of the scene until the playwright leaves him alone with his uncle for one of those man-to-man chats that must remind us of Hotspur being soothed by *his* elders. Mortimer Senior's advice, however, is only doubtfully effective. The last word rests with his nephew, and it is ominous:

> . . . whiles I have a sword, a hand, a heart,
> I will not yield to any such upstart.
> You know my mind; come uncle, let's away.   (I.iv.421–3)

It is the last time we see the uncle's restraining influence.

Young Mortimer's heart is written on his sword. In II.ii, it is he who wounds Gaveston in the presence of the king, intending to kill him, and sixty lines later draws his weapon on the king himself. By now his deeply choleric nature is fully revealed. The lines he speaks as he is led off to the Tower in III.iii intimate that this nature cannot be restrained:

> What, Mortimer! can ragged stony walls
> Immure thy virtue that aspires to heaven?
> No, Edward, England's scourge, it may not be;
> Mortimer's hope surmounts his fortune far.   (ll. 70–3)

During his imprisonment and foreign exile the rebel leader has time and means to cultivate his lonely ambitions. By the time Edward is defeated, Mortimer is addressing the queen as his equal: 'Fair Isabel, now have we our desire . . . ./Be ruled by me and we will rule the realm' (V.ii.1, 5). He becomes Lord Protector over the young Edward and commissions Matrevis and Gurney to torture the old in terms that are unashamedly hubristic: 'As thou intend'st to rise by Mortimer,/Who now makes Fortune's wheel turn as he please. . . .' (V.ii.52–3). Intoxicated with the sweet smell of power and his moral and emotional seizure of the queen, Mortimer gives way to an excess that is ironically reminiscent of Edward's own. He becomes, too, as thoroughgoing a Machiavel as Barabas himself (V.ii.78; V.iv.1, 19–20, 57–62), and as brazen. Never slow to resort to physical means to achieve his will, he threatens to carry off the young prince by force at the end of V.ii, and as I read the implied stage direction he makes good on his word forthwith. When Kent is being dragged off to execution at Mortimer's bidding, the luckless man cries out: 'Art thou king, must I die at thy command?'

(V.iv.102). Mortimer responds with a royal plural: 'At our command; once more away with him.' With Edward finally removed, Mortimer apostrophises himself:

> As for myself, I stand as Jove's huge tree,
> And others are but shrubs compared to me,
> All tremble at my name, and I fear none,
> Let's see who dare impeach me for his death?   (V.vi.11–14)

He goes to his own death unrepentant:

> Why should I grieve at my declining fall?
> Farewell, fair queen, weep not for Mortimer
> That scorns the world and as a traveller
> Goes to discover countries yet *unknown*.   (V.vi.63–6)

He remains a moral agnostic to the last. Hie severed head forms the play's final image: an emblematic warning against both the killing of a king and the spirit that would be king.

What I have tried to suggest in this account of Mortimer Junior is that the extreme behaviour revealed in Act V has been latent from the beginning in the man's isolated and suppressed energy, an energy primarily of anger. (At I.iv.418 he confesses his 'impatience' to his uncle.) When the chance is ripe, the anger will out, the sword its readiest instrument (cf. IV.ii.59). The actor of Mortimer may therefore plot his character from the opening scene, in which Warwick cautions him to 'bridle' his 'anger'. It is another written-in stage direction. Mortimer retorts:

> I cannot, nor I will not; I must speak;
> Cousin, our hands I hope shall fence our heads
> And strike off his that makes you threaten us.
> Come uncle, let us leave the brainsick king
> And henceforth parley with our naked swords.   (I.i.120–5)

It is only his second speech, but already the actor has the emotional and physical clues to sustain his impersonation to the end.

The title-page of the play's 1598 printing alludes to 'The troublesome raigne and lamentable death of Edward the second, King of England: with the tragicall fall of proud Mortimer: And also the life and death of Peirs Gaveston, the great Earle of Cornewall, and mighty favourite of king Edward the second. . . .' No mention of Isabel the queen.

The problem of Isabel may seem to disappear if the actress takes Edward's account of her at face value and presents her as the court slut, Mortimer's cohort and paramour from the start. But such a reading must collide with the text itself. When, for example, in I.iv, Edward accuses her of being the means of Gaveston's latest exile (l. 155), we are in a position to contradict him, having — unlike Edward — witnessed scene ii, in which she pleads against Mortimer for a peaceable solution and amnesty for the royal minion, much as she abhors him. Why does she do this? Because, I suggest, she loves her husband; and there is presumably nothing implausible about her continuing to love a man who does not love her, perhaps never has loved her, cannot love her, and indeed despises her. Spencer Junior says: 'Our lady's first love is not wavering' (II.i.27). He is describing Margaret's constancy to her wanton lord, Gaveston, surely no more responsive to his wife than Edward to his. What is true of one woman may well be true of the other. The queen's first soliloquy (in I.iv), like all soliloquies, carries privileged information: its message is clearly a wife's love of her husband, whom she will do anything to please, though he has just accused her of plotting against him. Again Marlowe's implicit stage direction describes her, through Lancaster: 'Look where the sister of the King of France/Sits wringing of her hands and beats her breast' (ll. 187–8): a stock demonstration of genuine grief in the code of Elizabethan acting. A hundred lines later her face lights up at the sight of the man she adores:

> . . . I love him more
> Than he can Gaveston; would he loved me
> But half so much, then were I treble blest.   (I.iv.301–3)

She gives him the good news of Gaveston's recall, and is thrilled with his evident response to it: 'O how a kiss revives poor Isabel' (I.iv.332). There is no reason to doubt the genuineness of her feeling for him.

But her happiness is shortlived. By II.ii Edward is again accusing her of troublemaking and of infidelity with Mortimer (ll. 223, 225), and this time Edward himself knows that he slanders her, since earlier in the same scene she twice took his part, in public, against Mortimer, condemning his 'fury' in wounding Gaveston, and exiting with the king's own party (ll. 85, 99). Edward's treatment of her, at the beginning of II.iv, when he takes leave of his niece and of Gaveston but ignores her, though she has consistently stood by him, is therefore simply intolerable. 'No farewell to poor Isabel, thy queen?' she asks. 'Yes, yes,' he replies, 'for Mortimer your lover's sake,' and abruptly exits. (Here, consciously or not, he is no doubt parroting Gaveston's rebuke of her at I.iv.147.) Isabella is left alone, and again the soliloquy justifies her absolutely:

> Heavens can witness I love none but you;
> From my embracements thus he breaks away;
> Oh that mine arms could close this isle about,
> That I might pull him to me where I would,
> Or that these tears that drizzle from mine eyes
> Had power to mollify his stony heart,
> That when I had him we might never part.   (ll. 15–21)

The lords enter. Mortimer roughly cuts short her lament and demands to be told where the king is. She will not tell him. He tries to get her first to stay in the castle and then to sail with the nobles to Scarborough. She vows instead to follow the king, and offers evidence of her fidelity to him:

> You know the king is so suspicious,
> As if he hear I have but talked with you,
> Mine honour will be called in question.   (ll. 53–5)

If Mortimer's reply — 'Madam, I cannot stay to answer you/But think of Mortimer as he deserves' — marks his exit, the queen's speech that ends the scene is another soliloquy. In it she resolves to 'importune' her husband once again 'with prayers'. If he continues to spurn her, she will defect, not to Mortimer, but to her brother, the King of France, and lay her just cause before him.

We are almost half-way through the play, and the queen's loyalty to her husband, though repeatedly tested and scorned, is intact. It is with this in mind, then, that we must consider her visible power over Mortimer in I.iv, when she calls for a private conference with him and in a mere eight lines wins him to her plan to recall Gaveston. The watching lords observe 'how earnestly she pleads' (l. 234). Tantalisingly, we never know for sure what her 'weighty reasons' are, but Mortimer with rare eloquence immediately expounds several to his peers which he may well have derived from her. At any rate they are wholly persuasive to the other lords. But if these are the queen's own reasons, why did she not declare them publicly herself? It seems that she must also have said something to Mortimer that was for his ear alone; and that could conceivably have been a hint, or interpreted by Mortimer as a hint, of personal favours to come. For it is not hard to believe that Mortimer's ambitions extend, even this early, to the queen herself, whether for private or political gain or both, and that she senses it; so that a whisper of encouragement from someone who knows her power over him would be enough to bend his public course. Granting that, however, is not to make Isabel unchaste but only duplicitous; at worst she offers Mortimer some private hope if Edward proves finally inaccessible. Meanwhile she wants more than anything to save her marriage, and if that can be accomplished only by tolerating Gaveston and enlisting Mortimer to support his recall, she will pay the price. It does not follow — indeed it seems out of the question — that she would, say, put her arms around her would-be lover during their mumbled colloquy, if only because all eyes are on them. This passage calls for a finely judged sensitivity in the actress.

Yet the queen does in the end become Mortimer's lover. The dispassionate Kent and Leicester attest to the fact (IV.v.22; vi.50), and she herself seems to admit it when she agrees to the king's deposition or worse: 'Sweet Mortimer, the life of Isabel,/Be thou persuaded that I love thee well' (V.ii.15–16). The shift of allegiance is plausible enough, if we accept that she is driven to it, despite her repeated resistance, by a husband who repeatedly disdains her. How, and where, does the actress make this shift palpable? The pivotal scene is the very one in which she finally protests her loyalty to Edward, II.iv, which I have already quoted. This scene is crucial because it shows us the queen at her rope's end. Her husband has ignored her at parting; the air is full of final leavetaking; she may never see him again; certainly it seems that he never wants to see her again; she is abandoned on stage. Enter Mortimer to the rescue. She defines herself as

> . . . the miserable queen,
> Whose pining heart her inward sighs have blasted
> And body with continual mourning wasted;
> These hands are tired with haling of my lord
> From Gaveston, from wicked Gaveston,
> And all in vain, for when I speak him fair,
> He turns away and smiles upon his minion   (ll. 23–9).

Her game is up. Mortimer chooses his moment to say 'think of Mortimer as he deserves' (l. 58), and whether or not he stays for her reply, it sounds unequivocal: 'So well hast thou deserved, sweet Mortimer,/As Isabel could live with thee for ever.' True, she immediately corrects that to something like 'I'll give Edward one last chance, and if he rejects it I'll home to my brother'; but the possibility of her replacing a husband with a lover is now in the open, and subsequent events will realise the change. The player of Isabel here, so far from embracing her fate with lascivious abandon, should seem what she says she is, a broken and exhausted woman. Yet she is now morally ready to replace not only her husband but the king, with troops rallied in France.

The title-page of *Edward II* mirrors the king's unkindness to Isabel in passing her over in favour of the male principals. Yet her tragedy is no less than theirs. She leads a better and more dignified life than they do, and she is more truly a victim of other people. She is not weak like Gertrude, even though her final state is similar to hers. Her lover is often callous to her:

> Cease to lament and tell us where's the king?   (II.iv.30)

> Nay, Madam, if you be a warrior
> Ye must not grow so passionate in speeches   (IV.iv.15–16)

> Madam, have done with care and sad complaint   (IV.v.75)

> In any case, take heed of childish fear   (V.ii.6)

This last taunt gathers poignancy from the fact that the Elizabethan actor of the queen was a child, out of his political depth. Isabel's new match is not a happy one. She may have credible doubts about the choice she has made. No wonder she stands 'in a muse', as her Belgian benefactor observes (IV.v.72). We need not question the sincerity of her compassion for Edward in his imprisonment — 'Alas, poor soul, would I could ease his grief' (V.ii.26); and the message she sends him that she is labouring to work his liberty (V.ii.69–72), though false, is not simply hypocritical. Desolate herself, she desperately wants him to think well of her, as indeed she mostly deserves. When her son commits her to the Tower, he should voice the feelings of all of us:

> Away with her, her words enforce these tears
> And I shall pity her if she speak again.   (V.vi.85–6)

Notes

1 *Marlowe and the Early Shakespeare*, the Clark Lectures for 1951, Oxford 1953, pp. 95ff. Judith Weil, one of the most perceptive critics of *Edward II*, tries bravely to mount the case for a consistent Mortimer: he is an opportunist throughout (*Christopher Marlowe*, Cambridge 1977, p. 153).
2 All quotations from the play are taken from the New Mermaid edition by W. Moelwyn Merchant, New York, 1968.

Muriel C. Bradbrook

THE ROSE THEATRE

The Rose Theatre (1587–1605) was dominated by Edward Alleyn and by the drama of Christopher Marlowe in the five years of its heyday, 1592–7. The arts of performance ruled throughout, as in the tradition that survived it. Yet here Elizabethan tragedy gained its poetic unity, its appeal to a popular mixed audience. The Rose lay at the opposite end of the theatrical spectrum from the choristers' theatres north of the river, which, however, had been closed for two years by October 1592, when Alleyn the tragedian, first star of the stage, and Philip Henslowe, owner of the Rose, established the most successful partnership among the eddying currents of theatrical London. Their tradition continued at the Fortune, branched into the Boar's Head and the Red Bull north of the river, with spectacle, roaring parts for the hero, clowning and atrocity plays, and, though seen as old-fashioned, it persisted even into the years of the Civil War after 1642. New styles emerged from the alliance of Burbage and Shakespeare at the Theatre and the Globe, and in the second wave (1600–8) of the choristers' plays, which widened the choice and developed the subtleties of this great decade; but the playwrights Henslowe first employed, and the actors Alleyn trained, fed the new theatres also. If the Fortune and the Red Bull became targets for the more sophisticated theatres, yet crowds swarmed to them. At Henslowe's latest theatre, the Hope on Bankside, in the Induction to *Bartholomew Fair* (1614), his old script-writer, Ben Jonson, ironically but jocularly proposed articles of agreement with the audience, before a play afterwards given at Court to King James:

> he that will swear *Jeronimo* or *Andronicus* are the best plays yet, shall pass unexcepted at here, as a man whose judgement shows it is constant, and hath stood still these five and twenty or thirty years.

These two plays had made their first appearances at the Rose just across Rose Alley from that Hope that Jonson ends by describing as 'as dirty as Smithfield and as stinking every whit'.

Another play, probably first performed at the Rose, Thomas Heywood's *The Four Prentices of London, with the Conquest of*

Jerusalem, was parodied by Francis Beaumont for the choristers' stage in *The Knight of the Burning Pestle* (1607). When Heywood, who had been bound covenanted servant to Philip Henslowe in March 1598, published the 1615 edition of his play, he explained that it was written 'in my infancy of judgement in this kind of poetry', though he maintained that 'as plays were then, some fifteen or sixteen years ago, it was in the fashion'. Heywood's service is recorded in Henslowe's *Documents* accompanying the *Diary*, which is really a memorandum, irregularly kept from February 1592 to 1603, offering the only records of how an Elizabethan theatre was run day by day. Much more meagre evidence remains for other theatres, from Court accounts and payments, other legal documents, and the Master of the Revels book. First used by Edmund Malone in 1790, and printed by W. W. Greg in 1904–8, Henslowe's *Diary* has been illuminated by the unearthing at Southwark in February 1989 of the foundations of the Rose Theatre. The discovery provides historians of the Elizabethan stage with a unique complementary set of evidence.

For scholars one thing is clear: the standard Globe, put together by evidence painfully assembled from many sources, must be replaced by multiple models. A tapering stage, which does not face the sunrise but faces south, a raked yard, an angled *scenae frons*, a polygonal form that grows a bulge behind the stage, are some of the new discoveries to be assimilated. The history of the Elizabethan theatre has become three-dimensional. A new model for a reconstructed Globe on Bankside had been set out fully by John Orrell (1983), but it has now to be seen in its context, as I suggested in my fourth volume of *Collected Papers* (1989). I shall look first at the history of the Rose in terms of performances, and then at the discovery of the Rose, a story still unfolding.

The late Bernard Beckerman's study of Philip Henslowe (1971) was followed by Ernest L. Rhodes's survey (1976), and a chapter by Scott McMillin (1987). Two other recent studies of the *Diary* act as further guides. Carol C. Rutter (1984) rearranges the material chronologically, with an introduction defending Henslowe from earlier pictures of a Mr Gradgrind, and appendices on wages, prices, apparel. Neil Carson's *Companion* (1988), with tables and analyses of performances, expenses, and consolidated accounts, but based on Greg rather that the later Foakes and Rickert, has been sharply criticised by S. P. Cerasano in *Shakespeare Quarterly*, vol. 39, no. 4 (Winter 1988), yet provides useful material for other workers.

Philip Henslowe, whose Protestant father was the bailiff of the Catholic Lord Montagu from Hampshire, might have been named for the King of Spain if he was born between 1554 and 1558, when Philip II was Queen Mary's husband. Lord Montagu's town residence, Waverley House, was on Bankside; so here Henslowe was apprenticed to a rich dyer, married his master's widow, Agnes Woodward, became a churchwarden, and carried on the business, investing in a tavern, eating houses, and a brothel. His father had been Master of the Game to Lord Montagu, so perhaps the son knew about bears. The Queen's bears were kept by her Master of the Game just east on land belonging to the Manor of the Bishop of Winchester. The Rose lay nearby, in what was then Bridge Ward of the City.

Glynne Wickham's suggestion (1972) that bears could have appeared at the Rose seemed to be ratified in August 1989 by the archaeologists (usually concerned with earlier 'digs') who discovered a brown bear's skull outside the foundations of the theatre. The bears lived on the border between the Liberty of the Clink and Paris Garden, together with about one hundred mastiff dogs, as shown on Norden's map of 1593, just north-west of the Rose. If Shakespeare played at the Rose in 1593–4, his notable disgust of dogs (first commented on by Whiter in 1794) would have been roused here; the stench of so many animals and their food must have made the rose garden which gave its name to the theatre site a refuge for visitors to the nearby brothels. The Rose stood in a centre of entertainment. In March 1585 the ground had been leased by Henslowe from the powerful city church of St Mildred Bread Street for thirty-one years at £7 a year. By Simon and Jude's Day complaints had been lodged against performances on Sundays.

It was in September 1592 that Robert Greene in *Greene's Groatsworth of Wit* wrote of 'the only Shakescene of the country', the player who could 'as well bombast out a blank verse as the best of you', in his appeal to Marlowe and others. While Lord Strange's Men were at the Rose, fifteen performances of 'harey the vj' between 3 March and 19 June 1591–2 are recorded by Henslowe. The links between these plays and Marlowe have been noted by Harold Brooks (1968). 'harey the vj' was still playing in January 1594, and *Titus Andronicus*, marked 'new', was given by the Earl of Sussex's men on the 23rd of that month. The Rose was really starry then; on Norden's map of 1600 it was labelled The Star, perhaps from the 'Blazing Star' of tragedy, or from its polygonal form.

The vital entry in Henslowe's *Diary* comes on page 2 of the text:

> Edward Alleyn was married unto Joan Woodward the 22 of day of October 1592 in the four and thirty year of the Queen Majesty reign Elizabeth by the grace of God of England France and Ireland defender of the faith.

Its legal formality marks the event's importance. Alleyn impaled Henslowe's arms with his own, though incorrectly, as Joan was only a step-daughter. It was Alleyn who brought to his father-in-law's Rose Theatre the plays of Christopher Marlowe. Shakespeare, the new star, moved with Burbage to the Theatre north of the river. Here, continuing his history plays, he gained a new reputation for a kind of love comedy which owed more to Lyly than to Marlowe, whose style continued to support the image of Alleyn's supremacy. Henslowe's list supplies lost plays such as *Cutlack* and *Tamer Cham* (or *Tambercame*) which, along with *Tamburlaine*, provided the 'scenical strutting and furious vociferation' that later Jonson, at first one of Henslowe's team, would reject. But Jonson also said of Alleyn: 'others speak, but only thou dost act'. He was larger than life; his commanding presence, energy, and mesmerising power found fit expression in Marlowe's 'drumming decasyllabon'. Marlowe cut out the clowning from the text of *Tamburlaine*, printed well in 1590; this was an Aeschylean moment. 'All air and fire, that made his verses clear', Marlowe through Alleyn kindled poetic drama in a little theatre about the size of two tennis courts. The ephemeral art gave birth to a Phoenix that still glows today. A shepherd driving kings in animal harness, Tamburlaine was succeeded by 'Alleyn playing Faustus with a cross upon his breast', challenging the King of Kings. Struggles in the corridors of power were dramatised in *The Jew of Malta*. (The theological implications of its staging were expounded by G. K. Hunter in 1964.) Machevil, its Prologue, could have been read by Marlowe at Cambridge, but the political battles reflected contemporary court conflict.

The Massacre at Paris, Marlowe's last drama, produced at the Rose in January 1593, was played ten times after Marlowe's death in May of that year, and depicted events as recent as 1572. Henslowe entitled it *The Guise*, and costumed it carefully. The early undated Quarto assigns it also to the Lord Admiral's Men; *Edward II* in 1594 was attributed to the Earl of Pembroke's Men, a company that broke, and sold its books the year before. (Mortimer the younger is not a very large role in *Edward II*, but the only one that would have suited Alleyn.) Henslowe's *Diary*, which records the change of repertory every day, runs from 19 February 1591–2 to December 1593 with Lord Strange's Men (there is

some muddle over calendar years); December 1593 to February 1593–
4 with Lord Sussex's Men; then with the Queen's Men that April; in
June 1594 with the Lord Admiral's and the Chamberlain's Men at
Newington; then from mid-June at the Rose the Admiral's Men
continuing, with occasional intervals, till November 1597.

Carson's analysis of the list offers a quick way of judging here. Most
of the plays are lost, and must have been burned in the disastrous fire at
the Fortune in 1622, when all playbooks were destroyed and the
company was quite broken. (By then it was termed the Palsgrave's
Men.) Marlowe's plays were later published by collateral groups, as
when Heywood issued in 1633 *The Jew of Malta*, first entered in 1594
in the Stationers' Register, with new prologues and epilogues for a
revival at the Cockpit to challenge the memory of Alleyn's performance.

Henslowe's longest run was *The Wise Man of West Chester*, which
may be Anthony Munday's *John a Kent and John a Cumber* (*c.* 1587–
90); thirty-two performances were recorded. References to *Warlam-
chester* may be to the same play, or to a lost twin. The theatre's
audience was drawn from the immediate neighbourhood, from its
trades of shipbuilding, brewing, and tanning — the brewers are still
there — and from the local taverns and brothels, catering to disbanded
soldiers and sailors wandering from the channel ports. Some audience
might come from the Southwark prisons, since they were run mildly
compared with the dread fastness of Newgate on the north bank, or the
royal fortress of the Tower. In 1595, the lawyer John Davies observed:

> For as we see at all the playhouse doors,
> When ended is the play, the dance, and song,
> A thousand townsmen, gentlemen, and whores,
> Porters and servingmen together throng.

Another lawyer, John Marston, later added that in the tiny theatres of
the choristers he was not in danger of 'being pasted to the barmy jacket
of a beer brewer'. Michael Drayton, one of Henslowe's writers, in a
sonnet of about 1600 described 'the thronged theatre' with

> shouts and claps at every little pause,
> When the proud round on every side hath rung . . . ;

whilst Philip Gawdy, another lawyer, described the City's attempt in
1602 to impress soldiers, when 'all the playhouses were beset in one
day', along with bawdy-houses, bowling-alleys, and ordinaries, where
officers pressed not only 'gentlemen, and serving men, but lawyers,
clerks, countrymen that had law causes, aye the Queen's men, knights,

and as it was credibly reported one Earl . . . in all there are pressed four thousand' (*Letters of Philip Gawdy*). Davies' verses are endorsed.

All could be charmed by Alleyn; but in 1597 he retired to a sleeping partnership in the Lord Admiral's Men, becoming managerial, selling his apparel from stock. On the stage of the rival Theatre his style began to be mocked by the Lord Chamberlain's Men, as Shakespeare's Pistol, drunk on Marlowe and malt beer, roared:

> Shall packhorses,
> And hollow pampered jades of Asia,
> Which cannot go but thirty mile a day,
> Compare with Caesars and with Cannibals,
> And Troyant Greeks?   (*2 Henry IV*, II.iv.159–61)

The success of the Rose on the south bank drew competitors round it. I have written elsewhere (*Collected Papers*, vol. 4, paper 10, 1989) of the combat on Bankside. In 1595 or 1596 Francis Langley, Lord of the Manor of Paris Garden, a very crooked City man who had bought his way up, built the Swan Theatre west of the Rose, hoping to entice the Lord Chamberlain's Men, whose badge, the flying swan, they would wear on their coats. In August 1597 his theatre came under ban from the Privy Council, for what was termed 'A lewd play . . . containing very slanderous and seditious matter'; an anonymous informer gave warning to Topcliffe about *The Isle of Dogs* by Nashe and Jonson. Jonson and two actors (Shaa and Spencer), who had deserted Henslowe for the Swan, were gaoled. The case did not stand up to investigation, but Langley's licence was not renewed. If the question 'Cui bono?' ('Who benefits?') is asked, the answer is clearly Henslowe and Alleyn. The poor, needy, anonymous informer had done them good service. On 19 February 1598 the Privy Council authorised two companies only, the Lord Chamberlain's and the Lord Admiral's, to play one north, one south, of the river. Naturally the order had only limited effect. Henslowe and Alleyn had known what strings to pull; Langley, though quite unscrupulous, was ignorant of theatrical manoeuvring and removed his enterprise to a third theatre, the Boar's Head in Whitechapel. Meanwhile Burbage, Shakespeare, and company left their Shoreditch Theatre in a dispute with the ground landlord, moving first to its little neighbour, the Curtain, and then, in a bold venture, to rented land just east of the Rose, where they erected, with timbers from the Theatre, the first Globe, which was open at the latest by September 1599, when Thomas Platter saw *Julius Caesar* there. The Lord Chamberlain's flying swan had taken wing and landed in Henslowe's back yard. It could not be dislodged or beaten; the Globe was larger than the Rose, which had two years earlier seen its star actor withdraw from the boards. Alleyn then moved his troupe in the opposite direction, across the river, and slightly further west, nearer the Inns of Court and the royal quarters at Westminster. The conflict is like nothing so much as the territorial squabbling of birds.

In their last years at the Rose, the Admiral's Men began to succeed in a different style. *Two Angry Women of Abingdon* (1598) was so popular that in February 1599 Henslowe paid 'Mr. Porter' for 'the second part of The Angry Women of Abingdon', and later that month for *Two Merry Women of Abingdon*, perhaps the same piece under another name. Henry Porter had been at Brasenose College, Oxford, two years before Marlowe went up to Cambridge, and might have written this farce originally in a local setting, like the Cambridge *Gammer Gurton's Needle* thirty years before. It is very long, with the comic servants' parts extended. The plot turns on eloping lovers. The two angry women were probably parts for men, who ended fighting with torches when lost in a wood chasing the runaways. Men sometimes played the older women — they danced in drag in jigs; Shakespeare may have exploited the possibilities in tragedy in Queen Margaret, and later in Juliet's Nurse.

Thomas Dekker, a cockney of cockneys, supplied Henslowe's theatre with a comedy still often revived in Oxford, Cambridge, and London. A riotous version appeared at the Mermaid Theatre in 1964, another at the National Theatre in 1981. The record in the *Diary* reads:

> Lent unto Samuel Rowley and Thomas Downton the 15 of July 1599 to buy a book of Thomas Dekker called The Gentle Craft the sum of £3.

Henslowe did not always allow his plays to come into print but, although not registered in the Stationers' Register, this one was published within a year under its new title:

> *The Shoemakers' Holiday or The Gentle Craft* . . . as it was acted before the Queen's most excellent Majesty on New Year's Day at night last by the right honourable the Earl of Nottingham Lord High Admiral of England, his servants . . . 1600.

The flourish of titles betrays the hand of Henslowe; the Preface 'To all good fellows, professors of the Gentle Craft of what degree soever' reads as Dekker's. It is followed by two three-man songs, and by the prologue given before the queen, appealing to the 'dear Goddess', the 'bright mirror of true chastity', that her 'sun-like eyes' would smile on the offering.

Simon Eyre, 'shoemaker and Lord Mayor of London', stars on the title-page as the 'humorous' hero, probably played by Samuel Rowley. He belongs with the Host in *Sir John Oldcastle*, published the same year. His boisterous patter, with his catchword 'Prince am I none, yet am I princely born', maintains the legend of the shoemaker princes, and glorifies the crafts of London. The London legend could appeal to the queen — her grandfather had been of the Grocers' Company — and when at the end an unnamed king, clearly the future victor of Agincourt 'on the day of Crispin Crispianus', granted trade privileges to the Shoemakers, he would echo the recent concession to the Lord Admiral's Men.

Dekker boasts in his Preface that the play was 'for the mirth and pleasant matter by her Highness graciously accepted, being indeed no way offensive'; and, though Henslowe does not record receipts, the five seventeenth-century reprints suggest that it was also a success in the public theatre. The contrast of style between *The Shoemakers' Holiday* at the Rose and *Twelfth Night* (Christmas 1600) at the other theatre makes them feel as if they belong to different eras.

The Rose was allowed to run down when the Admiral's Men left for the Fortune's square auditorium constructed for Alleyn for a modest sum (maybe from an innyard) by Peter Street, builder of the Globe. A company calling itself Pembroke's Men acted at the Rose for two days in 1600, and Worcester's Men from August 1602 to May 1603, when they went back to the Boar's Head, which they preferred. In 1603 Henslowe's *Diary* ends. In June that year he conferred with a 'Mr Pope' (perhaps Thomas Pope of the King's Men, who had been at the Rose in 1593), to discuss the lease of the Rose. The landlord was now asking £20 a year, plus 100 marks a year 'upon building' (presumably maintenance). Henslowe told his friend Pope: 'I would rather pull down the playhouse', and 'he bade me do, and said he gave me leave and would bear me out for it was in him to do it'. The plan was presumably to take the valuable timber, as Burbage had done from the Theatre, but Pope died before it could be carried out. The Rose, moreover, stood on very marshy ground, and Henslowe was liable for drainage. By October 1605 he told the Commissioners of Sewers that it was 'out of his hands', and in 1606 the ground landlord paid for 'the late playhouse in Maid Lane'. The 'glory of the Bank' was now the Globe.

In February 1989 the foundations of the Rose came to light. Its site had been known to theatre historians from various records, including two maps by John Norden, of 1593 and 1600. An earlier survey of the area reported that there might be significant remains; but this survey was not kept in the Ministry of the Environment, and clearance was given for Imry Merchant Developers to build an office block on the site. The planning permission allowed some exploration by archaeologists. The story of the five months' struggle for the site of the Rose was fully reported in *The Times*, and may be followed there; the findings were described by John Orrell and Andrew Gurr in *The Times Literary Supplement* of 9–15 June 1989 with a diagram of the foundations. An expanded version in *Antiquity* (September 1989) was accompanied with English Heritage's account of the procedure by G. J. Wainwright, an expert on Stonehenge. The editor of *Antiquity* added a judicial survey of the controversy. Near the Rose, Sam Wanamaker had already secured the site of the old Hope for his new model of the Globe; his Bear Garden Museum is already housed in an old warehouse on the other side of Rose Alley, overlooking the Rose on Maid Lane (now known as Park Street). One hundred yards east from the Rose, the site of part of the old Globe is now exposed; part remains under the approach to Southwark Bridge and Anchor Terrace.

The foundations of the Rose Theatre have supplied important new evidence, whilst the proposed 'dig' at the nearby Globe is likely to yield little. If the remains reveal only a ghostly outline of half the Rose, it does include the stage. It is the western half of a theatre much smaller than was expected, a fourteen-sided polygon whose outer diameter was laid by the builder John Grigg at about 74 ft. The depth of the galleries can be measured from their inner walls, which begin at a radius of 24 ft 9 in. from the centre of the yard. The ground is raked down toward the stage, which is set at the north, opposite the entry from Maid Lane (now Park Street). Two successive stages have been revealed, showing that the improvements of 1592 pushed the stage back to give more audience space, and extended the backstage area into a bulge beyond the circle. The back wall of the stage was curved, unlike that in the Swan drawing. One stage-post of the second stage was located at the front right edge of the platform, which is not rectangular but tapers to about two-thirds of its rear width. It is smaller than that of the Fortune, of which the builder's measurements survive. The roof was thatched, the ground of the yard mortared. The depth of three galleries, about 10 ft 6 in. each, would carry about 1,400 people, the yard about 600. Even after the enlargement of 1592, the capacity would be only some 2,425 compared with the 3,000 or more of the Globe. Such is our new knowledge of the theatre of Alleyn and Henslowe.

In *Shakespeare Survey*, 43 (1991), R. A. Foakes writes on 'The Discovery of the Rose Theatre' confirming my statement that the model of the public theatres has now become more diversified; he includes diagrams of the Rose, relying on Orrell and Gurr, and adds several suggestions on form and capacity.

References

Beckerman, Bernard (1971) 'Philip Henslowe', in *The Theatrical Manager in England and America*, ed. J. W. Donohue Jr., Princeton, NJ, USA: Princeton University Press.

Bradbrook, Muriel C. (1989) *Collected Papers*, vol. 4, London: Harvester-Wheatsheaf.

Brooks, Harold (1968) 'Marlowe and the Early Shakespeare', in *Christopher Marlowe*, ed. Brian Morris, London: Ernest Benn.

Carson, Neil (1988) *A Companion to Henslowe's Diary*, Cambridge: Cambridge University Press.

Davies, Sir John, ed. Krueger, Robert (1975) Epigram 17, 'In Cosmum', *Poems*, Oxford: Clarendon Press.

Drayton, Michael, ed. J. William Hebel (1931) *Idea*, Sonnet 47, *Works*, vol. 2, Oxford: Shakespeare Head Press.

Edmond, Mary (1990) 'The Builder of the Rose Theatre', *Theatre Notebook*, vol. XLIV, no. 2, London: Society for Theatre Research.

Foakes, R. A. and Rickert, R. T. (1961) *Henslowe's Diary* ed., Cambridge: Cambridge University Press.

Gawdy, Philip, ed. Jeayes, I. H. (1906) *Letters*, London: J. B. Nichols.

Greene, Robert (1592) *Greenes Groats-worth of Witte*, reprinted (1970), Westport, Connecticut, USA: Greenwood Press.

Greg, Walter W. (1904–8) *Henslowe's Diary*, ed., ii vols., London: A. H. Bullen; and (1907) *Henslowe Papers*, London: A. H. Bullen.

Gurr, Andrew and Orrell, John (1989) (1) *Rebuilding Shakespeare's Globe*, London: Weidenfeld & Nicolson; (2) 'What the Rose can tell us', *Antiquity*, vol. 63, no. 240, September 1989, London: Oxford University Press.

Herford, C. H. and Simpson, Percy and Evelyn (1938 and 1947) *Ben Jonson*, vol. VI; vol. VIII, Epigram LXXXIX, Oxford: Oxford University Press.

Hunter, George K. (1964) 'The Theology of Marlowe's *The Jew of Malta*', *Journal of the Warburg and Courtauld Institutes*, xxvii; reprinted in 1978, *Dramatic Identities and Cultural Tradition*, Liverpool: Liverpool University Press.

Marston, John, ed. H. Harvey Wood (1939) *Jack Drum's Entertainment*, *Plays*, vol. 3, Edinburgh: Oliver & Boyd.

McMillin, Scott (1987) *The Elizabethan Theatre and 'The Book of Sir Thomas More'*, Cornell: Cornell University Press.

Orrell, John (1983) *The Quest for Shakespeare's Globe*, Cambridge: Cambridge University Press.

Rhodes, Ernest L. (1976) *Henslowe's Rose: the Stage and Staging*, Lexington, USA: University Press of Kentucky.

Rutter, Carol C. (1984) *Documents of the Rose Playhouse* ed., Manchester: Manchester University Press.

Wainwright, G. J. (1989) 'Saving the Rose', *Antiquity*, vol. 63, no. 240, London: Oxford University Press.

Wickham, Glynne (1972) *Early English Stages, 1300 to 1660*, vol. ii, 1576–1600, Part II; London: Routledge & Kegan Paul.

LIST OF CONTRIBUTORS

Jonas Barish has taught English at the University of California, Berkeley, since 1954. He is the author of *Ben Jonson and the Language of Prose Comedy*, *The Antitheatrical Prejudice*, and various articles chiefly on English Renaissance drama. He is currently at work on a study of closet drama.

Murray Biggs is Adjunct Associate Professor of English and Theater Studies at Yale University where he teaches acting, directing, and dramatic literature, and writes about performance on stage and screen. His own stage directing includes a dozen plays by Shakespeare, as well as the American première of Wordsworth's *The Borderers* (1987), and the first 20th-century production in English of Byron's *Sardanapalus* (1990).

Muriel C. Bradbrook, Fellow of the Royal Society of Literature, Fellow of the British Academy, and Member of the Norwegian Academy of Sciences and Arts, is Professor Emerita of English Literature at Cambridge University, and Fellow and former Mistress of Girton College. Her 26 books include works on Shakespeare and other Elizabethan as well as modern dramatists, on poets of various periods, and four volumes of *Collected Papers*. She is a Life Trustee of Shakespeare's Birthplace.

Tony Church played these roles in *Love's Labour's Lost*: Holofernes in Peter Hall's Cambridge production in 1953, the Argo Recording in 1957, and John Barton's 1965 production with the RSC; Don Armado in David Jones's 1973/75 production, and John Barton's 1978/9 production, both with the RSC. He has directed the play twice, in 1986 at the Guildhall School of Music and Drama, and in 1989 at the Santa Cruz Shakespeare Festival in California.

He played Quince in Peter Hall's 1962 production of *A Midsummer Night's Dream* with the RSC, Theseus in Robin Phillips' 1968 production at the Northcott Theatre, Exeter, and directed the play at the National Theatre Conservatory in Denver in 1989.

Philip Edwards retired in 1990 as King Alfred Professor of English Literature at Liverpool University. He was formerly Professor of English Literature at Trinity College, Dublin, and at Essex University. He is the author of *Shakespeare and the Confines of Art* (1968) and *Threshold of a Nation* (1979). He has edited *The Spanish Tragedy* and *Hamlet* and was co-editor of the Clarendon Press edition of Philip Massinger. His more recent work has been on voyage narratives. He is a Fellow of the British Academy.

(211)

Inga-Stina Ewbank, Professor of English Literature at Leeds, grew up in Sweden (née Ekeblad). Since her first book (on the Brontës), she has specialised in the drama, Elizabethan, Jacobean, and Scandinavian, and is currently at work on a book on Ibsen, Strindberg, and Shakespeare called *The Word in the Theatre*. She has translated both the Scandinavian masters for the English-speaking stage, most recently *The Wild Duck* directed by Sir Peter Hall.

Ernst Honigmann was Joseph Cowen Professor of English Literature in the University of Newcastle-upon-Tyne, 1970–89. His books include *The Stability of Shakespeare's Text* (1965), *Shakespeare: Seven Tragedies* (the dramatist's manipulation of response) (1976), *Shakespeare's Impact on his Contemporaries* (1982), *Shakespeare: the 'lost years'* (1985), *Shakespeare and his Contemporaries: essays in comparison* (1986), *John Weever: a biography* (1987), *Myriad-Minded Shakespeare* (1989), and editions of *King John* (1954) and *Milton's Sonnets* (1966). He is joint general editor of *The Revels Plays*.

Kenneth Muir, Vice-President of the International Shakespeare Association, former editor of *Shakespeare Survey*, sometime King Alfred Professor at Liverpool University (1951–74), has edited five of Shakespeare's plays, written a number of critical studies of his works, discovered hitherto unknown poems of Wyatt, and made verse translations of plays by Racine, Corneille, and Calderón.

A. D. Nuttall read first Classical Moderations and then English at Oxford. From 1962 he taught at the University of Sussex, becoming Professor of English in 1973 and Pro-Vice-Chancellor in 1978. In 1984 he became a Fellow of New College, Oxford.
   His books include *A Common Sky* (1974, on solipsism and literature), *Overheard by God* (1980), *A New Mimesis* (1983), *Timon of Athens* (1989), and *The Stoic in Love* (1989).

Lois Potter is Ned Allen Professor of English at the University of Delaware. Her publications include *A Preface to Milton, Twelfth Night: Text and Performance*, and *Secret Rites and Secret Writing, Royalist Literature 1641–1660*. She is also one of the editors of the Revels History of Drama in English, and a frequent reviewer of plays.

Claude Rawson is George M. Bodman Professor of English at Yale University, and an Honorary Professor at the University of Warwick. His books include *Henry Fielding and the Augustan Ideal under Stress, Gulliver and the Gentle Reader, Order from Confusion Sprung: Studies in Eighteenth-Century Literature from Swift to Cowper*, and (with F. P. Lock) an edition of the *Collected Poems of Thomas Parnell*. He is at present General Editor of the Yale Editions of the Private Papers of James Boswell.

Marion Trousdale, professor of English at the University of Maryland at College Park, is the author of *Shakespeare and the Rhetoricians* and editor of *Texts and Pretexts in the English Renaissance*. Her articles on Shakespeare and

Renaissance theory have appeared in *ELH, English Literary Renaissance, Shakespeare Quarterly*, and *Renaissance Drama*. She is presently finishing a book on Shakespeare's social poems.

Eugene M. Waith is the Douglas Tracy Smith Professor of English Literature Emeritus at Yale University. The author of *The Pattern of Tragicomedy in Beaumont and Fletcher* (1952) and *The Herculean Hero* (1962), he has recently edited *Titus Andronicus* and *The Two Noble Kinsmen* for The Oxford Shakespeare. A collection of his essays, *Patterns and Perspectives in English Renaissance Drama*, was published in 1988.

Robert Weimann is professor of English and literary theory at the Berlin Academy of Sciences, and president of the Deutsche Shakespeare Gesellschaft in Weimar. He is currently engaged in a revised and enlarged English edition of his book in German on authority and representation in the Elizabethan theatre. His previous publications in English include *Shakespeare and the Popular Tradition in the Theater* and *Structure and Society in Literary History*.

Stanley Wells, Professor of Shakespeare Studies and Director of the Shakespeare Institute of the University of Birmingham, is also General Editor of The Oxford Shakespeare and editor of *Shakespeare Survey*. His writings on drama in performance include *Royal Shakespeare: Four Major Productions at Stratford-upon-Avon* (1976, 1977) and many reviews in the *TLS, Shakespeare Survey*, and elsewhere.

The editors of this book gratefully acknowledge the help and advice of Shelagh Hunter and Andrew Gurr.

BIBLIOGRAPHY OF G. K. HUNTER'S WORKS
(COMPILED BY SHELAGH HUNTER)

BOOKS

Shakespeare, *All's Well that Ends Well*, ed. G.K.H., The New Arden Shakespeare. London: Methuen, 1959.

Shakespeare: The Later Comedies. London: Longman, for the British Council, 1962.

John Lyly: The Humanist as Courtier. London: Routledge, 1962.

John Marston, *Antonio and Mellida*, ed. G.K.H., Regents Renaissance Drama Series. Lincoln, NE: U. of Nebraska Press, 1965.

John Marston, *Antonio's Revenge*, ed. G.K.H., Regents Renaissance Drama Series. Lincoln, NE: U. of Nebraska Press, 1965.

Shakespeare, *Macbeth*, ed. G.K.H., New Penguin Shakespeare. Harmondsworth: Penguin Books, 1967.

Lyly and Peele. London: Longman, for the British Council, 1968.

F. P. Wilson, *The English Drama 1485–1585*, ed. with a bibliography G.K.H., The Oxford History of English Literature, vol. IV(a). Oxford: Oxford UP, 1969.

John Webster, ed. G.K.H. and S. K. Hunter, Penguin Critical Anthologies. Harmondsworth: Penguin Books, 1969.

A Casebook of Shakespeare's Henry IV, ed. G.K.H. London: Macmillan, 1970.

Shakespeare, *King Lear*, ed. G.K.H., New Penguin Shakespeare. Harmondsworth: Penguin Books, 1972.

John Marston, *The Malcontent*, ed. G.K.H., The Revels Plays. London: Methuen, 1975.

Dramatic Identities and Cultural Tradition: Studies in Shakespeare and his Contemporaries, Liverpool English Texts and Studies. Liverpool: Liverpool UP, 1978.

Shakespeare's Styles: Essays in Honour of Kenneth Muir, ed. Philip Edwards, Inga-Stina Ewbank and G.K.H. Cambridge: Cambridge UP, 1980.

Milton's Paradise Lost, Unwin Critical Library. London: Allen & Unwin, 1980.

John Lyly, *Campaspe*, ed. G.K.H., with *Sappho and Phao*, ed. David Bevington, The Revels Plays. Manchester: Manchester UP, 1991.

English Drama 1586–1642. The Oxford History of English Literature, vol. VI. Oxford: Oxford UP, forthcoming.

ESSAYS

'The Cocktail Party', *The Month* ns II (1949), 337–9.

'The Marking of *Sententiae* in Elizabethan Printed Plays, Poems and Romances', *The Library*, 5th Series, VI (1951/2), 171–88.

(214)

'The Dramatic Technique of Shakespeare's Sonnets', *Essays in Criticism* III (1953), 152–64.

'*Henry IV* and the Elizabethan Two-Part Play', *Review of English Studies* V (1954), 236–48.

'Isocrates' Precepts and Polonius' Character', *Shakespeare Quarterly* VIII (1957), 501–6.

'The Structure of Milton's *Areopagitica*', *English Studies* XXXIX (1958), 117–19.

'A Survey of Modern *Hamlet* Criticism', *Critical Quarterly* I (1959), 27–32.

'Shakespeare's Politics and the Rejection of Falstaff', *Critical Quarterly* I (1959), 229–36.

'The Romanticism of Pope's Horace', *Essays in Criticism* X (1960), 390–404.

'English Folly and Italian Vice', in *Jacobean Theatre*, ed. John Russell Brown and Bernard Harris, Stratford-upon-Avon Studies. London: Arnold, 1960, 85–111.

'Bibliography of Sir Philip Sidney', in *Sir Philip Sidney* by Kenneth Muir. London: Longman, for the British Council, 1960, 36–40.

'The Heroism of Hamlet', in *Hamlet*, ed. John Russell Brown and Bernard Harris, Stratford-upon-Avon Studies. London: Arnold, 1963, 90–109.

'The Theology of Marlowe's Jew of Malta', *Journal of the Courtauld and Warburg Institute* XXVII (1964), 211–40.

'Six Notes on *Measure for Measure*', *Shakespeare Quarterly* XV (1964), 167–72.

'The Five-Act Structure of *Doctor Faustus*', *Tulane Drama Review* VIII (1964), 77–91.

'English at Warwick', *Critical Survey: The Journal of The Critical Quarterly Society* (Summer, 1965), 128–31.

'Elizabethans and Foreigners', *Shakespeare Survey* XVII (1964), 37–52.

'Ironies of Justice in *The Spanish Tragedy*', *Renaissance Drama* VIII (1965), 89–104.

'*Macbeth* in the Twentieth Century', *Shakespeare Survey* XIX (1966) 1–11.

'The Transition from the Sixth Form to the University' (with S. K. Hunter), *Aspects of Education* IV (1966), 102–9.

'The Last Tragic Heroes', in *Later Shakespeare*, ed. John Russell Brown and Bernard Harris, Stratford-upon-Avon Studies. London: Arnold, 1966, 11–28.

'Seneca and the Elizabethans: a Case-Study in "Influence"', *Shakespeare Survey* XX (1967), 17–26.

'Othello and Colour Prejudice', *Proceedings of the British Academy* LIII (1967), 139–63.

'A. C. Bradley's *Shakespearean Tragedy*', *Essays and Studies 1968*, collected for the English Association by Simeon Potter. London: John Murray, 1968, 101–17.

'Drab and Golden Lyrics of the English Renaissance', in *Forms of Lyric*, ed. Reuben Brower, Selected Papers from the English Institute. New York: Columbia UP, 1970, pp. 1–18.

Introductions to three facsimile reprints of *King Lear* in the editions of 1820, 1831 and 1858. London: Cornmarket Press, 1970.

'English Drama, 1900–1960', in *Sphere History of English Literature in the English Language: Vol. VII, The Twentieth Century*, ed. Bernard Bergonzi. London: Sphere Books, 1970, 310–35.

'The Discipline of Literary Criticism', in *English: an Outline for the Intending Student*, ed. Angus Ross. London: Routledge, 1971, 9–26.

'Shakespeare's Reading', in *A New Companion to Shakespeare Studies*, ed. Kenneth Muir and S. Schoenbaum. Cambridge: Cambridge UP, 1971, 55–66.

'T. S. Eliot and the creation of a symbolist Shakespeare', *Twentieth-Century Literature in Retrospect*, Harvard Studies in English II (1971), 191–204.

'Spenser's *Amoretti* and the English Sonnet Tradition', in *A Theater for Spenserians*, ed. Judith M. Kennedy and James A. Reither. Toronto: Toronto UP, 1973, 124–44.

'Italian tragicomedy on Shakespeare's stage', *Renaissance Drama* ns VI (1973), 123–48.

'Shakespeare's earliest tragedies: *Titus Andronicus* and *Romeo and Juliet*', *Shakespeare Survey* XXVII (1974), 1–9.

'Seneca and English Tragedy', in *Seneca*, ed. C. D. N. Costa. London: Routledge, 1974, 166–204.

'Unity and numbers in Spenser's *Amoretti*', *Yearbook of English Studies* V (1975), 39–45.

'The beginnings of *Hamlet* and *King Lear*', *Theoria* XLIV (1975), 1–10.

'Were there Act-Pauses on Shakespeare's Stage?', in *English Renaissance Drama: Essays Presented to Madeleine Doran and Mark Eccles*, ed. Standish Henning, Robert Kimbrough, Richard Knowles. Carbondale, IL: Southern Illinois UP, 1976, 15–35.

'A Roman Thought: Renaissance Attitudes to History Exemplified in Shakespeare and Jonson', in *An English Miscellany: Presented to W. S. Mackie*, ed. B. S. Lee. Capetown: Oxford UP, 1977, 93–117.

'*Troilus and Cressida*: a Tragic Satire', *Shakespeare Studies* (Japan) XIII (1977), 1–23.

'Shakespeare's Tragic Sense as it Strikes Us Today', in *Shakespeare: Pattern of Excelling Nature*, ed. David Bevington and Jay Halio. Newark, DE: Delaware UP, 1978, 81–7.

'The Royal Shakespeare Company Plays *Henry VI*', *Renaissance Drama* ns IX (1978), 91–108.

'The Idea of Comedy in Some Seventeenth-Century Comedies', in *Poetry and Drama in the English Renaissance: Essays in Honor of Jiro Ozu*, ed. Nakanori and Tamaizumi. Tokyo: Kinokuniya, 1980, 71–91.

'Poem and Context in *Love's Labour's Lost*', in *Shakespeare's Styles: Essays in Honour of Kenneth Muir*, ed. Philip Edwards, Inga-Stina Ewbank and G.K.H. Cambridge: Cambridge UP, 1980, 25–38.

'Flatcaps and Bluecoats: Visual Signals on the Elizabethan Stage', *Essays and Studies 1980*, collected for the English Association by Inga-Stina Ewbank. London: John Murray, 1980, 16–47.

'Tyrant and Martyr: Religious Heroism in Elizabethan Tragedy', in *Poetic Traditions of the English Renaissance*, ed. Maynard Mack and George deForest Lord. New Haven: Yale UP, 1982, 85–102.

'Political Theater in Shakespeare — and Later', *Mosaic* XVI.4 (1983), 1–14.

'Sources and Meanings in *Titus Andronicus*', in *Mirror up to Shakespeare: Essays in Honor of G. R. Hibbard*, ed. J. C. Gray. Toronto: Toronto UP, 1984, 171–88.

'Comedy, Farce, Romance', in *Comedy from Shakespeare to Sheridan: Essays in Honor of Eugene M. Waith*, ed. A. R. Braunmuller and J. C. Bulman. Newark, DE: Delaware UP, 1986, 27–52.

'Shakespeare and the Traditions of Tragedy', in *The Cambridge Companion to Shakespeare Studies*, ed. Stanley Wells. Cambridge: Cambridge UP, 1986, 123–41.

'Bourgeois Comedy: Shakespeare and Dekker', in *Shakespeare and his Contemporaries: Essays in Comparison*, ed. E. Honigmann. Manchester: Manchester UP, 1986, 1–15.

'The Beginnings of Elizabethan Drama: Revolution and Continuity', *Renaissance Drama* ns XVII (1986), 29–51.

'How Greene Was My Shakespeare? K. M. Revisited', in *KM 80: A Birthday Album for Kenneth Muir, Tuesday, 5 May, 1987*. Liverpool: Liverpool UP, 1987, 76–8.

'The Pleasures of Renaissance History', in *L'Europe de la Renaissance: Cultures et Civilisations: Mélanges offerts à Marie-Thérèse Jones-Davies*. Paris: Jean Touzot, 1989, 315–23.

'*Truth and art in History plays*', *Shakespeare Survey* XLII (1990), 15–24.

'The History of Styles as a Style of History', in *Addressing Frank Kermode: Essays in Criticism and Interpretation*, ed. Margaret Tudeau-Clayton and Martin Warner. London: Macmillan, 1991.

'Religious Nationalism in Later History Plays', in *Literature and Nationalism*, a Festschrift for Philip Edwards, ed. Vincent Newey and Ann Thompson, 1991.

INDEX